Ecomodernism

Ecomodernism

Technology, Politics and the Climate Crisis

Jonathan Symons

polity

First published in 2019 by Polity Press

Polity Press
65 Bridge Street
Cambridge CB2 1UR, UK

Polity Press
101 Station Landing
Suite 300
Medford, MA 02155, USA

ISBN-13: 978-1-5095-3119-6 (hardback)
ISBN-13: 978-1-5095-3120-2 (paperback)

A catalogue record for this book is available from the British Library.

Library of Congress Cataloging-in-Publication Data

Names: Symons, Jonathan, 1976- author.
Title: Ecomodernism : technology, politics and the climate crisis / Jonathan
    Symons.
Description: Cambridge, UK : Polity Press, [2019] | Includes bibliographical
    references.
Identifiers: LCCN 2018054235 (print) | LCCN 2019002440 (ebook) | ISBN
    9781509531226 (Epub) | ISBN 9781509531196 | ISBN 9781509531202
    (pb)
Subjects: LCSH: Climate change mitigation. | Environmental protection–
    Technological innovations. | Environmental degradation–Prevention | Green
    technology. | Nature–Effect of human begins on.
Classification: LCC TD171.75 (ebook) | LCC TD171.75 .S96 2019 (print) |
    DDC 363.738/74–dc23
LC record available at https://lccn.loc.gov/2018054235

Typeset in 11 on 13 pt Sabon
by Toppan Best-set Premedia Limited
Printed and bound in Great Britain by CPI Group (UK) Ltd, Croydon

For further information on Polity, visit our website: politybooks.com

Contents

Acknowledgements

When it was first conceptualized, this book was to have been coauthored with Rasmus Karlsson. Although I ended up writing the book alone, I am grateful to Rasmus for hosting me for some memorable weeks at Umeå University where we formulated the book's central themes, for reading and commenting on the manuscript, and for his ongoing friendship. I also thank Macquarie University's Outside Studies Program for supporting my visit to Umeå.

I am indebted to the commissioning editor Louise Knight and her team at Polity for their constant encouragement and insight; to two anonymous readers and five reviewers of the book proposal; to Susan Beer and Sandey Fitzgerald for assistance with editing; to Dennis Altman, Emma Brush, Sophie Cunningham, Kate Gleeson, Maryam Khalid, Ted Nordhaus and Jessica Whyte for commenting on sections of the text; to a great many friends and colleagues for discussions that have found their way into the book, including Lee Archer, Govand Azeez, Noah Bassil, Leigh Boucher, Barry Brook, Carol D'Cruz, Peter Eckersley, Kingsley Edney, Anna-Karin Eriksson, Roger Huang, Sung-Young Kim, Stephanie Lawson, Lavina Lee, Adam Lockyer, Stephen Luntz, Terry Macdonald, Kate Macdonald, Bryan Maher,

Andrea Maksimovic, Andrew McGregor, Clare Monagle, John Morgan, Steven Noble, Jonathan Corpus Ong, Spiros Panigirakis, Carol Peterson, Dominic Redfern, Robert Reynolds, Anna Schurmann, Chris Schurmann, Ben Skidmore, Hsu-Ming Teo, Shaun Wilson and Hendri Yulius; and to my family and especially Matthew Masiruw for their love and support.

The sections of Chapter 6 that discuss solar geoengineering have previously been published as, 'Geoengineering justice: who gets to decide whether to hack the climate?' in the *Breakthrough Journal*. I thank Ted Nordhaus, director of the Breakthrough Institute, for allowing republication. I also thank the Breakthrough Institute for allowing me to attend the 2016–2018 Breakthrough Institute Dialogues. I am indebted to many Dialogue participants, but especially Ted Nordhaus, Oliver Morton and Rachel Pritzker, for insights that have influenced this book.

Most of the book was written either at Macquarie University or at the Kings Cross Library in Sydney. The university is named after Lachlan Macquarie who was the Governor of New South Wales between 1810 and 1821. Macquarie is now remembered both for his work as a progressive reformer and for his genocidal acts – at one point ordering that slain Aboriginal warriors be 'hanged up on trees in conspicuous situations, to strike the survivors with the greater terror'. The Kings Cross library sits in an historically queer and red light district. Its establishment and its deliberate embrace of homeless patrons is a tribute to the social democratic impulse. Nevertheless, as I sit at the library's windows gazing eastwards I am aware that this land, and all I can see, were stolen from the Gadigal people of the Eora Nation whose rightful ownership I acknowledge.

Abbreviations

ACT UP	AIDS Coalition to Unleash Power
AIDS	Acquired Immune Deficiency Syndrome
AZT	first HIV drug
BI	Breakthrough Institute
BP	British Petroleum
BSE	Bovine spongiform encephalopathy
CCP	Chinese Communist Party
CCS	Carbon capture and storage
CCU	Carbon capture and utilization
CDM	Clean Development Mechanism
CRISPR	Clustered Regularly Interspaced Short Palindromic Repeats (genome editing)
DNA	Deoxyribonucleic acid (molecule)
EU	European Union
GATT	General Agreement on Tariffs and Trade
GDP	Gross Domestic Product
GHG	Greenhouse gas
GJC	Geoengineering Justice Coalition (a fictional entity used for illustrative purposes)
GM	Genetically modified
GMO	Genetically modified organism
G77	Group of 77

HIV	Human Immunodeficiency Virus Infection
ICAO	International Civil Aviation Organization
ICISS	International Commission on Intervention and State Sovereignty
IEA	International Energy Agency
IMF	International Monetary Fund
IPCC	Intergovernmental Panel on Climate Change
MI	Mission Innovation
MNC	Multi-National Corporation
NIEO	New International Economic Order
OECD	Organization for Economic Co-operation and Development
OPEC	Organization of the Petroleum Exporting Countries
PV	Photovoltaic (solar)
RtoP	Responsibility to Protect principle
R&D	Research and Development
RD&D	Research, Development and Deployment
SRM	Solar Radiation Management
TCP	Technology Collaboration Programmes
UNEP	United Nations Environment Programme
UNFCCC	United Nations Framework Convention on Climate Change
US	United States of America

Introduction

Restraint or Innovation?

In 1982 when press secretary Larry Speakes was first asked for President Reagan's response to the AIDS epidemic, he replied, 'I don't have it. Do you?' This contempt set the tone for years, during which, as tens of thousands of Americans died, the word 'AIDS' never passed the President's lips. Faced with an unprecedented epidemic, Reagan chose to ignore, moralize and exclude rather than to enlist science or include affected communities in public-health responses. Emphasizing the immorality of drugs and homosexuality, officials urged educators to 'teach restraint as a virtue'. Reagan's first budgets actually cut medical research alongside renewable energy research programmes.

The Republican Party of the 1980s, committed both to 'supply-side economics' and the ascendant 'moral majority', was perhaps especially ill equipped to respond to an illness whose first victims included homosexuals, injecting drug users and sex-workers. Some religious conservatives described HIV as God's work and redoubled their efforts to sanction homosexuality and drug use. America was not exceptional. Sweden passed compulsory quarantine laws, Chinese

Communist Party officials denied that the epidemic had reached their shores, and many thousands of South Africans died unnecessarily because President Mbeki promoted traditional herbal cures and challenged the connection between HIV and AIDS. Each of these countries has since made giant strides towards inclusive and effective public health programmes. However, in the face of ideologues promoting simplistic solutions, it was at first unclear how affected communities should respond. Even some in the gay community chose to question whether HIV was really the cause of AIDS, to moralize against promiscuity, or to ask if the CIA had covertly spread the disease. Only slowly did activists formulate a response that was tailored to the challenge: inventing and promoting safe-sex and safe-injecting practices; demanding access to state-funded medical research; enhancing public services; and producing and distributing generic drugs in the developing world.

It was not until 1987 that Congress began to earmark funds for the work that ultimately produced effective antiretroviral treatments for HIV (Danforth 1991). Although state-funded innovation was necessary to counter the epidemic, so too were social reforms. In the first instance, activist groups like ACT UP fought repressive attitudes and discriminatory laws, reshaped clinical drug trials and demanded increased medical research-funding (France 2016). Later, people in the developing world accessed life-saving treatment, but only after a global, civil society campaign successfully demanded that intellectual property regulations allow low-cost manufacture of generic drugs. More inclusive public health programmes, in which George W. Bush's President's Emergency Plan for AIDS Relief played a big part, eventually brought further progress. Although the HIV epidemic is far from over and some political divisions remain, new infection and treatment rates have improved dramatically during the twenty-first century.

Why begin a book about ecomodernism, technology and climate change by recalling historical debates over AIDS? Most practically, the analogy underscores the value of innovation. State-funded, democratically controlled innovation has yet to gain the prominence it deserves within climate activism. By contrast, HIV activists fought not only for a dramatic increase in spending on HIV research, but to open drug-trial registers, eliminate the use of placebo medications for control groups, and make medical services accessible to all (France 2016, p. 253). In retrospect, it may seem obvious that medical innovation should have been a central political demand. Yet the gay community was beset by vigilante attacks, media neglect, and discriminatory health-care providers. AIDS activists might easily have focused on these adversaries and ignored the slow and complex processes of medical research. Yet, as historian David France describes in *How to Survive a Plague*, on the same day in 1987 that pharmaceutical company Burroughs Wellcome obtained FDA approval for the first HIV treatment, the company also announced that the drug, AZT, would cost $10,000 per year – far above many insurance plans' coverage caps. ACT UP's fury at this exploitative pricing prompted activists to seek to reform medical innovation. Among other things, this book is something of a call to arms for a similar climate response – and a rejection of the idea that innovation should be viewed as somehow belonging outside of politics.

A second reason to compare climate change with HIV is because, amid the challenges of resurgent nationalism, international inequality and climate-denial, this story offers hope. It reminds us that communities have faced intractable, 'wicked' problems before, and have eventually found their way to an inclusive and scientifically engaged response. However, it was only by treating AIDS as a medical illness, rather than as a judgement on the society it struck, that a coherent response became possible (Sontag 1989). It is remarkable how many of the flawed cultural logics that thwarted early HIV responses persist within climate discourse. For example, while few now propose abstinence education as a useful response to HIV, Reagan's pro-celibacy mantra 'teach restraint as a virtue' has been repurposed by people who promote virtuous individual behaviour change as a coherent climate response. Denial, which is so often the twin of abstinence, has also blighted both debates.

Third, HIV and climate change have both challenged pre-existing paradigms. Just as HIV activism needed to move beyond gay liberation, a politics capable of addressing climate change may look very different from twentieth-century environmentalism, whose foundational beliefs were formed before the climate crisis was well understood. For example, opposition to hydroelectricity and nuclear power – which even today are the two largest sources of zero-carbon electricity and the only technologies that have allowed any country to decarbonize their electricity grid (Finland's remarkable geothermal resources make it the only exception) – was central to the emergence of modern Green movements. A climate-focused politics might take a very different view on these mature, low-carbon technologies. Green taboos against 'intervention in nature' are also challenged by advances in genetic technology. For example, milk brewed from genetically modified yeast, low-methane GM rice crops, or genetically engineered algae-derived biofuels might potentially achieve significant cuts in greenhouse gas (GHG) emissions (Shuba and Kifle 2018). As climate change gathers pace, those strands of twentieth-century Green ideology that oppose all such interventions may provide an imperfect guide to effective responses.

Whereas perceptions of elite greed and corruption galvanized AIDS activists to politicize innovation, in climate politics the reverse has happened. Allegations of elite corruption have fuelled a fruitless culture war over the reality of climate change. On one side, 'climate change deniers' allege a vast conspiracy in which grant-hungry scientists are working with the United Nations to promote socialist world government. Many conservatives find the whole warming hypothesis inherently suspicious. The discovery that capitalist–consumerist modernity is destroying the biosphere seems to have too convenient a fit with left-wing agendas (Uscinski et al. 2017; for an example of conspiratorial thinking see Inholfe 2012). Thus, early efforts by fossil-fuel lobbyists to seed doubt over climate science have bloomed into a genuine movement of denial (Hamilton 2013). Although denial of climate science is intellectually groundless – the evidence is increasingly there to be seen and experienced – conservative nationalists are right about one thing. Many climate activists really do think an effective climate response will require a move towards much deeper forms of international cooperation and assistance. This book is an example – I argue that social services and emergency assistance must be guaranteed universally if the most vulnerable people are to be protected from climate harms. My call for a rethinking of international obligations, although radical, mirrors that of many climate justice activists. If the lifestyles of ordinary first-world people are indirectly and accidentally impoverishing people in far-away places, then political institutions should ideally reflect the new ways in which our fates are connected.

On the progressive side of politics people overwhelmingly accept the reality of climate change, yet many are preoccupied with a different conspiracy. Consider Naomi Klein's analysis of the root cause of climate change:

> We are stuck because the actions that would give us the best chance of averting catastrophe – and would benefit the vast majority – are extremely threatening to an elite minority that has a stranglehold over our economy, our political process, and most of our major media outlets. (2015, p. 18)

Klein is right that carbon-intensive industries (which include energy, industrial, agricultural and transport sectors), like cigarette companies before them, really have set out to oppose regulatory responses and to muddy the public's understanding of the science. However, her argument takes a conspiratorial form: it alleges that an elite minority is secretly plotting to harm the wider community. Fixation with conspiratorial dynamics can distort analysis even when the basic outline of a conspiratorial belief is accurate. For example, some people have become so obsessed with the US's significant moral failings that they overlook the flaws of the despotic regimes that oppose it – one has to assume that contemporary left-wing apologists for Assad's Syrian regime are caught in this dynamic (Hasan 2018).

I worry that preoccupation with the immorality of fossil fuel industries might similarly distort our understanding of climate mitigation. To be sure, extractive industries have worked hard to delay climate action, but we should also recognize that GHG emissions are the unintended consequence of the technologies that well-meaning people depend upon in their everyday lives. The frame we adopt – whether of 'elite corruption' or 'unintended consequence' – will influence our political responses. In believing that renewable energy is already superior and that fossil fuels are kept alive only by the political power of incumbent industries, many climate activists conclude that political mobilization is all that's needed. They propose that we must divest and resist, blockading mines, pipelines and power plants, one campaign after another, until we break the power of the fossil fuel industries. Valuable as these campaigns may be, I argue that climate activism should also think in more strategic, global terms. I worry that if the underlying demand for fossil fuels remains, these blockades may resemble efforts to deflate a mattress without opening the valve. Roll on one part of the mattress, and pressure escapes elsewhere. Force one coal mine to close and, if the demand for fossil fuels persists, production will simply expand at another.

A more effective way of undermining extractive industries would be to use the institutional power of the state to develop radically better technologies. When new technologies are profoundly more attractive than established alternatives, incumbents either lose their power or embrace change. Kodak's swift decline following the rise of digital photography, and DuPont's development of substitutes for ozone-layer destroying chlorofluorocarbons in the late 1980s are examples. Protection of the ozone layer under the Montreal Protocol (negotiated during the less-than-Green Reagan

Administration) is probably the single most successful example of global environmental action. It was achieved in part because DuPont, seeing an opportunity for technological advantage, became an advocate for international regulation (Haas 1992).

When zero-carbon technologies become cheaper and more dependable than fossil fuel alternatives, similar transformations will become possible. Wind, solar power and electric cars have all made dramatic and sustained gains in the last decade. Yet, they have not attained the kind of advantage that rapidly reshapes markets. Shortly before I completed this book, British Petroleum (BP 2018) released its annual summary of world energy statistics for 2017. Solar and wind enjoyed a record year in 2017, but their success was insufficient to halt the steady increase of oil and gas production. Global coal consumption also increased in 2017, with a net increase in energy generated that was just a little greater than that achieved by solar (coal had declined slightly in previous years). Even in countries like Germany and Denmark where renewable industries have gained the upper hand politically and won aggressive government support, GHG emissions have remained far above levels that would be consistent with averting dangerous climate change.

Recognizing the difficulty of decarbonization, the Intergovernmental Panel on Climate Change (IPCC) has argued that the development of 'new technologies is crucial for the ability to realistically implement stringent carbon policies' (Somanathan et al. 2014, p. 1178). Bizarrely, some climate activists disagree. They insist that we already 'have the technical tools we need to get off fossil fuels' and propose that all that is needed is a collective struggle against the privileged 'extractivist' elites (Klein 2015, p. 16). The possibility that low-carbon innovation might be a desirable goal of collective struggle, or that new technologies might help reconcile the twin challenges of eliminating GHG emissions and advancing the welfare of what will most probably soon be ten billion people, is rarely considered. Calls for collective struggle against an oppressive elite are attractive because they fit climate change into a paradigm that is familiar from many previous social justice campaigns. Addressing climate change, however, is not like a civil rights movement – it calls into question the technological constitution as well as the political and cultural organization of human society. Just as ACT UP activists responded to HIV by politicizing the process of medical research, so too should climate activism seek to transform zero-carbon innovation.

The idea that state-backed technological innovation is a necessary precondition for both human and ecological flourishing is commonly associated with a strand of environmentalism that has come to be called *ecomodernism*. This philosophy has been most publicly articulated by the environmental think-tank, the Breakthrough Institute, which was established in Oakland, California, in 2003. The term *ecomodernism*, however, has only been in common use since 2013 (see Kloor 2012; Asafu-Adjaye et al. 2015). Ecomodernism's argument for innovation is not the familiar demand that governments must simply support deployment of renewable energy, nor is it a celebration of capitalist creative destruction (Schumpeter 2010). Rather, it is a call for state investment in mission-oriented research to accelerate the development and deployment of an array of breakthrough low-emissions technologies that can transform industry, transport and agriculture as well as electricity generation. Ecomodernists welcome the emerging twenty-first-century trend towards convergence of global living standards (Milanovic 2011), and wish to hasten progress towards universal human flourishing. They argue, however, that their vision of 'universal human development' on an 'ecologically vibrant planet' also necessitates a second core principle, that of *intensification*. The idea here is that a global modernity will only spare space for nature if most people live in high-density cities, utilize high-density energy sources and draw on all available technologies to minimize the footprint and maximize the efficiency of agricultural production.

The difficult reality is that today's technologies necessitate a close link between GHG emissions and human development (Bazilian 2015). This creates tough choices. Which should be the higher priority: expanding third-world energy access or reducing emissions? A community's resilience to climate harms is closely linked to the state of its hard infrastructure. If poorer countries are to adapt to climate harms by constructing robust housing, hospitals, sewage systems, road and rail, they will need emissions-intensive steel, concrete and oil. Should the rich world use its power to influence development choices? Naomi Klein's beguiling account of collective struggle against elite extractivists pretends that there is no tension between human flourishing and ecological protection and elides the question of which technologies a population of eight billion people will use to supply food, shelter, health care and travel in a post-capitalist future. Addressing these challenges really will require collective struggle. Third-world communities are already rising up and demanding better standards of living and more equal energy access. As they do so, their allies in the rich world should be mobilizing to increase public investment in low-carbon innovation so that these expectations can be satisfied without compounding climate harms. Attempting to block the third world's rise would be both monstrous, given the deprivation in which the majority of the world's population still live, and stupid, because they will demand their time in the sun regardless.

Back in 2006, Harvard psychology professor Daniel Gilbert (2006) wrote an opinion piece provocatively titled 'If Only Gay Sex Caused Global Warming'. Gilbert argued that humans are social animals whose minds are specialized for thinking about people and their intentions, and that we are particularly exercised by threats that prompt disgust, or moral outrage. Conversely, if a story lacks scheming villains, we tend to ignore it. I think this explains why both reactionaries and progressives tell conspiratorial stories. Both the conservatives' fiction of fraudulent scientists bent on 'one-world' government and the progressives' (more plausible) fables of rapacious, extractivist elites serve the same function. We humans are enraged by the thought of immoral, privileged cliques. Without these villains, a slow-burn problem like climate change becomes about as interesting as retirement-planning. So perhaps I shouldn't be too critical of Naomi Klein. Propagandists who spin morally compelling stories expand public interest in climate change. Although their arguments are flawed, the partisan outrage they inspire may be a necessary stage in societal reckoning with a complex challenge. If we hope, however, to take effective climate action, then we also need narratives that connect to the main feature of the problem: that the technologies that enable modern lives also inadvertently imperil the planet.

Social psychology also tells us that people are generally much more likely to acknowledge the existence of a threat if they believe that others have caused it. Consider the 2015 Paris Agreement's aspirational target of limiting warming to 1.5°C. This goal was always a fantasy whose adoption suggests a collective desire to avoid difficult truths. Even if all emissions ceased today, warming might eventually exceed 1.5°C (Hansen et al. 2008). The more ambitious 2°C target now also looks practically unfeasible. Full implementation of the Paris Agreement pledges would bridge only about twenty-two percent of the gap between our current emissions trajectory and a pathway consistent with limiting this century's warming to 2°C (UNFCCC 2015b, p. 44). At the time of writing, no major developed economy is on track to meet even these feeble pledges (Victor et al. 2017). If we must acknowledge that temperature rises in the vicinity of 3°C by 2100 are now likely (with more warming in the twenty-second century), it feels better to blame this on a nefarious elite than to accept our collective failure. The reality is more unsettling. When I fly from Sydney to Melbourne to visit family at Christmas, when a rice farmer seeds a methane-emitting paddy, or when builders pour the concrete foundations and erect the steel girders of a new hospital, we intend no harm. Yet, climate change arises as an unintended side-effect of each of these well-meaning actions.

'Dangerous climate change' is now such a familiar phrase that we generally pay it little attention. In the near-term, many climate harms will be hard to distinguish from the everyday atrocities created by global inequality. People who lack access to high-quality shelter and health care are always the most vulnerable to extreme weather events, crop failures, infectious disease and floods. Already there are incremental shifts in these harms that reflect the worsening climate. In time, impacts will become obvious to richer communities too – especially as cities such as Venice and Miami battle rising seas. Even as the impacts worsen, however, the underlying process of climate change is unlikely to become a key focus. People will always be preoccupied with immediate concerns like employment, education, health care and costs of living. When we confront unseasonal wildfires, droughts and flooding cities, political focus is likely to turn to emergency measures and local resilience rather than to reducing global emissions. If the very worst climate scenarios eventuate, in which melting permafrost in Canada, Russia and Greenland release trapped methane and trigger runaway warming, we will be concerned only with survival.

And so we arrive at a tragic dilemma. On the one hand, warming has the potential to imperil the entire human enterprise (most other species are already suffering at our hands). On the other hand, climate change seems likely to remain a secondary political concern. Current policies suggest the Anthropocene will see planetary conditions quite unlike those under which our species evolved. The 'Anthropocene' is a controversial term that refers to a geological epoch in which human activities have become a dominant force shaping our planetary environment. Debate surrounds whether the Anthropocene is a helpful concept, and when the proposed epoch commenced. When atmospheric chemist Paul Crutzen and limnologist Eugene Stoermer (2000) proposed the term, they suggested it should be dated from the Industrial Revolution, owing to the increased use of fossil fuels that began at this time. Today, there can be little debate that human activities are inadvertently reshaping the planet's biomes and climate. Our challenge is to place our ecological impacts under democratic control.

Outline of the Argument

In searching for a politics that might effectively respond to climate change, this book advances three arguments. First, I outline the case for states to take on the mission of driving low-carbon innovation. Historically, innovation has been only a peripheral concern of social theory. Today, democratizing and accelerating the pace of technological change is an essential element of any effective response to Anthropocene challenges. Ultimately, low-carbon technologies need to become so attractive that they are widely deployed even under governments that repudiate Green values. While policy instruments like carbon prices are valuable, they are politically fragile. As the election of the Trump Administration has made clear, wider political currents will not always advance climate change mitigation. How, then, to achieve this accelerated technological progress? I argue that the state is the only actor with the capacity and social mandate to take on such a role, and that climate activists should make a demand for innovation central to their work.

   This first argument is by no means innovative. The necessity of low-carbon innovation has been recognized by the IPCC (Somanathan et al. 2014, p. 1178), and by a wide variety of scholars (e.g. Garnaut 2008; Prins and Rayner 2007; Victor 2011; Brook et al. 2016) and public intellectuals (Asafu-Adjaye 2015; Gates 2015). Nevertheless, many Green activists are hostile towards technologically oriented environmental arguments, such as those advanced by ecomodernists. Therefore the book's second theme addresses ecomodernism's political character and prospects. I argue that ecomodernism is best understood as a *social democratic* response to global ecological challenges. Social democracy is an ideology that advocates state regulation and intervention in a capitalist economy in order to promote equality, human development and other shared public interests. Ecomodernists, like most social democrats, are materialists in the sense that their concern for human welfare includes a focus on material comfort. Today, this materialism has been rejected by many Greens and consequently, ecomodernists' advocacy of traditional progressive values can seem conservative. The book's third argument emerges from an effort to extend ecomodernism by critiquing it against its own social-democratic and humanist values. Chapters 5 and 6 argue that if 'universal human flourishing' is to be possible during an era of mounting climate harms, then ecomodernism's social agenda will need to be broadened into a vision of 'global social democracy'. Universal provision of social services and global democratic control over earth systems governance will be needed.

The book thus has a dual purpose. First, it seeks to rethink whether social democratic principles can support global human flourishing in the Anthropocene. Second, it critically examines the connections between ecomodernism, social democracy and other strands of progressive thought. Specifically, I advance these goals by (1) outlining key drivers and threats associated with the climate crisis; (2) situating ecomodernism politically and connecting ecomodernist thinking with contemporary debates over social democracy, development and democratizing global governance; and (3) identifying emergent practices of ecomodernism and sources of momentum towards an ecomodernist future. While I am broadly sympathetic to ecomodernism, this book aspires to produce a critical reframing of ecomodernist ideas that connects them more explicitly with social democratic thought. My aim is to develop ideas that might help guide progressive climate policy and activism.

Innovation and Ecomodernism

How should social democrats respond to climate change? Warming has placed new burdens on governments and added impetus to calls for a Greening of the nation-state. To date, however, climate mitigation has not generally been seen to require a fundamental change to the state's role in society. Governments have used the same policy tool-kit developed for responses to local environmental challenges such as air pollution: they have priced carbon, raised efficiency standards and subsidized the deployment of renewable energy. These measures have proven woefully inadequate. The carbon-intensity of global energy supply is almost the same today as it was in 1990. Owing to the growth of the global economy, however, global CO_2 emissions from fossil fuels in 2017 were 57% higher than in 1990.[1] Keeping in mind that our goal must be to achieve net zero emissions, the scorecard from the first three decades of climate policy-making is derisory (IPCC 2014a).

Fossil fuels still support virtually every economic activity, and supply around 79% of global energy. Since we lack adequate zero-carbon replacements for many technologies, and since major industrial emitters are well organized, political constraints have always weakened carbon pricing signals, while the private sector has declined to take on the enormous risks of financing breakthrough innovation. These factors suggest that our best path towards a good Anthropocene lies in a more distinctly social democratic response: *states* must drive the innovation and deployment of breakthrough technologies that completely transform the economy's technological metabolism. The challenge is immense.

---

[1] Figures drawn from the BP Statistical Review of World Energy; in 1990 world fossil fuel emissions were 21,295 million tonnes and in 2017, 33,444 million tonnes. Data available at: https://www.bp.com/content/dam/bp/en/corporate/excel/energy-economics/statistical-review/bp-stats-review-2018-all-data.xlsx

Innovations must make clean energy universally abundant, reduce GHG emissions arising from agriculture, industry and transport, achieve negative emissions, and begin to rectify wider environmental harms.

Ecomodernist ideas are controversial among environmentalists. This often surprises outsiders, who correctly note that ecomodernists and traditional environmentalists share most of the same concerns. Nevertheless, some respected Green political theorists advocate 'resisting ecomodernism' and describe its call for states to deliberately transform the technological metabolism of human society as a defence of neoliberalism (Fremaux and Barry 2019, p. 18 n. 1; see also Collard et al. 2015). Since neoliberalism commonly refers to an ideology that advocates a smaller role for government in the economy, and since ecomodernism's central argument is for a larger innovation-driving state, this critique seems confused. The underlying claim, however, seems to be that corporate capitalism is intrinsically ecocidal, and so any climate response that is not explicitly anti-capitalist is doomed to failure (Wright and Nyberg 2015, p. 167). A second set of critiques focuses on ecomodernists' desire to universalize human freedom and material prosperity. Some radical ecologists argue that human freedoms rest on the domination of non-human natures; so, they argue, we must curtail these freedoms and reduce human populations (Crist 2015). An alternative Green perspective decries the waste and over-consumption of Western culture and argues, with a neat obfuscation of agency, that the poor world should choose a different path. In this view, ecomodernists' support for third-world peoples' entitlement to an equal share of modernity ignores the ecological reality of 'limits to growth' and reflects contempt for non-Western cultures.

Chapters 1 and 2 seek to think through the issues that are at stake in disputes between 'Greens' and ecomodernists, and to promote some degree of reconciliation or at least respectful disagreement among progressive environmentalists. Although there is some empirical evidence of divergence between the worldviews of ecomodernists and other cohesive Green ideologies (Nisbet 2014; Bernstein and Szuster 2018), environmentalism has always encompassed a diverse group of movements (see Gottlieb 2005) and lines of contention shift over time. Nevertheless, since my interest concerns the relationship between environmentalism and innovation, I'll tend to emphasize these divisions. I'll generally use the term 'environmentalism' to refer to a general concern for the environmental protection of species and ecosystems which is shared by Greens and ecomodernists. I'll use the term 'Green' to refer to political movements that advocate mending the rift between humans and nature by choosing humble, small-scale technologies, reducing consumption and re-localizing production. Ecomodernism, by contrast, is a form of environmentalism that rejects Green localism and which advocates reducing human impacts on the non-human world through the intensification of production and continuous technological innovation.

In Chapter 2 I argue that ecomodernism's role in the contemporary environmental debate in some ways parallels the social democrats' position in twentieth-century conflicts with Marxist, fascist, conservative and laissez-faire alternatives. Like earlier generations of social democrats, ecomodernists promote a 'third way' between laissez-faire and anti-capitalism, and they defend humanist ideals of scientific reasoning, liberal democracy and equality against post-liberal strands of environmentalism. Indeed, just as the pioneering social democratic thinker Eduard Bernstein's close association with Marx and Engels made it harder for early Marxists to ignore Bernstein's social democratic ideas, the involvement of iconic Green figures like James Hansen and Stewart Brand has provided some cover for ecomodernism. I argue, however, that ecomodernism also has much to learn from its critics. Given that disagreements among climate activists encompass both differing values and rival accounts of the facts, Chapter 3 seeks to review some of these debates. It argues that warming in excess of 2°C is now nearly inevitable, that stabilizing temperatures at any level will require considerable technological innovation, and that although responsibility for climate change is radically unequal, blame cannot solely be attributed to a tiny elite. Instead it is the technological metabolism of modernity – in which both ordinary first-world people and the developing world middle class are implicated – that drives climate harms.

Ecomodernism's focus on innovation is sometimes described as elitist. Many climate activists are doubly sceptical because an innovation-led climate response has often been advanced by conservatives as a cover for inaction. Others complain that a focus on technology is 'apolitical', since it casts 'scientists, inventors and engineers' as the only relevant actors in climate politics (Hamilton 2015). Chapter 4 explores the politics of innovation, and argues that innovation is never apolitical; it destroys some people's lifeworlds even as it creates new possibilities. Innovation's distributional consequences mean that it almost always faces political resistance. However, the trade union movement's campaign for a 'Just Transition' for coal-miners and power station workers provides a valuable example, albeit at a local scale, of how innovation can be incorporated into a programme of progressive change. The Just Transition campaign recognizes that even the most socially beneficial forms of innovation can have devastating consequences for displaced workers, and that deliberate social policy is needed to embed innovation in a wider political bargain (Sweeney 2012). Ecomodernism's great challenge is to develop forms of solidarity that enable progressive social and technological change to be pursued on a global scale. While ecomodernism repudiates many of the Green movement's prescriptions, it is also a product of Green political thought. Writing before the climate crisis was well understood, Langdon Winner (1986, p. 55), one of the leading Green thinkers on technology, argued that 'society's technical constitution' must be brought under deliberate, critical, democratic control and that we should 'seek to build technical regimes compatible with freedom, social justice, and other key political ends'. Ecomodernists share Winner's aspiration. They argue, however, that it is now the climate crisis rather than the goal of local, participatory democracy that should shape our technological choices.

Rethinking Social Democracy for the Anthropocene

Is social democracy well suited to driving a global techno-logical transition? As Swedish political economist Jenny Andersson has written, social democrats have repeatedly played an active role in bringing new economic configura-tions into existence (Andersson 2009). Yet, the earlier itera-tions of social democratic thought that Andersson describes have all been embedded in national narratives and have responded to national economic and social challenges. Eco-modernism differs in two dimensions. First, its animus is ecological – ecomodernists recognize the potentially cata-strophic threat posed by climate change and seek to reconcile climate governance with global human progress. Second, the ecomodernists' vision is global, rather than national. Although they view high-capacity states as the agents of transformation, ecomodernists are primarily concerned with solving global ecological and developmental challenges. They seek to increase the efficiency of global production systems, promote universal access to plentiful food and energy, and extend greater freedom of movement to all people, not just to members of specific national communi-ties or to first-world elites. This cosmopolitanism begs two questions – am I wrong to characterize ecomodernism as social democratic? And what source of thick solidarity could support a move towards global social democracy?

Ecomodernists reject the idea that capitalism is either the ultimate source or solution to ecological harms. Instead they propose that wealth generated by capitalism should be applied to transforming human society's technological basis. Thus, ecomodernism clearly embraces what political scientist Sheri Berman describes as one of social democracy's central insights: that while capitalism is useful for generating the material prosperity on which a good life can be built, markets should be collectively managed in order to advance societal goals (Berman 2006, p. 211). So far so good. However, social democracy's second distinctive element is its democratic *communitarianism*. Here, ecomodernism's position is slightly contradictory. Certainly, ecomodernists have emphasized that developing countries have the right to choose their own development pathways, even if this means the construction of coal and gas fired power stations that set back global climate action. And they have argued that environmental protection, economic development and global equity are mutually supporting and inseparable goals (Nordhaus and Shellenberger 2007, p. 269). Chapter 5 interrogates these communitarian arguments against 'Green conditionality' and draws out ecomodernism's precursors within the postcolonial movement's call for a *new international economic order* and the integrated development of the globe.

Ecomodernists, however, also call on affluent democracies to prioritize global ecological goals above narrow national economic interests. Is this consistent with communitarian nationalism? Or is communitarian social-democracy ill-suited to Anthropocene challenges? Chapter 6 takes up the challenge of thinking about how the metaphor of global social democracy might guide ecomodernism's climate response. Historically, there have been many highly egalitarian small-scale communities. However, as the size of political units grew through the emergence of city-states, kingdoms and empires, so did inequality. Earlier generations of social democrats discovered how to organize a large, complex society so that it was also egalitarian. They nurtured national, communitarian social bonds which meant that people felt trust and solidarity across the national community, and so gave their support to government policies that promoted equality and universally available public services.

By contrast, climate-linked inequalities arise internationally, and so are quite unlike those that have previously been resolved by social democracies. The key barrier to achieving climate justice arises because predominantly national bonds of social solidarity do not correspond with the distribution of climate impacts. The world's most vulnerable people – overwhelmingly living in the formerly colonized 'third world' – are the primary victims of climate change. However, the actors who are most responsible and who have the greatest capacity to avert the climate crisis, are affluent states whose people are least vulnerable. Over time, climate harms will amplify global inequality. Since there are no global democratic political institutions, and only minimal bonds of communal solidarity outside the state, ecomodernists face profound questions. Can national communities be motivated to prioritize global goals? Can universal human flourishing be secured amid worsening climate harms? Can global ecological governance be brought under global democratic control?

Chapter 6 argues that the goal of universal human flourishing necessitates a global social democratic compact. To put this another way, ecomodernism will be an elitist, Western project if it primarily focuses on climate-change mitigation and environmental protection. First, this is because climate-linked water shortages, sea-level rise, crop failures and extreme weather events are already imposing severe hardship on vulnerable populations. Those people whose access to the benefits of modernity is now most tenuous are at greatest risk of being re-impoverished. If ecomodernism responds only to the technological causes of climate change without also addressing these climate harms, then its commitment to *universal* human flourishing is insubstantial. Advancing universal human freedom in the Anthropocene will only be possible if social services such as health care, education and built infrastructure are provided universally; when states are unable to do so, the international community should offer assistance. Given that climate change is primarily caused by the lifestyles of the richest 20% of humanity, such assistance is consistent with widely accepted standards of fairness. In the language of normative theory, climate change is creating a 'global community of fate' that generates obligations of justice: richer people have obligations to compensate and assist the vulnerable people they have indirectly harmed. However since social democrats prioritize *political* self-determination, they will also seek to preserve national autonomy.

Throughout this book I use the term 'third world' to describe the developing and (in nearly all cases) formerly colonized countries of Asia, Africa and South America that are now more commonly called 'the global South'. I use this slightly old-fashioned sounding term for two reasons. First, given the diversity of wealth and historical experience of non-OECD countries, catch-all phrases such as 'the global South' or 'developing world' promote a reductive view of politics. Where I am trying to emphasize these distinctions, I use the World Bank's classification of low-income, lower-middle-income, middle-income and high-income countries. However, I also use the term 'third world' to describe middle-income countries because, as Chapter 5 explores, ecomodernist developmentalism resonates with aspects of the anti-colonial Third World Project which, historically, has been the most significant political movement that aspired to a world in which all people would live modern lives.

The idea that the future should be democratically chosen rather than allowed to emerge from unmediated market interactions has always been a central element of social democracy. This is what Sheri Berman has termed 'the primacy of politics' as against 'the primacy of economic forces' (Berman 2006). Still, how can this social democratic principle be applied today when many decisions about ecological governance are inherently global, but politically significant sources of identity are mostly national, and the institutions of global governance are far from legitimate or democratic? The growing literature on 'earth systems governance', a term which refers to efforts to steer societies' responses to environmental change, shows that the absence of democratic institutions is not necessarily an insurmountable problem. Governance may be achieved by networks of non-state actors, through multilateral cooperation or by 'nested' institutions (Ostrom 2012). However, ecomodernist advocates of universal human flourishing must advocate at least for thicker global institutions that ensure equal representation to all people.

While scholars have shown some interest in ideas of 'progressive globalization', 'global democracy' and 'earth systems governance', these debates have often failed to acknowledge the full gravity of the ecological crisis (see Jacobs et al. 2003; Rockström et al. 2009). For example, the dominant discourse within the earth systems governance literature concerns efforts to limit human ecological impacts by controlling GHG emissions, resource harvesting, nitrogen run-off, habitat destruction and so on. The goal of these efforts is commonly understood as being to remain within ecological boundaries that delimit the 'safe operating space' for humanity. However, at least in the case of climate change, it is clear that we are already outside this safe operating space and are hastening into the unknown (Rockström et al. 2009). Some now advocate research into solar geoengineering techniques such as ocean cloud brightening to help negate some of the impacts of climate change (Reynolds 2014). Most environmentalists reject geoengineering as they correctly believe that preventing climate change would be preferable to masking its symptoms. Unfortunately, anthropogenic warming is now a reality, so the choice we face is not between virtuous mitigation and hubristic geoengineering, but between different bundles of harms. In Chapter 6 I point out that the well-meaning Western assumptions that solar geoengineering should be prohibited conceals a cruel double standard. Western opponents are insisting that rules governing intentional actions through which developing countries might protect their people from climate harms, should be very different from the rules governing the unintentional actions that create those harms. Instead, I argue that since developing world people will be most affected by climate change, developing countries should dominate decision-making about solar geoengineering.

While the pathway to enhancing the democratic legitimacy of global climate governance will doubtless be long, the two elements of a global social democratic compact are likely to be mutually reinforcing. Historically, high levels of social trust have arisen within societies following the expansion of social services rather than the other way around. It thus seems probable that creation of a global social safety net might prompt similar advances in international trust. Greater social trust could in turn be conducive to the deepening of global political institutions. Implausible as the idea of global social democracy sounds, its infeasibility is a consequence of social and political barriers, rather than material limits. For example, average global per capita GDP is today higher than was Great Britain's per capita income in 1948, when the National Health Service was established. Yet, there is also a real possibility that ecomodernist strategies of innovation and intensification will be successfully utilized to protect affluent people from the worst impacts of climate change in the absence of a wider social vision. Moreover, it would be easy to interpret China's current development trajectory as an instance of authoritarian innovation-led environmental governance. An authoritarian ecomodernism, or one that fails to democratize innovation and earth systems governance will fail to achieve ecomodernism's vision of universal human flourishing (Symons and Karlsson 2018).

Finally, a note: this is a book about ecomodernist ideas rather than about ecomodernists. Since my focus is on climate change, I have emphasized the ecomodernist ideas that are most relevant to climate policy. In Chapter 2 I offer a synopsis of key ecomodernist ideas that primarily draws on the Breakthrough Institute's publications and on the earlier co-authored works of Ted Nordhaus and Michael Shellenberger. In January 2016 Shellenberger left the Breakthrough Institute and founded a new, more aggressively pro-nuclear organization named Environmental Progress.

Environmental Progress and its ideology of 'atomic humanism' are not discussed in this book. Although I have deliberately not investigated the factors that led Shellenberger to leave the Breakthrough Institute, the two organizations are adopting divergent policy-positions and styles. In 2018 Shellenberger welcomed the Trump Administration's decision to provide policy support for both nuclear and coal-fired generation, while the Breakthrough Institute condemned the move (Shellenberger 2018). Shellenberger argued that the Trump Administration policy would bolster nuclear production much more than coal, and therefore would provide a net climate benefit. Even if Shellenberger's maths is accurate, I view offering support for coal-fired power or a climate-denying President as a strategic and ethical lapse. Rather than in such specific debates, however, my interest is in the conceptual underpinnings of innovation-focused environmentalism.

1

The Thirty Years' Crisis

Ecomodernists are often called techno-optimists. The term puzzles me. Most ecomodernists are pessimistic about the likely trajectory of climate change – they think warming far above 2°C is now inevitable. Most are pessimistic about the potential for existing technologies to achieve decarbonization – they argue that we lack mature technologies to eliminate emissions from industry, transport and agriculture. They are pessimistic about proposals for intermittent renewable energy such as wind and solar to supply all our power, as they think a stable grid requires sources of dispatchable firm capacity. They worry that the proven sources of zero-carbon dispatchable electricity – nuclear and hydroelectric power – lack public support and so are unlikely to be constructed at scale. They think it improbable that whole communities will give up aviation, meat, dairy, cars, steel, concrete or choice over family size in order to avert climate harms. Finally, ecomodernists are pessimistic about the prospects for international cooperation – they doubt that states will agree to high carbon prices, to binding emissions pledges, or to overcoming the limitations of local intermittent generation by constructing a planet-straddling hyper-grid.

So why are ecomodernists called optimists? I think it's because, despite the real risk that climate change will prove catastrophic, they argue that through the wise use of science a 'good Anthropocene' could be possible. Whereas many Greens offer narratives of decline and promote a return to more humble technologies, ecomodernists point to continuing advances in human welfare and urge us to keep faith with technology and science. Given the tendency for scientific advances to bring unintended consequences, ecomodernism's position does involve an optimistic leap of faith. However, some ecomodernists have described this optimism as strategic; they believe positivity enables progressive change. Moreover, ecomodernists' promotion of technological innovation reflects a comparative judgement. Far from believing that technology will unlock a utopian future, they propose that a climate response that draws on scientific ingenuity alongside social change is likely to achieve more than strategies that reject 'hubristic' technologies and interventions in nature out of hand. Finally, ecomodernists can seem optimistic because, although they recognize the deep inequalities of the contemporary world, they insist that human welfare is advancing steadily. Here, ecomodernists 'hold two ideas at the same time: that bad things are going on in the world, but that many things are getting better' (Rosling et al. 2018, p. 248). Some people are critical of this 'celebration' of progress. Given the depth of international equality they believe it is premature and self-serving for Western elites to express optimism. I am sympathetic to this critique. However, I think the more important debate concerns how we might accelerate advances in human welfare while also preserving a habitable planet. Ecomodernists offer some important insights into reconciling these desirable yet potentially contradictory goals.

Before we consider ecomodernism's response to these challenges, I first want to set the scene by outlining some of the key trends shaping global climate politics, some of the systematic ways in which we might misperceive these trends, and some of the prior commitments that have shaped the Green movement's climate response. This chapter will then conclude by arguing that Green scepticism concerning innovation, large-scale technology and the state, has created a barrier to effective climate action. This is not to deny that the Green cultural critique has real value. Where Green movements have been influential they have often created more inclusive, safe and resilient communities. However, Green thinking has proven more valuable for achieving qualitative improvements in wellbeing, than for guiding climate responses. Effective climate action must enable a massive expansion in the third world's access to modern energy alongside an unprecedent technological transformation of the global economy. Despite the slogan 'think globally, act locally', the Green response to climate change has rarely seemed commensurate with the scale of this challenge.

A Temperature Check

It's now been three decades since climate change gained a central place on the global political agenda. In 1988 world leaders met at the Toronto International Conference on the Changing Atmosphere and pledged to cut GHG emissions by 20% by 2005. That same year, 1988, the Intergovernmental Panel on Climate Change (IPCC) was established and Professor James Hansen, head of the NASA Goddard Institute for Space Studies, testified to a US Congressional committee that climate change was already occurring. World leaders were thus fully briefed on climate risks. How much progress have we made in the ensuing three decades? Indulge me by taking a pen and noting your answers to the following questions:

1. In order to halt continuing human-induced climate change, global GHG emissions will eventually need to be brought to zero. Between 1988 and 2017,

annual global carbon dioxide emissions from fossil
fuels:
(a) decreased by about 60%; (b) remained stable;
(c) increased by about 60%.

2. In 2017, what proportion of global final energy
   consumption (for electricity, heating, transport,
   industry etc.) was sourced from fossil fuels?[2]
   (a) roughly 40%; (b) roughly 66%; (c) roughly
      80%.

3. About one quarter of global GHG emissions come
   from electricity production. In 2017, which of the
   following near zero-carbon sources generated the
   most electricity:
   (a) hydroelectricity; (b) nuclear; (c) wind; (d) solar
      photovoltaic.

4. At the end of 2017, solar provided what percentage
   of global electricity production?
   (a) less than 2%; (b) less than 10%; (c) about 20%.

5. In 2017, non-OECD (developing) countries
   accounted for what proportion of global CO_2 emissions from fossil fuels:
   (a) less than 10%; (b) about 33%; (c) over 60%.

6. In 2017 coal accounted for 27.6% of global final
   energy consumption. In 1988 coal's share was:
   (a) about 50% higher; (b) roughly the same; (c)
      about 50% lower.

7. Between 1988 and 2018, the proportion of people
   living in extreme poverty worldwide has:
   (a) increased by about two thirds; (b) stayed about
      the same; (c) decreased by about two thirds.

---

[2] According to BP's data, fossil fuels supplied 86% of energy
sourced from tradeable fuels and renewable energy generation
in 2017. If we also include traditional biomass, fossil fuel's share
of world energy is about 79.5% (Ren21 2018, p. 31).

8. After adjusting for price differences, the majority
   of the world's population have incomes of:
   (a) less than $2 per day; (b) less than US $10 per
   day; (c) more than $10 per day?[3]

When I ask my students at Macquarie University, Sydney,
they answer these questions according to a fairly consistent
pattern. Although deeply pessimistic about climate inaction
generally, they think renewable energy is making better
progress than is actually the case, and they underestimate
progress towards eliminating extreme poverty, although
most students guess correctly that a majority of people
earn less than $10 per day. I helpfully order the sources of
low-carbon energy from highest (hydroelectricity) to lowest
(solar PV). However, my students typically identify solar
(or sometimes nuclear) as the largest source. In fact, hydroelectricity's 16.4% share of global electricity supply is more
than double that of wind (5.6%) and solar (1.9%) combined. I suspect my students' exaggerated perceptions of
renewable energy's progress partly reflect the Green movement's enthusiasms. While it is true that wind and solar
are being deployed at record rates, their success has not
yet halted the growth of fossil fuels. Meanwhile, significant
advances in human welfare are connected to the fact that
nearly all of the increases in emissions are occurring *outside*
the OECD. Consequently, most countries and most people
are now much better placed to withstand climate harms.
Thus, the three decades since 1988 have seen both rapidly
increasing emissions and unprecedented advances in human
material welfare. Arguably these trends define our era.

Growing emissions, declining poverty and rising national
inequality are not simply emergent properties that have
arisen unintentionally through the aggregation of individual
self-interested behaviour. They reflect deliberate political
choices. On the one hand, affluent communities have been

---

[3] Answers: (1)c; (2)c; (3)a; (4)a; (5)c; (6)b; (7)c; (8)b.

reluctant to price carbon or invest in low-carbon innovation; on the other hand, third-world communities are intensely motivated to achieve greater energy access. In 2014 the world's second and fourth most populous countries both saw dramatic elections. International media have portrayed Narendra Modi as a right-wing Hindu nationalist with a chequered human rights record, and Joko Widodo (Jokowi) as a comparatively liberal reformer who, having been born in a slum, was challenging the Indonesian elite's stranglehold on power. However, these two leaders' electoral platforms had one thing in common – they both promised a dramatic expansion of electricity generation and grid connections. To be sure, both leaders advocated a growing role for renewable energy. Prime Minister Modi has gained a reputation as a solar enthusiast, while President Widodo's achievements include reforming regressive fuel subsidies that at times have consumed as much as one quarter of the national budget. However, fossil fuels remain central to each country's development. For example, in 2017, coal consumption increased by 4.8% in India and 7.4% in Indonesia (BP 2018). With per capita electricity consumption well under one tenth of that in affluent countries like the United States, Australia or Singapore, no one should be surprised if ordinary Indians and Indonesians prioritize accessing modern energy over climate mitigation.[4] Unfortunately, the consequence is increasing GHG emissions. Although India and Indonesia are both what the World Bank terms 'lower-middle-income' countries, they are also much too powerful to have their energy choices determined by outsiders.

Any effective global climate response needs to reflect an understanding that the era of Western dominance is over, and that the formerly impoverished communities of the Third World Coalition are demanding their time in the sun.

---

[4] IEA Atlas of Energy, http://energyatlas.iea.org/#!/tellmap/-1118783123/1

Perhaps the most promising present-day development is that the global middle-class is swelling rapidly as manufacturing and service industries expand outside the OECD. However, even after decades of steady progress, there are still around four billion people who earn less than $8 a day (adjusted for purchasing power parity) and whose current climate impact is minimal. As more and more people achieve modest prosperity and lead longer lives, their climate impact will grow. This is why I'm not persuaded by the argument that an effective climate response should focus on economic *de*-growth and reduced consumption. If we were only discussing the world's richest billion people such strategies might be valuable, as we in the rich world could probably lead happier lives while consuming less climate-damaging products (for example, substituting vegetables for meat and driving less). But climate responses need to have a global perspective which takes account of the billions of people whose basic material needs are not yet adequately met.

The Thirty Years' Crisis: the Era of Knowing Climate Inaction

In September 1939, Edward Hallett Carr, an English foreign office official turned scholar, published a book that has become a classic text in the discipline of International Relations. *The Twenty Years' Crisis: 1919–1939* examined the League of Nations' failure to manage international tensions during the two decades prior to the outbreak of the Second World War. Although Carr's concern was with national security, his analysis concerned a general tendency for policies to be built on utopian aspirations and naive hopes rather than on an accurate understanding of underlying forces. Carr wrote that 'when the human mind begins to exercise itself in some fresh field, an initial stage occurs in which the element of wish or purpose is overwhelmingly strong' (Carr 2001, p. 6). Carr was writing at a time when the community of states had only recently gained the technological capacity for *intentional* self-destruction, and he was interested in the kinds of political institutions and strategies that might prevent recourse to war. In climate change the challenge is a little different. We have now gained the technological capacity for *unintentional* self-destruction, and our search is for global political institutions and strategies that might govern the unintended consequences of economic activity. Just as Carr described the inter-war period as a 'twenty years' crisis', we could view the three decades since the Intergovernmental Panel on Climate Change was created in 1988 as a thirty years' crisis for climate governance.

Once again, the international community's failures reflect an excessive 'element of wish'. To date, global mitigation efforts have failed even to stop annual growth in emissions. In the 1980s, global emissions grew at an average rate of 1.9%. Growth fell to about 1.1% in the 1990s as energy efficiency improved in China and as the former USSR deindustrialized. However, China's rapid coal-based industrialization drove emission increases of an astonishing 3.1% per year in the twenty-first century's first decade. Now, in the 2010s, we are doing a little better. Average growth of 1.1% per year between 2010 and 2017 approximates that of the 1990s (see Peters et al. 2017). Why this inaction? I argue that the central problem has been a failure at every level – from environmental activism to diplomatic negotiations – to understand climate change as a *technological* challenge, requiring the development and deployment of entirely new zero-carbon technologies. Instead, climate change has been treated like any less challenging environmental problem, by negotiating international agreements that set national targets.

If GHG emissions were akin to nuclear warheads, and reductions could be negotiated via reciprocal pledges, this approach might work. If your country has 1,000 warheads and mine has 500, we might both agree on a 90% reduction down to 100 and 50. If we figure out monitoring and compliance mechanisms, we could shake hands confident that our diplomacy has made progress. The same logic can be applied in environmental negotiations, but only if a *technological* solution is at hand. For example, ozone layer depletion was successfully tackled via a similar framework of reciprocal pledges in the late 1980s. States committed to a gradual phase-out of ozone depleting substances (initially 50% cuts under the 1987 Montreal Protocol), 'essential uses' exemptions guaranteed that costly cuts could be avoided, and cleverly designed incentive schemes ensured near-universal participation (Victor 2011, pp. 43–7). When the United Nations Framework Convention on Climate Change (UNFCCC) was negotiated in 1992, negotiators had the same model in mind. However, the climate challenge is entirely different to ozone layer depletion (or to nuclear disarmament). The Montreal Protocol on Substances that Deplete the Ozone Layer's success was possible only because technological alternatives were available or could be readily developed by the chemical companies without government assistance. Climate negotiations face a higher hurdle – how to eliminate emissions when, in many parts of the economy there is no available technological substitute?

If climate change were a faster-moving challenge, the need for innovation might have been more obvious. During the West African Ebola epidemic of 2013–16, for instance, no-one questioned that state funded research would be a priority. By contrast, innovation policy has been strangely peripheral to climate negotiations. Moreover, the delay between GHG emissions and their environmental impacts has allowed a gap to open between talk, decisions, and the implementation of climate policy (Geden 2016). International agreements have come one after another – the UNFCCC (1992); Kyoto Protocol (1997); Copenhagen Accord (2012); Paris Agreement (2015) – and all the while global emissions have crept steadily higher. Just as the bold emission cuts pledged at Toronto in 1988 have faded into memory, so might the Paris Agreement's promise to keep warming well below 2°C. Successive generations of politicians have made ambitious long-term pledges for which they will never be held to account. A few countries, such as Sweden and the United Kingdom, have made real progress towards reducing locally sourced emissions. However, their nationally focused thinking means they have made only a minimal contribution to developing globally scalable responses. Although there have been a few exceptions such as the Obama Administration's initiative, *Mission Innovation*, most troubling has been the general failure to invest in research and innovation that would make decarbonization politically and socially feasible.

Another problem befuddling climate politics is the tendency to compare our performance not with where we need to get to, but with how we did last year. We pat ourselves on the back when we install more solar panels, build more electric cars or stabilize our emissions from one year to the next. However, if our goal is to halt warming we must bring emissions to zero. Comparative targets are a distraction from this goal. Consider how some media reports celebrated the stabilization of global emissions between 2014 and 2016 – stable emissions mean that CO_2 is accumulating in the atmosphere at a roughly constant rate. Another misleading milestone arrived in 2015, when installation of new renewable *capacity* exceeded that of new fossil fuels *capacity* for the first time (Randall 2015). Since 'capacity' is a measure of maximum potential generation (i.e. generation when the sun is shining, or when a coal plant is operating at full capacity) comparing installed capacity tells us very little about energy generation. Unfortunately, electricity generated by fossil fuels is continuing to expand. In order to limit warming at any level, accumulation of warming gases in the atmosphere must end, and global emissions of greenhouse gases must zero out. Only then will atmospheric concentrations of greenhouse gases stabilize and, through the slow process of natural absorption, start to *fall*. Every year that passes in which we fail to cut emissions, the goal of avoiding dangerous climate change slips further from our grasp.

One way to guess future emissions is by measuring 'emission commitments'. If all the existing CO_2-emitting power infrastructure world-wide continued to operate for its expected lifespan, what emissions would result? One 2018 analysis suggested that if currently operating generators were not shuttered before the end of their expected lifespan, they would commit the globe to emissions of around 300 $GtCO_2$ (Pfeiffer et al. 2018). Since the quantum of emissions consistent with limiting warming to 1.5°C–2°C is in the vicinity of 240 $GtCO_2$, and since there's a wide variety of emissions sources outside the power sector, these numbers don't inspire confidence. There is also a pipeline of further coal and gas plants planned for construction. The world's dilemma is all the more acute because most of this additional construction is in lower-middle-income countries like India and Indonesia, which are anxious to increase their energy capacity in order to enhance the living standard of their populations. Facilities that are scheduled to be built will almost double future emissions, adding an additional 270 $GtCO_2$ (Pfeiffer et al. 2018). To be sure, the pipeline of coal and gas construction has begun to shrink, and some of the planned infrastructure will probably not be built. Unfortunately, lower-middle-income countries may not have the option of alternatives. Coal and gas plants are still being built at scale and their owners and financiers will be assuming a lifespan of 30–60 years. The inertia associated with built infrastructure is such that even if every country meets the pledges it made as part of the Paris Agreement, global emissions will still be higher in 2030 than today, and temperature rises exceeding 3°C by 2100 would still be likely (UNFCCC 2015b, p. 44).

The IPCC's Fifth Assessment Report included a series of 'carbon budgets'. These budgets were supposed to provide a simple guide for policy-makers by specifying the total amount of carbon that could be emitted while still avoiding 1.5, 2 or 3°C of warming. They suggested that if emissions continued at their current rate (approximately 37 billion tonnes of CO_2 in 2017), the budget that would preserve a two-thirds chance of avoiding 1.5°C warming would be exhausted by around 2021. The budget consistent with 2°C would be blown about fifteen years later. That is to say, even if emissions ceased completely after 2037, warming of around 2°C would still be probable. Of course, you can stretch any budget by economizing. In the case of the 2°C budget, if emissions decline towards zero at a steady rate, the budget will be exhausted only in the 2050s. Yet, since GHG emissions from almost every source are still increasing, it seems unimaginable that we could approach zero emissions in forty years (necessary to avoid 2°C warming) let alone by 2024 (for 1.5°C). As a result, scenarios that limit warming to 2°C almost all require significant negative emissions later in the century. At present there is no mature or socially accepted technology that could achieve negative emissions at the necessary scale. Tree planting or increases in soil-carbon, which in Australia might potentially be achieved by drawing on traditional indigenous farming practices could help (Pascoe 2014). However, the scale of negative emissions needed means these 'natural' strategies alone will be insufficient. The IPCC's reports (2014b, 2018) suggests that, barring miracles or scientific error, warming well in excess of 2°C is now all but inevitable.

Do the IPCC's 'budgets' provide an accurate guide? Several papers published since 2017 have suggested that the remaining carbon budget may be several times larger than the IPCC estimates. Other studies using different assumptions and modelling methods suggest that the 1.5°C target has already been exhausted. Obviously, these perspectives can't all be right. However, they are all scientifically defensible. We may already have blown the 1.5°C budget, or else CO_2 emissions between 2016 and 2100 of up to 475 Gt CO_2 may be possible (Peters 2018, p. 378). The scientific uncertainty concerning a 2°C budget is even greater. Thus, it is possible that this century's warming might be anywhere in a range from extremely challenging (1.5°C) to apocalyptic (>4°C). As a result, some experts now suggest we should abandon the whole carbon budget concept. Since we know that stabilizing the climate at any level will ultimately require bringing global emissions to zero, our goal should be to achieve zero emissions as soon as possible. Glen Peters (2018, p. 378) of Oslo's Center for International Climate Research has argued that:

> [C]arbon budgets are not all that relevant for policy. Carbon budgets are global and need translation to country pathways. Regardless of the carbon budget, emissions need to reach zero between 2050 in 2100 (as specified by the Paris Agreement). An earlier achievement of this goal will lead to lower temperature. And equity requires rich countries to reach zero before poor countries. The carbon budget concept has perhaps served its purpose, time is short.

Taking zero emissions as our target also removes any ambiguity over what level of emissions is acceptable. If an activity creates emissions it must eventually be replaced with a zero-carbon alternative (or eliminated). Consider the International Civil Aviation Organization's 2016 agreement to stabilize aviation emissions after 2020 through gradual efficiency improvements and 'carbon offsets' – most probably tree planting. Such an approach is incommensurate with avoiding dangerous warming as it fails the zero emissions test. The goal – assuming that we do not wish to ban aviation – must be to develop and utilize a zero-carbon jet fuel. One reason I emphasize the zero emissions target is that it makes clear why innovation is so crucial to effective mitigation.

Agreeing on zero emissions as a target doesn't mean that the size of emissions budgets and the level of anticipated warming become irrelevant. As we make decisions about how to adapt to climate change, it is important to have a sense of the likely scale of warming, sea level rise and other harms. For example, my understanding of how emissions are tracking against the carbon budget makes me think that warming of 3°C, which would have catastrophic consequences, is nearly inevitable. My expectations are that the associated sea-level rise will threaten major cities like

Shanghai, Mumbai and Miami and displace tens of millions of people from low-lying areas of countries like Bangladesh later in the century. Given these looming dangers, I've reluctantly concluded that we should carefully consider the possibility of using solar geoengineering to artificially halt warming. It's my deep pessimism about the climate future that leads me to contemplate this hubristic, planetary scale intervention. I would take a different view if I thought our carbon budget were larger.

An Era of Human Flourishing

In the three decades since 1988, little progress has been made towards averting climate change. However, the era of knowing climate inaction has been a time of unprecedented human flourishing. In the three decades to 2018, child mortality rates have roughly halved, the proportion of the global population living in extreme poverty (under $1.90 per day) has dropped from about 37% to about 10%, global literacy rates have lifted from about 68% to about 83%, and as China has pursued coal-fired industrialization, the proportion of Chinese people living in extreme poverty has dropped from around two in every three people (66%), to around one in every fifty (2%) (World Bank 2018). Chinese GDP per capita has lifted from around US$318 in 1990 to around $US7328 in 2017. Thanks largely to the rise of China and East Asia, global income inequality has declined even as inequality has increased in many individual countries (Milanovic 2011).

As a result of this rapid progress, communities are today much better placed to adapt to climate harms. Discussion of climate adaptation often focuses on physical infrastructure, such as sea walls and buildings that can withstand extreme weather events. However, improvements in health care are equally vital as they boost resilience against a wide variety of climate threats. For example, floods are worsening and in relatively poor countries like Bangladesh and

Pakistan, floods are routinely followed by outbreaks of infectious disease. As these countries grow richer, improved public health responses and storm water management will begin to address these challenges. Further up the income ladder more expensive forms of adaptation become possible. For example, heat wave deaths are currently increasing in India but declining in the United States even though heat waves are becoming more extreme in both countries. The key difference is the growing prevalence of air conditioning in the United States (Mazdiyasni, et al. 2017). Wealth insulates, literally, against climate harms.

Although the era of knowing climate inaction has been a time of unprecedented human flourishing, gains in human welfare have lagged far behind gains in wealth. Since labour-based income has achieved the vast majority of poverty reduction, those left outside the workforce often remain in poverty. Some people believe that growing inequality is an almost inevitable consequence of rapid growth and industrialization. However, judged against historical standards, the countries now approaching middle-income status have been unusually slow to develop public services and social welfare. As Raj Desai observes:

> In per-capita income terms (in 2005 purchasing power parity adjusted for international dollars), India today is richer than Germany was in the late 1880s, when Bismarck created contributory social insurance programs for all workers. Indonesia is as rich as the United States was in 1935, when it passed the Social Security Act. And China is richer than Britain was in 1948, when it inaugurated the National Health Service. (Desai 2015, p. 315)

The forms of social policy adopted in lower-middle-income countries will play a significant role in determining how fast extreme poverty is eliminated, and how well the poorest communities can withstand climate harms. Although I've celebrated the decline in the proportion of the global population living in extreme poverty, the gap between the level of poverty and our capacity to address it is greater than ever.

Later, I argue that ecomodernism takes up some of the developmentalist economic theories that were advanced by newly decolonized countries in the post- Second-World-War decades. During this era, 'Third World' economic ideology assumed that state development, industrialization and promotion of economic equality were interconnected. For example, the Mexican statesman and economist Raul Prebisch (1962, p. 24) believed that 'inequality of income distribution would inhibit the appearance of mass production industries, an essential step in the process of development'. Today, the economic and social policies of emerging economies are not nearly as focused on equality and poverty reduction. However, there is one area of continuity with 1960s' developmentalism: third-world governments still prioritize economic growth and industrialization over global environmental challenges. In a 1993 article, political scientist Marc Williams identified four positions that the Third World Coalition had been taking to global environmental negotiations since 1972: (1) 'that responsibility for global environmental problems lies with the industrialized countries'; (2) 'that any ameliorative measures taken should not hinder their [the third-world's] development prospect'; (3) that environmental protection be supported through 'free transfer of technology from North to South'; (4) that 'Third World countries demand the transfer of additional resources to enhance environmental protection' (Williams 1993, p. 21). These same four points also offer a decent summary of these states' positions in the subsequent decades of climate negotiations. However, attitudes have softened since 1993, and most developing states now accept a measure of shared responsibility for environmental challenges (Najam 2005).

Perhaps the biggest change has been in China's role. After it was widely blamed for the failure of the Copenhagen Accord in 2009, China began to nurture a reputation as a responsible environmental citizen. The Chinese party-state is still reluctant to take on binding or verifiable emissions limits, still insists that the West must lead the way in providing international adaptation and mitigation assistance and has become a major funder of international fossil fuel development through its 'belt and road' initiative. However, as the world's largest emitter of greenhouse gases, and self-styled leader of the G77 (the group of countries that Williams refers to as the Third World Coalition), China also acknowledges its responsibilities to limit its own emissions. Indeed, China's Paris agreement pledge for emissions to peak before 2030 has been reasonably well received. For example, the Climate Action Tracker initiative ranks this target as 'highly insufficient' and consistent with warming of between 3 and 4°C, which compares favourably to the US or Russia's 'critically insufficient' scores. Other rising powers have followed China's example – pledging reductions in carbon intensity but emphasizing their right to prioritize economic growth. Nevertheless, developing world leaders still occasionally lapse into an older style of third-world rhetoric. For example, when he was India's chief economic adviser, Arvind Subramanian repeatedly condemned Western efforts to shape India's energy choices as 'carbon imperialism' (Subramanian 2015).

The Failure of Environmental Politics

Considering the thirty years' crisis of global climate inaction, we might ask: is the problem that environmentalism is insufficiently strong, or that it has made the wrong demands? Climate change is such an enormously difficult challenge that our progress would probably have been inadequate with even the wisest strategies. However, I argue that progress has been *slowed* because the Green movement, although presenting as a single-minded proponent of aggressive climate action, actually has a set of prior commitments that it values above climate mitigation. This is not necessarily a criticism. If we are not monsters, we all prioritize other values over climate mitigation. Impoverishment, genocide, infanticide and economic crisis, for example, are all proven paths to reducing GHG emissions.

Serious as climate threats are, they must be balanced against other priorities. However, I think it is useful to distinguish between measures we advocate on account of climate mitigation, and measures that are inspired by our other values. For example, Germany's *Energiewende* (energy transition) policy is often justified with reference to climate change, however the decision to close zero-carbon nuclear power stations before emission intensive coal and lignite, which has driven increases in GHG emissions, is clearly motivated by other concerns.

Environmentalism was already a mature movement with a broad-ranging political agenda when it became apparent that climate change was a paramount environmental challenge. Green thinking began to shift to take account of this new reality in the 1990s. For example, opposition to coal now joined opposition to nuclear power as a key Green concern. Generally though, Greens have responded to climate change by promoting their ideas with renewed urgency, rather than by reconsidering their existing commitments. Given the extent to which Green ideas have come to dominate climate discussion, these Green values – such as disdain for technological innovation and for nuclear power – have had an outsized and negative influence on our entire society's climate response.

The Green response to climate change has certainly been well intended. The problem is that their response – like all human responses to new information – reflects a psychological tendency known as 'confirmation bias' or 'politically motivated reasoning' (Nickerson 1998; Kahan 2015). Humans have a strong tendency to interpret new information in ways that are consistent with their pre-existing beliefs. For example, after discussing her opposition to nuclear power, Naomi Klein reflected on the possibility that she, much like climate deniers, might be 'rejecting possible solutions because they threaten my ideological worldview'. However, she then refuted this possibility, explaining that 'I was propelled into a deeper engagement with it [climate change] partly because I realized it could be a catalyst for forms of social and economic justice in which I already believed' (Klein 2015, p. 50). Although her book is titled *This Changes Everything*, Klein makes clear that climate change has only amplified her existing beliefs.

So, what was it that Greens believed before the arrival of the climate crisis, and why? Modern environmentalism became an influential social force in the 1970s, but this newly influential ideology drew on a wide variety of pre-existing movements and impulses. I'll try to describe how the pre-climate-change Green movement looked by drawing on two landmark texts, Anna Bramwell's *Ecology in the 20th Century* (1990), and Robyn Eckersley's *Environmentalism and Political Theory* (1992). Both books were published just as climate change was becoming a major concern (the term appears in neither index) and both sought to map the tributary streams whose confluence had created the modern 'ecological' or 'ecocentric' movement (both books use this precise metaphor). Bramwell's project was historical. Tracing the ecological movement's origins to German, British and North American thinkers in the second half of the nineteenth century, she identified two distinct strands of Green thought:

> One was an anti-mechanistic, holistic approach to biology, deriving from the German zoologist, Ernst Haeckel. The second strand was a new approach to economics called energy economics. This focused on the problem of scarce and non-renewable resources ... [and] has come to mean the belief that severe or drastic change within [a closed] system ... is seen as wrong. Thus, ecological ideas have come to be associated with the conservation of specific patterns of energy flows. (Bramwell 1990, p. 4)

Bramwell argued that by the late nineteenth century, German ecologists' desire for a 'more "authentic", earth-bound identity' had solidified into a set of anti-mechanistic values that included 'opposition to big institutions and size as an end in itself'. Thus, nineteenth-century ecological thought contained precursors to most of the ideas that have been rearticulated within modern environmentalism. For example, Ernst Haeckel's desire to reform the relations between human society and the natural world, and to show 'reverence before the beauty and order of nature' seems to have been recapitulated in Joanna Macey's argument for the 'greening of the self' (Bramwell 1990, p. 43); the desire to conform to the natural energy flows of biotic systems is reflected in Murray Bookchin's proposal to 'rescale communities to fit the natural carrying capacity of the regions in which they are located' (Bookchin 1989, p. 185); and E. F. Schumacher's book *Small is Beautiful* reprises the critique of mechanistic technology. Asking, '[w]hat is it that we really require from the scientists and technologists?' Schumacher (1973, p. 21) answered, '[w]e need methods and equipment which are – cheap enough so that they are accessible to virtually everyone: suitable for small-scale application; and compatible with man's [sic] need for creativity'. This celebration of 'small-scale', 'non-violent' technology seems to explain why the Green movement embraces some technological advances but not others. The distinction concerns *scale*, or at least, imagined scale. Greens typically embrace solar PV, electric cars and lithium-ion batteries because each technology can take a household-scale form. By contrast, carbon capture and storage, hydroelectric dams and nuclear power are commonly imagined to be inherently big and thus anathema to Green values. Of course, if solar and wind are to account for a substantial proportion of global energy consumption, they will need to be installed at vast scale.

Schumacher describes the inherent 'wisdom in smallness' as emerging from its positive impacts on the 'relationship of man to nature', the greater potential for democratic control, and reduced consequences if things go wrong. He explains that the 'greatest danger invariably arises from the ruthless application, on a vast scale, of partial knowledge such as we are currently witnessing in the application of nuclear energy' (1973, p. 22). Instincts to suspect state power, to prefer autarky (local self-sufficiency) and to reject depersonalizing mechanistic technology were reinforced by the twentieth-century experience. War, holocaust and the threat of thermonuclear destruction all pointed towards the wisdom of technological modesty. During its emergence as an influential movement in the 1970s, Green thinking must have seemed to offer a refuge against the insanity of the Cold War order.

Robyn Eckersley's stocktake of environmental thought was written at the same juncture as Bramwell's but with a different purpose – Eckersley sought to contribute to an explicitly 'ecocentric' politics that integrated its concerns with those of other 'new social movements, particularly those concerning feminism, peace, and Third World aid and development' (1992, p. 20). Since Eckersley was seeking to consolidate the connections between ecocentric and progressive politics, she first carefully acknowledged the commonalities between environmentalism and conservatism. She describes these as including:

> [A]n emphasis on prudence or caution in innovation (especially with respect to technology), the desire to conserve existing things (old buildings, nature reserves, endangered values) to maintain continuity with the past, the use of organic political metaphors, and the rejection of totalitarianism. (Eckersley 1992, p. 21)

While embracing each of these conservative impulses, Eckersley's goal was to deepen the connections between ecologism and emancipatory thought. She wished to confirm ecologism's place on the political left.

Eckersley identified five streams of environmental thought: resource conservation, human welfare ecology, preservationism, animal liberation, and ecocentrism. She divided these into two categories: anthropocentric and ecocentric (ecology focused). However, since her specific interest was in developing emancipatory ecopolitical thought, she described ecocentric impulses most carefully. First, was a belief that the environmental crisis should be understood not only as a matter of survival, but also as a 'crisis of culture' which created cultural opportunities and emancipatory potential.

Eckersley illustrated this point by quoting William Leiss's (1978, p. 112) argument that:

> [E]verything depends upon whether we regard such limits [to growth] as a bitter disappointment or as a welcome opportunity to turn from quantitative to qualitative improvement in the course of creating a conserver society.

Eckersley agreed and noted that:

> Surely, more of us (human and nonhuman) can live richer and fuller lives if humans can become less dependent on this kind of technological infrastructure and the kinds of commodities and lifestyles it offers. (1992, p. 20)

Since emancipatory ecopolitical thinkers viewed culture as the central problem and opposed all forms of domination (including by the state), they also emphasized the revitalization of civil society as a key task of ecocentric politics.

There is much that is attractive in Eckersley's account of emancipatory Green theory, and its opposition to all forms of domination (class, patriarchy, imperialism, racism, totalitarianism, and the domination of nature) explains how Green thinking became allied with a wide variety of progressive movements. However, the Green critique of 'human needs', technology and the state have proven to be detrimental to the Green climate response. Eckersley herself has since argued that the 'Green State' must be recognized as a central agent of environmental transformation (2004, p. 144). Most environmentalists are also at pains to acknowledge the material needs of impoverished people: arguments promoting 'survival emissions', aid and fair trade reflect these commitments. However, scepticism concerning material needs predisposes the Green movement to misunderstand the material scale of climate and energy challenges. Were all of humanity to converge on a standard of living typical of middle-income countries – replete with mattresses for sleeping, cooking stoves, reliable electricity and refrigerators, but excluding Western luxuries like long-distance travel, private washing machines or cars – this would still entail a massive increase in consumption. Finally, Green scepticism concerning large-scale technology has promoted opposition to highly effective decarbonizing tools, such as nuclear power (Cao et al. 2016, p. 548).

Ecomodernists' advocacy of nuclear power as a zero carbon energy source is central to their public image. However, debate over nuclear power is perhaps a distraction from the more urgent need to focus on innovation policy. The belief that existing nuclear technologies can resolve climate change is today scarcely more credible than faith in renewable energy. Even if policy-makers were now single-mindedly to pursue a nuclear-based strategy, it would take at least three decades to eliminate fossil fuels from global electricity supply, and thus eliminate one quarter of global GHG emissions (Qvist and Brook 2015). Such a flawless roll-out of nuclear power might also assist with some industrial and transport emissions. However, political resistance and economic costs mean that any nuclear renaissance will in fact be much more gradual. It is therefore clear that although nuclear power is a valuable decarbonizing tool, it is not a 'magical silver bullet' that can address global climate change.

Nevertheless, if there is any one issue that might destabilize the public association between the Green movement and climate action, it is nuclear power. The near-zero-carbon grids of Sweden and France provide a powerful illustration of nuclear's mitigation potential. In fact, in Finland, some prominent Green politicians and party members have become nuclear advocates. Elsewhere, a small but passionate pro-nuclear climate movement is building – for example, pro-nuclear climate networks have formed among Australian and American university students. Despite these stirrings of support though, the Green movement generally remains opposed. Not only is nuclear a mechanistic, large-scale technology, but it harnesses energy sources that are external to natural ecosystem flows. Naomi Klein touches on these themes where she writes that, far from being a solution, nuclear power represents 'a doubling down on exactly the kind of reckless, short-term thinking that got us into this mess. Just as we spewed greenhouse gases into the atmosphere thinking that tomorrow would never come' nuclear is a 'hugely high-risk' technology that 'would create even more dangerous forms of waste' and which lacks a 'discernible exit strategy' (Klein 2015, p. 63).

Advocates of nuclear power dispute each of Klein's claims. Measured in loss of human life per unit of electricity, nuclear is by far the safest energy source (Markandya and Wilkinson 2007). Fast-breeder nuclear reactors could reprocess spent nuclear fuel, and even without fast-breeder reactors nuclear waste is a much smaller environmental hazard than coal ash. But the key argument put forward by nuclear proponents is that nuclear power has to date been the *only* universally available technology (other than geographically constrained hydroelectricity or geothermal power) with the proven capacity to decarbonize entire grids. Moreover, the Swedish and French nuclear roll-outs have deployed zero-carbon energy several times more rapidly than any subsequent renewables deployment. (Denmark has seen the most rapid deployment of renewables; see Cao et al. 2016, p. 548.)

It is true, however, that nuclear has not lived up to its early promise. While the costs of nuclear power fell and deployment accelerated until the early 1970s, over the ensuing decades new reactors have experienced 'negative learning rates' meaning that costs have risen rather than fallen. Consequently, nuclear's share of global energy has slowly declined (South Korea is an exception where costs continued to fall). According to some nuclear advocates, the Green movement is to blame for the excessive safety precautions and unnecessary red-tape that have ended nuclear's ascent. This critique underestimates the impact that events like the Chernobyl disaster would have had on public attitudes and costs even without Green opposition. It is also clear, however, that nuclear's decline has been a lost opportunity for climate action. For example, one analysis suggests that if the learning rates and deployment rates of the 1960s had continued, by 2015 nuclear could have displaced all coal-fired generation and consequently, gas and emissions from fossil fuels would have been cut by over one third (Lang 2017, p. 216).

Since Green opposition to nuclear power emerged long before climate change was well understood, the idea that the Green movement is in some way responsible for the severity of the climate crisis is unfair. Before the era of climate change, the Green movement's anti-nuclear argument must have seemed unimpeachable. After the Chernobyl disaster, nuclear power became conflated with fears of irradiated landscapes, nuclear conflict and even with nuclear weapons tests. Much uranium mining also seemed to violate the rights of indigenous land-owners. It is true that nuclear's risks for human health are trivial when compared with the many thousands of lives lost each year through the routine operation of coal-fired power plants. However, the fears and negative associations of nuclear are also real. From a Green perspective the reasons to resist nuclear power vastly outweigh its mitigation potential, even if nuclear power has historically been the technology that has achieved the fastest emissions reductions.

Conclusion

Stewart Brand, the Green pioneer who was both a publisher of *The Whole Earth Catalogue* in the 1970s and a co-author of the *Ecomodernist Manifesto* in 2015 is typical of most ecomodernists in that he is also a lifelong environmentalist. Brand recounts how, as a ten-year-old in 1948, he took the Conservation Pledge, which he found in the magazine *Outdoor Life:* 'I give my pledge as an American to save and faithfully defend from waste the natural resources of my country – its air, soil, and minerals, its forest, waters and wildlife' (2009, p. 21). Brand observes that he has now rejected the national parochialism and anthropocentrism implicit in that pledge, but not its commitment to wild nature. I could tell a similar story, except that my own conversion to environmentalism came a little later, as a twelve-year-old reading Tim Flannery's articles in the *Australian Natural History Magazine* in the late 1980s. As I deepened my engagement with Green politics I was attracted by its opposition to all forms of domination, and its vision of a more just and harmonious world remains attractive.

Unfortunately, the Green movement's defining instincts meant that, as Greens responded to climate change, they rarely focused on the potential value of state-backed innovation or took adequate account of the third world's irrepressible demand for development. In short, the Green movement's desire to create a better society and a different relationship with nature has proved stronger than its desire to reduce GHG emissions. From the perspective of Green ideology, this choice is justified. However, these priorities mark a fundamental distinction between Greens and eco-modernists. Of course, the two groups disagree on many specific topics – on the need for innovation, the desirability of urban density versus small-scale farming, and the value of scale and efficiency versus traditional technologies. However, the fundamental difference concerns which should be accorded a higher priority – the Greening of society, or the decarbonization of production.

2

Ecomodernism and its Critics

Encircled by state troopers and with the Grand Canyon yawning behind, Geena Davis looks to Susan Sarandon in the final scene of *Thelma and Louise* and suggests 'let's keep going'. If this scene were a metaphor for humanity's ecological predicament, then the choice between surrender and flooring the accelerator might capture the comparison between the Green 'politics of limits' and an ecomodernist 'politics of innovation'. While we might theoretically avoid dangerous warming by limiting global consumption, an austerity based response would require such severe restraints on third-world development and such a transformation of the lives of the global middle-class as to only be possible if enforced by an illiberal and authoritarian power. But what is the alternative? Given my sympathy for ecomodernism this metaphor – in which an ecomodernist future is represented by a Thunderbird convertible arcing into the Grand Canyon – might seem ill judged.[5] Nevertheless, I think Thelma and

---

[5] Ecomodernists commonly utilize acceleration metaphors involving vehicles, like planes, that are designed for safe landing (Karlsson 2016).

Louise's death-or-glory defiance (against patriarchal oppression in their case) explains the appeal of turning to hubris in the face of catastrophe. Only by increasing our momentum, say the ecomodernists, will it be possible to accelerate the tendencies towards ecological decoupling that are already emergent in the contemporary global economy. Steering to safety requires that we first extend modernity's line of flight. Ecomodernists hear Theodor Adorno and Max Horkheimer's warning that 'the fully enlightened earth radiates disaster triumphant' (1979, p. 3) but, seeing no alternative, hasten further into the enlightenment.

By comparing ecomodernism to Thelma and Louise, I've implied that technological acceleration might be justified as a lesser evil. Ecomodernists rarely speak in such terms. Instead, they promise the possibility of a 'good or even great Anthropocene' (Asafu-Adjaye et al. 2015, p. 31). But is this language not tone-deaf to the deep inequalities and ecological tragedies that actually characterize the Anthropocene? Ecomodernists argue that a politics capable of mobilizing a global, zero-carbon civilization must speak not of despair and limits, but to our capabilities and dreams. Indeed, Ted Nordhaus and Michael Shellenberger argue that the challenge of global warming is so enormous as to 'require a kind of greatness – even hubris – humankind has never before seen' (Shellenberger and Nordhaus 2007, p. 273). The term *hubris* is generally used to describe prideful behaviour that challenges the natural order, and which must, in the formula of Greek tragedy, inevitably be punished. By embracing hubris, Shellenberger and Nordhaus seem to be recognizing that the 'great Anthropocene' is an improbable prospect and that, like Thelma and Louise, we have reached a precipice from which there is no easy escape.

Ecomodernists argue that the climate crisis is so serious that our response must draw on every available tool. Believing that avoiding dangerous warming is politically infeasible with today's technologies, they see a central role for the state in deliberately accelerating the pace of low-carbon innovation. Since ecomodernists are also environmentalists who love wild nature and wish to prevent dangerous climate change, their embrace of radical technological innovations may be confusing. The modern environmental movement that emerged in the 1970s often feared technology, fretted over third-world population growth and, despite its affinity for the political left, tended to distrust the state. Some Greens thus critique ecomodernism for its hubristic faith in science and technology, and for its promotion of state-led development and universal human affluence.

If it seems that these disagreements don't fit neatly onto a left/right political spectrum, that's because they don't. Navigating the climate crisis involves questions of technology, ideology, politics and psychology, and ecomodernists tend to believe that climate mitigation will only become possible by transcending many contemporary political divisions. Here, I will do my best to explain these contradictions and the relationship between ecomodernist climate responses and those advocated by other kinds of Greens. After first outlining some of the core ideas associated with ecomodernism, the chapter's second section will seek to situate ecomodernism politically, and to explain why ecomodernists have sometimes fallen out with the wider environmental movement. My answer is simple: ecomodernists and Greens have often been in conflict because, although preoccupied with many of the same problems, they have different frames of cultural reference. Many Greens reject the meta-narratives of modernity such as faith in reason, and progress through scientific and technological development, and promote a transition to more natural, small-scale and local patterns of life. By contrast ecomodernists and their sympathizers celebrate enlightenment reason, science and material progress, and seek to achieve environmental benefits through increased intensity and the technological sophistication of production. Perhaps it is not surprising that as the two groups' cultural values have diverged, ecomodernists and Greens have sometimes forgotten how much they hold in common.

Greens and ecomodernists can probably agree that the climate-changed future will look radically different from the present. What is not clear is whether the transformation will involve enforcement of limits, climate catastrophe or intentional planetary interventions and technological acceleration. Ecomodernists argue that we are so far down the path of technological transcendence that to go back is more dangerous than to go on. Thus, accelerating the pace of technological innovation now offers our best path forward. Rasmus Karlsson (2013, p. 1) crystallizes a key ecomodernist insight when he writes that:

> In ideal-typical terms, there are two ways that the current crisis of environmental sustainability can be [safely] resolved, either: (1) through the development of advanced technologies that would allow humanity to transcend its planetary boundaries or; (2) through the political and economic enforcement of those boundaries.

One reason that ecomodernists emphasize technological progress is that they believe that most third-world people prioritize improving their material standards of living over climate mitigation. Any climate mitigation strategy must therefore take account of the third world's legitimate hopes of accessing a modern material standard of living. Ecomodernism's belief that material comfort is a universal human desire aligns it with a long tradition of progressive materialist thought (Chibber 2014, p. 179). In fact, ecomodernists typically believe that egalitarian economic growth and politically directed technological change are key, not only to addressing climate change, but also to a broader progressive agenda that might push back against rising ethno-nationalism, economic stagnation and national inequality.

Defining Ecomodernism

What kind of politics can best address global climate change? The attempt to answer this question has taken ecomodernists on an intellectual odyssey. Most ecomodernists have histories in the environmental movement but, at some point, have rejected the Green critique of technology. Since ecomodernism is not yet a stable ideology, defining its differences with traditional Green thinking is slightly difficult, though. Ecomodernists commonly describe themselves as 'pragmatists' who are responding to climate change by seeking 'positive and politically achievable steps that yield discernible benefits, which in turn provide the rationale for the next steps' (Atkinson et al. 2011, p. 23). However, the moniker 'pragmatist' seems ill-fitting, as ecomodernists frequently criticize the most politically feasible climate policies such as state subsidies for renewable power, and they sometimes promote exotic schemes such as solar geoengineering and nuclear fusion. Perhaps the word pragmatic suggests that ecomodernists view climate change as primarily an engineering problem, rather than a political or cultural problem.[6] This seems plausible – focus on technological solutions rather than cultural change does seem central to ecomodernism. However, most mainstream environmentalists also seek technological change, for instance towards renewable electricity and electric cars. At the same time, ecomodernists do advocate some cultural changes – they promote the environmental benefits of urban density over suburban sprawl, for example. It seems that ecomodernists' self-image as science-oriented, progressive pragmatists neither accounts for all of their beliefs, nor for their relationship with the wider environmental movement. For that, we need a sense of ecomodernism's origins.

---

[6] This explanation was offered to me by Stewart Brand. While Brand is best known for his achievements in the twentieth century as a publisher of the *Whole Earth Catalog* and instigator of Californian 'digital utopianism' he has also been a central figure in the development of ecomodernism. In *Whole Earth Discipline* (2009, p. 1), Brand defines pragmatism as 'a practical way of thinking concerned with results rather than with theories and principles'.

Ecomodernist worldviews were first clearly articulated in the 1990s in isolated works by scholars such as Martin Lewis (1994) and Jesse Ausubel (1996). While ecomodernism also draws on many earlier varieties of environmental thought, including 'ecological modernization' and 'human welfare ecology' (Eckersley 1992, pp. 35–48; Wissenburg 1998), its emergence as a self-conscious movement is very recent. As has been noted, the think tank with which the term is associated – the Breakthrough Institute – was only established in 2003, and only began to use the word ecomodernism in 2013.[7] A landmark essay, *The Death of Environmentalism: Global Warming Politics in a Post-environmental World*, published in 2004 by the Breakthrough Institute's founders Ted Nordhaus and Michael Shellenberger, contains almost none of the specific policy ideas now associated with ecomodernism. Instead, the essay excoriates the environmental movement for its inadequate response to 'the world's most serious ecological crisis' (climate change) and for its failure to offer an 'inclusive and hopeful vision for America's future' (2004, p. 27).

The Death of Environmentalism's ideas were developed further in Nordhaus and Shellenberger's subsequent book, *Break Through* (2007). The two texts outlined a mission which seems to have guided the Breakthrough Institute's subsequent work: to articulate a vision of the future that is simultaneously 'inclusive ... hopeful' and 'commensurate with the magnitude of the climate crisis' (Nordhaus and Shellenberger 2004, p. 6) The impulse to address climate change without being constrained by the Green movement's traditions, which at times may verge on deliberate contrarianism, has also found a supportive audience among progressive donors. The most influential of these has been Rachel Pritzker, who has chaired the Institute's board since

---

[7] Ted Nordhaus credits Keith Kloor (2012) for being the first to identify the emergence of a distinct intellectual movement (encompassing figures such as Emma Marris and Mark Lynas) around the Breakthrough Institute.

2011, was a co-author of the *Ecomodernist Manifesto* (Asafu-Adjaye et al. 2015) and was previously a founding board member of the (Democratic party aligned) Democracy Alliance. Breakthrough's tendency to challenge Green assumptions also brought notoriety. One prominent critique dismissed Nordhaus and Shellenberger as attention-seeking opportunists, motivated by the discovery that 'ex-hippies punching hippies' garners media attention and donor funds (Roberts 2011).

A distinct ecomodernist agenda crystallized slowly, primarily through the Breakthrough Institute's work. Publication of Stewart Brand's book *Whole Earth Discipline* in 2009 was pivotal. Brand's subtitle, *Why Dense Cities, Nuclear Power, Transgenic Crops, Restored Wildlands and Geo-engineering are Necessary* summarized many of the specific ideas which, by attacking the shibboleths of modern environmentalism, have deepened division between ecomodernists and mainstream Greens. However, the most deliberate effort to define ecomodernist ideas was the *Ecomodernist Manifesto* (the Manifesto) of 2015 (Asafu-Adjaye et al. 2015). Drafted by a group of nineteen authors including environmental activists Nordhaus, Shellenberger, and Steward Brand, scientists Pamela Ronald, Barry Brook and David Keith, economists Joyashree Roy and John Asafu-Adjaye, and filmmaker Robert Stone, the Manifesto affirms the idea that 'humanity must shrink its impacts on the environment' but rejects one of the central propositions of modern environmentalism, that 'human societies must harmonize with nature'. Instead it calls for 'conscious acceleration of emergent decoupling processes' that can 'liberate the environment from the economy' (Asafu-Adjaye et al. 2015, p. 18). The Manifesto identifies two key strategies through which to promote this decoupling: (1) *intensification* of all human activities, but particularly in agriculture, energy, forestry and urban form; and (2) *technological innovation*, which it suggests can allow humanity to avoid imposing an increasing burden on natural systems or being constrained by ecological limits (Asafu-Adjaye et al. 2015, p. 9).

Of course, even if the skilful deployment of science and technology can ensure that people continue to enjoy better lives, the costs for non-human nature may continue to mount. Here too, ecomodernists reverse conventional Green thinking. They argue that ecological goals are best advanced by putting universal human development at the centre of politics. Assuming both that communities are generally most willing to protect the environment once their material needs are securely met, and that the majority of the world's people will aspire to 'modern' living standards, ecomodernists suggest that global environmental challenges can only be addressed as a co-benefit of egalitarian human development (Nordhaus and Shellenberger 2007, p. 269). There may seem to be a contradiction here, as ecomodernists also accept that the technological metabolism of the contemporary global economy is ecocidal. However, ecomodernists claim to embrace growth precisely to enable technological transformation. Nordhaus and Shellenberger (2007, p. 113) explain:

> And herein lies the anomaly that most frustrates the environmentalists' pollution paradigm: the fact that overcoming global warming demands something qualitatively different from limiting our contamination of nature. It demands unleashing human power, creating a new economy, and remaking nature as we prepare for the future. And to accomplish all of that, the right models come not from [previous efforts to address] raw sewage, acid rain, or the ozone hole but instead from the very thing environmentalists have long imagined to be the driver of pollution in the first place: economic development.

This embrace of growth certainly utilizes language that is currently associated with the political right. However, I think critics such as Rosemary-Claire Collard (Collard et al. 2015) who describe this 'Green' developmentalism as a defence of neoliberalism misread ecomodernism completely. Neoliberalism is a term that is often used quite loosely to refer to free-market oriented economic thinking. However, a more precise definition distinguishes neoliberalism from neo-classical economics on the basis that neoliberals propose that the state's *only* significant role, apart from providing security, should be in creating markets and sustaining competition. The neoliberal state should therefore create and defend property rights, enforce contracts, prohibit anti-competitive behaviour and maintain price stability (Srnicek and Williams 2015, p. 53). A neoliberal response to climate change might thus centre on pricing carbon and creating carbon markets. By contrast, ecomodernism argues that instead of relying on market instruments, the state should play an active economic role shaping the trajectory of technological and economic change. Ecomodernism thus repudiates the defining feature of neoliberal thought.

Historically, the idea that the state should intervene in the economy to promote economic growth and technological progress has been shared by a wide variety of economic theories and political ideologies. European social democracies, third-world developmental states and the East Asian 'state developmentalist' models have all subscribed to these general goals.[8] I'll use the term *state-led developmentalism* to describe this broader category of pro-growth interventionist states. Of course, advocates of de-growth will find state-led developmentalism every bit as problematic as neoliberalism. However, those critics who describe ecomodernism as neoliberal are very confused.

Admittedly, my argument that ecomodernism should be understood as a social democratic response to climate change is harder to reconcile with the *Ecomodernist Manifesto* than with many other Breakthrough Institute (BI) publications. Consider my earlier claim concerning ecomodernism's theory of change – that it identifies democratic states as the only actors with the capacity and social license to drive

---

[8] The term *state developmentalism* is generally used to describe states that have 'transformative goals, a pilot agency and institutionalized government business cooperation' (Weiss 2000, p. 23).

the necessary low-carbon innovation. These ideas are discussed at length in Nordhaus and Shellenberger's 2007 book *Break Through* (pp. 118–24), and are developed in multiple subsequent BI publications (e.g. Jenkins et al. 2010) including Fred Block's *Breakthrough Journal* articles (e.g. Block 2011, 2018). These ideas also form the central argument of Mariana Mazzucato's *The Entrepreneurial State* (2015), which is included in the Breakthrough Institute's 'syllabus' for fellowship recipients. Indeed, this account of the state's role in innovation is one of the key ideas that distinguishes ecomodernism from earlier theories of *ecological modernization* (see Wissenburg 1998). However, the *Ecomodernist Manifesto* skates over the state's role. Only on its penultimate page does the Manifesto explain that accelerated innovation requires 'aggressive participation of private sector entrepreneurs, markets, civil society, and the state':

> While we reject the planning fallacy of the 1950s, we continue to embrace a strong public role in addressing environmental problems and accelerating technological innovation, including research to develop better technologies, subsidies, and other measures to help bring them to market, and regulation to mitigate environmental hazards. (Asafu-Adjaye et al. 2015, p. 30)

Instead, the Manifesto's most striking themes are its celebration of modernization and liberal humanism – both of which emphasize divergence from Green cultural values. The Manifesto defines modernization as 'the long-term evolution of social, economic, political and technological arrangements in human societies towards vastly improved material well-being, public health, resource productivity, economic integration, shared infrastructure and personal freedom'. Meanwhile, it advocates 'liberal principles of democracy, tolerance and pluralism', both for their own sakes and as keys to achieving human flourishing on an ecologically vibrant planet (Asafu-Adjaye et al. 2015, p. 31). In the ecomodernist imagination, achieving a 'great

Anthropocene' requires the globalization of modernity, liberal freedoms, the rule of law, material prosperity and the preservation of wild nature. Emphasizing gradual global improvements in life expectancy, public health, gender equity and declining inter-state violence, the Manifesto argues that the current era is one of *both* human flourishing and mounting ecological damage.[9] Ecomodernists seem to view optimism concerning human progress both as a response to empirical evidence, and also as a political commitment (see also Pinker 2018). They argue a belief in progress can be self-fulfilling or, at the very least, that belief in the possibility of progress generates the kind of social trust that is a prerequisite for progressive change.

Ecomodernism's claim that modernization has benefited humanity even as it has harmed non-human nature supports its distinctive perspective on at least another four aspects of environmental politics. First, since ecomodernists understand climate change as an unintended consequence of well-motivated communities seeking to improve their lives, they view polluting technologies rather than the capitalist growth dynamic as the root cause of climate harms: explicitly anti-capitalist ecomodernists like Leigh Phillips (2015) are a minority. Although Nordhaus and Shellenberger have written at length about how inequality and financial insecurity undermine support for environmental policies (2007, pp. 13–37), ecomodernists generally advocate reforming, rather than overthrowing, capitalism. They instead seek to invest wealth generated by capitalism in low-carbon innovation. However, support for an innovation-led climate response does not mean that climate mitigation is technocratic and apolitical. Instead, ecomodernists argue that political mobilization must promote and shape innovation policies.

---

[9] I'd suggest the destruction of indigenous cultures also deserves a place on any checklist of modernity's impacts. Not all humans are flourishing.

Second, although ecomodernists are sometimes critical of wasteful consumption, critiquing consumption is not at all central to their politics. One reason, developed at length in Nordhaus and Shellenberger's book *Break Through* (2007), is that they view economic security and the provision of material needs as a precondition for the development of postmaterialist values that include environmental protection. That is to say, ecomodernists view tackling economic insecurity as a higher priority than moralizing against consumption. Moreover, they view the material poverty of the developing world as harmful for both human and environmental welfare. Consequently, even if it is true that the richest billion should ideally consume less, ecomodernists anticipate that aggregate global material consumption needs to increase. If a significant increase in global consumption is desirable, then working to eliminate the environmental impacts of production will seem more pressing than advocating first-world 'de-growth'. Ecomodernists also worry about how to nurture the capacity for collective action more than about flaws in individual behaviour. For example, when Fred Block (2011) critiqued 'consumer culture' his worry was not for its direct environmental impacts, but that it has 'nurtured a focus on the sovereignty of the individual' that has 'corroded the solidaristic foundations that provide the basis for liberal democracy'.

Social anthropologist Daniel Miller discusses consumer culture with an empathy that ecomodernists might share. Miller writes that '[l]eft-wing critics claim consumption is largely fostered by advertising and demand is created by commerce. These goods then contribute to practices of status emulation, which in turn can be related back to capitalism's other consequences in fostering of class and social inequality' (Miller 2012, p. 182). In the Green imagination the same excessive consumption that drives climate change also drives inequality. Miller rejects this logic and, after a career studying consumption in both capitalist and non-capitalist settings, has reached what he believes is an unpopular conclusion: that 'social relations are the primary cause of consumption' which would remain elevated even if all advertising were banned. As against Thorstein Veblen's view that status competition motivates 'conspicuous consumption', Miller argues that most consumption is governed by a morality that seeks to provision the household while reserving resources for the future, and that rather than by status competition, most consumption is oriented around the goal of achieving 'normality' (Miller 2012). While ecomodernists don't necessarily share Miller's exact understanding of consumption, neither have they made a critique of excessive consumption or 'affluenza' central to their politics. Since universal human development is an urgent priority, ecomodernists think it is desirable for aggregate consumption to continue to increase.

This brings me to ecomodernism's third distinctive perspective on modernization. Ecomodernists typically defend third-world developmentalism and even increased fossil fuel use as a means of addressing poverty and building resilience against climate harms. Curiously, the Manifesto emphasizes universal human development rather than equality. Although the two impulses are interconnected, the choice of language seems intended to avoid politically partisan framing. Ecomodernists have been particularly critical of Western efforts to control energy development choices. Targets have included World Bank lending rules that restrict finance for polluting energy sources (Pritzker 2016) and European NGOs' campaigns against biotechnology across the third world (Lynas 2018). Ecomodernists reject aid-conditionality both because they view relationships of domination (among humans) as inherently unethical and because of their belief that prosperity is a stepping stone to climate resilience and environmental concern. Where there is an unavoidable tension between third-world development and GHG emissions, ecomodernists support national communities' right to make their own choices. The close link between carbon emissions and human development provides one more reason for ecomodernism's focus on technological innovation. If zero-carbon transport, industry and electricity became cheaper than fossil fuel alternatives, tensions between mitigation and development would be resolved.

Fourth, ecomodernists propose distinctive metaphors of ecological transition. The ecomodernist metaphor of *decoupling from nature* rejects the Green vision of small-scale, traditional and local production that grounds human communities in local ecosystems. Consider the example of efforts to commercialize milk-proteins that are brewed from genetically engineered yeast rather than milked from cows. Many traditional environmentalists will oppose both the hubris of biotechnology and the social implications of capital-intensive production, and so will prefer traditional farming. By contrast, ecomodernism celebrates cow-free milk's potential to reduce methane emissions, land use, water requirements and animal cruelty.[10] Several decades before the emergence of ecomodernism as a self-conscious movement, Martin Lewis articulated this ecomodernist view, writing in respect of human material needs that 'the separation of the human economy from natural systems turns out to offer profound environmental benefits, while the continued immersion of our apparatus of production into the intricate webs of nature is itself highly threatening to the natural world of nonhuman species' (1993, p. 797). Thus, in the ecomodernist imagination, the key attraction of nuclear power is its potential to provide humanity with abundant energy from a source that neither generates greenhouse gases nor extracts energy from natural ecosystems.

Finally, consistent with their liberal humanism, ecomodernists have rejected the idea that there is any one, ideal understanding of the relationship between humanity and nature. Instead, the Manifesto argues that the treatment of non-human nature will inevitably reflect human priorities and that these will change over time. There seems to

---

[10] Dairy production involves a constant cycle of impregnation, separation and slaughter, in which bobby calves (new-born calves less than 30 days old who are not with their mother) are killed as surplus soon after birth.

be some tension between this respect for pluralism and the Manifesto's stated desire to preserve ecological diversity and vibrancy. Indeed, perhaps the Ecomodernist movement lacks a coherent perspective on the idea of nature – the Breakthrough Institute's early exploration of the inherent hybridity of nature and culture (see Latour 2011) fits poorly with the more recent insistence on 'separation from nature' which seems to accept the traditional human/nature division that earlier Ecomodernist work had challenged.[11] What is clear is that ecomodernism doesn't fit perfectly onto a spectrum that divides environmentalism into anthropocentric (human-centred) and ecocentric (ecology centred) strands. While sharing the ecocentric hope that the nonhuman world should be accorded moral standing and allowed 'to unfold in its many diverse ways' (Eckersley 1992, p. 26), ecomodernists seem to have settled on the assumption that all environmental thought will necessarily derive from human culture.

Emma Marris has offered perhaps the most nuanced ecomodernist reflection on the future of 'nature' in her book *Rambunctious Garden* (2013). Since ecosystems have always been in a state of flux, Marris argues that efforts to restore some 'baseline' of untrammelled nature are misguided. Moreover, aspirations to restore wild nature often prompt the dispossession of relatively powerless people who live in forests and other areas marked for protection. Neither, she notes, is there any stable pre-industrial climatic baseline to which we should aspire to return, even though it is clear that the current pace of climatic change is unprecedented and ecologically harmful. Where does this leave conservation? Marris canvases a variety of defensible, but partially inconsistent conservation goals that include respecting the intrinsic rights of other species, preserving charismatic mega-fauna and maximizing ecosystem services, before proposing that we think of the future earth as a

---

[11] I am grateful to an anonymous reader for this observation.

human-tended 'rambunctious garden'. However, Marris offers few definitive prescriptions other than the need to preserve open land: 'Don't ignore green, growing land just because it isn't your ideal native landscape. Protect it from development, even if it is just a "trash ecosystem". Build your cities in tight and up high, and let the scenery take over the suburbs' (Marris 2013, p. 170).

While ecomodernists generally refuse to prescribe a specific relationship with nature, ecomodernist imagery unsettles the distinction between humility and hubris that informs much Green thinking about technology (Niemann 2017). For example, Bruno Latour, writing in the *Breakthrough Journal,* revisited Mary Shelly's *Frankenstein* and argued that hubris lay not in the creation of new technologies, but in a failure to care and attend to scientific creations:

> The goal of political ecology must not be to stop innovating, inventing, creating, and intervening. The real goal must be to have the same type of patience and commitment to our creations as God the Creator, Himself. (Latour 2011)

Ausubel expressed the same idea in more prosaic language. He suggested that the potential for 'unanticipated consequences' to diminish technology's value could be managed via feedback systems that '[a]ssess technologies early in their prospective social penetration, watch them thereafter for surprises, and tailor designs to fit changing needs and tastes' (1996, p. 167).

In the course of reviewing debates over using science to revive extinct species, Marris argues that 'to be truly humble is to put other species first, and our relationship with them second ... A truly bio-centric ethic puts the sea turtle's existence above the condition of the human soul' (2015, p. 49). Marris's approach might be applied more widely. Consider the example of brewed, cow-free milk discussed earlier. Is it more hubristic to insist on preserving the authenticity of humanity's relationship with cows and their lactation, as per Langdon Winner's argument against technologically complex processed milk in *The Whale and The Reactor* (1986), or to use genetic technology to end the industrialized cruelty of dairy production? Ecomodernists may have rejected the Green movement's critique of technology, but they remain attached to its wider ecophilic concerns.

Progressive Environmental Prometheans ... an Unfamiliar Constellation

One group that's gained much attention are the Ecomodernists who promise to lead us into a 'good Anthropocene'. Their tools are capitalism, technology and classical philosophy. More alienation, they argue, will fix the ills of current alienation. They are not worried about the hidden forces their interventions will let loose. Like other engineers before them they trust in man. I think of them as the inheriting sons; the ones who argue that the master's tools will allow us to refurbish the master's house. (Anna Tsing)[12]

Anna Tsing is typical of those who cast ecomodernism as an unreconstructed, techno-chauvinist response to environmental challenges. Is this fair? Here I want to revisit the question of where ecomodernism fits on a political spectrum. Describing a political spectrum is complex and the following definitions are very rough. I'll use the term 'conservative' to describe those who value tradition, are sceptical of the unintended consequences of change and are relatively untroubled by inequality; the term 'progressive' will be used to describe those who are open to change, believe in the possibility of improving society and wish to eliminate both wealth and identity linked forms of inequality. However, while conservatives are a dominant group on the 'right'

---

[12] Tsing, A. 2015. *A Feminist Approach to the Anthropocene: Earth Stalked by Man*. Barnard Center for Research on Women Public Lecture. https://www.youtube.com/watch?v=ps8J6a7g_BA

side of politics, the 'right' usually also includes economic liberals who embrace radical economic change, but who join conservatives in opposing socialist or strongly redistributive policies. Similarly, on the 'left', progressive side of politics, we will also find coalitions between socialists, Greens and cultural liberals. Meanwhile other important divisions, such as that between localist and globalist thinking, aren't captured by the left/right spectrum. Nevertheless, I'll use these terms as they are the most common ways in which we organize political ideas.

Like most progressives, ecomodernists advocate greater equality and an enlarged role for the state in shaping societal evolution. Like most environmentalists, their love for the natural world means they assert the intrinsic worth of non-human nature and wish to protect ecological systems for their own sake, and not simply for the services they provide to humanity. Why then do Green critics deride ecomodernists as right-wing apologists for corporate capitalism? I think the answer lies in ecomodernists' rejection of Green cultural politics. Had the *Ecomodernist Manifesto* been published in 1946 rather than 2016, it might have seemed unambiguously progressive. However, in the decades following the Second World War, a Green critique of power, progress, modernization, materialism and instrumental reasoning developed. Although these ideas initially challenged both socialism and capitalism, Green cultural ideals have now been largely integrated into progressive thinking and resisted by conservatives. Consequently, when ecomodernists argue that technological change, not cultural change, should dominate our climate response, they seem to be allied with conservative opponents of the Green cultural turn.

Ecomodernism's advocacy of efficient, universal service provision and of inherently collectivist technologies like the electricity grid has also fallen out of step with much progressive opinion. Whereas collectivism once belonged on the left and individualism on the right, the ideal of energy self-sufficiency and defection from the grid now captivates the Green-left. Rather than act as a metaphor for societal connection, the electricity grid has become a symbol of centralized authority and corporate power (Palmer 2014). Bizarrely, in the cultural politics of the West, even ecomodernism's defence of universal human prosperity now risks being interpreted as an imperialist assertion of Western values. Within much of the Green movement, commitments to localism and tradition have been elevated above material progress. As a result, ecomodernism's internationalism and materialism – values that once anchored the Marxian world-view – may now seem right wing.

One useful way to situate ecomodernism politically is by way of comparison with Alex Williams and Nick Srnicek's post-Marxist account of *accelerationism*. Consider Srnicek and Williams's *Accelerationist Manifesto* (2013):

> We believe the most important division in today's left is between those that hold to a folk politics of localism, direct action, and relentless horizontalism, and those that outline what must become called an accelerationist politics at ease with a modernity of abstraction, complexity, globality, and technology. The former remains content with establishing small and temporary spaces of non-capitalist social relations, eschewing the real problems entailed in facing foes which are intrinsically non-local, abstract, and rooted deep in our everyday infrastructure.

> Accelerationists want to unleash latent productive forces. In this project, the material platform of neoliberalism does not need to be destroyed. It needs to be repurposed towards common ends. The existing infrastructure is not a capitalist stage to be smashed, but a springboard to launch towards post-capitalism.

> We want to accelerate the process of technological evolution. But what we are arguing for is not techno-utopianism. Never believe that technology will be sufficient to save us. Necessary, yes, but never sufficient without socio-political action.

If the phrase 'ecologically destructive' replaced 'capitalism' and 'ecomodernism' were substituted for 'accelerationism', the above passage might encapsulate an ecomodernist critique of Green localism. The call to embrace the material platform of late capitalism and to deliberately yoke technological acceleration to socio-political action exactly mirrors ecomodernism. Only very occasionally do voices on the radical left articulate the same critique of Green politics (e.g. Battistoni 2015). However, since Srnicek and Williams engage the shortcomings of anti-capitalist localism (e.g. the *Occupy Wall Street* movement), they are generally received as sympathetic critics within the socialist tradition. By contrast, since localism has become constitutive of Green politics rather than incidental to it, ecomodernists are turncoats.

However, ecomodernism's 'betrayal' is not of the social-democratic left (or at least not of the moderate North American expression of this tradition). Instead, ecomodernists have rejected two of the ideas that typified post-1960s' Western environmentalism and which corresponded with the two strands of nineteenth-century ecological thought identified by Bramwell (1990):

1. The assumption that since environmental systems are unknowably complex, interventions are likely to have adverse unintended consequences and must be avoided at all costs;
2. The belief that ecological collapse can only be avoided by harmonizing with nature through a turn to simplicity, local production, economic 'degrowth' and a 'greening of the self'. Macy (1991)

The prohibition on intervention in complex systems

In the language of Green theory, we might summarize many of these distinctions by saying that, whereas most modern environmentalists are Malthusians, ecomodernists are Prometheans. The first group take their name from Thomas Malthus, a Scottish pastor who has become the patron saint of eugenics and overpopulation angst. In 1798, Malthus published a paper titled: 'An Essay on the

Principle of Population' which argued that since people are uniformly motivated by hunger and sexual passion, and since this aspect of human nature remains unchanged throughout time, populations will inevitably increase until they exhaust available food. Malthus argued that 'constant effort towards an increase of population ... tends to subject the lower classes of the society to distress and to prevent any great permanent amelioration of their condition' (Malthus 1888, p. 10). Believing overpopulation and impoverishment to be unchangeable laws of nature, Malthus argued that social reform was futile. Marx and Engels were appalled by Malthus's prejudice and ridiculed his theory of population throughout their work (Charbit 2009). It may therefore seem ironic that Malthusian logic has become a significant influence on the contemporary left via its application to global environmental politics. Paul Ehrlich's warning of a 'population bomb' and Donella Meadows's identification of 'limits to growth' have had such wide impact that Jared Diamond was simply articulating conventional wisdom when he wrote (2005, p. 511):

> [T]he larger danger that we face is not just of a two-fold increase in population, but of a much larger increase in human impact if the Third World's population succeeds in attaining a First World living standard.

Prometheans, on the other hand, anticipate that wise application of science and technology can potentially increase the abundance of resources and improve human welfare to such a point that third-world populations really do enjoy first-world livelihoods while also addressing environmental degradation. In Greek mythology, Prometheus was a divine being who stole fire from the gods and gave humanity a new ability to manipulate the world.[13] Green theorist

---

[13] Prometheus's ability to regrow limbs, although not relevant to our narrative, may presage developments in twenty-first-century medicine.

John Dryzek argues that from the Industrial Revolution on, the idea that the natural world could be manipulated to benefit humanity was so taken for granted in the West that it was rarely directly articulated (Dryzek 2013, p. 52). As William Meyer outlines in his history of *The Progressive Environmental Prometheans*, belief in the possibility of advancing human welfare through deliberate interventions in the biophysical environment was especially integral to collectivist, progressive (left) thought. Marx's embrace of the emancipatory potential of technological innovation is but one example.

However, Prometheanism's political valence began to change in the 1960s. Rachel Carson's 1962 book *Silent Spring*, which documented how the use of DDT to control insects harmed the environment, was perhaps the most influential text articulating a new message: that intentional interventions in nature often have unanticipated adverse consequences. Carson, who utilized scientific reasoning to point to hazards associated with excessive chemical use, offered an important corrective to a culture whose unalloyed enthusiasm for scientific progress lacked any real precautionary impulse.

Some contemporary Greens have gone further and have made the idea that 'intervention in nature' is inherently harmful into a moral principle. This belief has the virtue of allowing simple moral distinctions: traditional, small-scale and organic products are good; scientifically complex, capital-intensive or synthetic products are suspicious and probably harmful. But if the belief that natural is always better is elevated into a blanket prohibition on intervention in nature, it can become socially regressive. Movements rejecting water fluoridation and vaccination demonstrate as much. Of course, most Greens support these two public health measures and accept a wide variety of similar interventions in natural systems. For example, treatment of diabetes with synthetic insulin produced via recombinant DNA technology now attracts little controversy. However, use of genetic technologies in agriculture (where benefits are less personal) raises more Green ire. For example, if the new gene editing technology CRISPR allows insulin injections to be replaced with insulin secreting skin-patches, the benefits for individuals will be so significant that it will probably be quickly accepted. Meanwhile, CRISPR's application in agriculture – for example, to produce more nutritious and pest-resistant crops – faces resistance. The European Court of Justice's decision in July 2018 that plants created by gene-editing techniques that do not involve transferring genes between organisms should be subject to the same restrictive regulations as transgenic GM crops, entrenches Green influence. Ecomodernists' assertion that science, rather than non-interventionist rules of thumb, should guide decision-making about intervention in nature thus marks a major psychological and ideological break with mainstream environmentalism.

Rachel Carson died in 1964 soon after *Silent Spring*'s publication so we can only speculate as to how she would have engaged with contemporary debates. However, it is noteworthy that Carson was trained as a scientist and generally advocated a scientifically informed attitude towards intervention. In *Silent Spring*, she described the 'high hopes [that] Bacillus thuringiensis, found in Thuringia, Germany, that kills by poisoning larvae, can be used to stop crop damage' instead of DDT (1962, p. 289). One of the most widespread applications of genetic engineering to date has been the production of 'Bt crops' which, by adding Bacillus thuringiensis genes to plants cells, imparts intrinsic resistance to insect attack (Gerasimova 2016). Bt crops are just one of the technological advances that have allowed pesticide, herbicide and fertilizer use to all decline in absolute terms in the United States since the 1980s (Paarlberg 2010). Given that an overwhelming scientific consensus rejects claims that GM food presents health risks (Klümper and Qiam 2014) it seems possible that Carson might have approved of this use of science.

While the most acrimonious debates between ecomodernists and mainstream environmentalists concern scientific risk assessments, societal consensus has embraced much greater caution and scepticism about the limits of scientific knowledge and ecomodernists share this precautionary impulse. Their advocacy for scientific solutions is not without boundaries. They reject the Green prohibition on interference in nature only in circumstances where a choice must be made between competing environmental priorities. For example, they advocate nuclear power and carbon capture and storage because these could be important tools in mitigating climate change, and their advocacy of gene technologies has always been linked to goals such as improving human nutrition, creating space for nature through increased crop productivity, promoting food security, providing resilience against climate change and reducing animal suffering with in vitro meat or milk. Earlier I mentioned using CRISPR to create bio-available chickpeas. This could potentially bring significant environmental benefits. In India, for example, since just over half of all women are anaemic (Siddiqui et al. 2017) there is a strong public health argument for increased consumption of animal protein. A switch to bio-available chickpea crops could provide an alternative, more culturally sensitive solution.

Ecomodernism's Prometheanism does not fit neatly on a left–right spectrum because attitudes to intervening in nature do not have an inherent political valence. Even today, when belief in the inviolability of natural systems is primarily associated with the political left, some issues – such as stem-cell research – see conservatives become champions of inviolability. In fact, the Green critique of hubris may best be understood as a conservative position. As Meyer argues, the Green concern for unintended consequences is 'exactly the argument conservatives so often make with respect to the complex system of society' (Meyer 2016, p. 29). For example, conservative philosopher Michael Oakeshott has warned that '[w]henever there is innovation there is the certainty that the change will be greater than was intended' (Oakeshott 1991, p. 172). Arguably, the neoliberalism associated with Nobel-Prize-winning economist

Friedrich Hayek, which, confusingly, belongs on the right side of politics without being conservative, offers an even closer parallel with the environmental respect for the inviolability of natural systems. Both Hayek and Green theory promote an attitude of human 'submission' or 'humility' before complex systems, although Hayek sought to protect the inviolability of the market, while the Greens wish to protect ecological systems (Whyte 2017). Both have sought to prohibit intentional interventions in the functioning of these areas. Curiously, both neoliberalism and environmentalism also consolidated their political influence in the same historical juncture (post 1970s). Of course, progressive Greens generally reject neoliberal economic policies and resist Hayek's celebration of the spontaneous order of the market. Yet, to the extent that each philosophy prohibits progressive intervention, they also inculcate submission to the inequalities generated by colonial legacies or a market-governed order.

Harmonizing with Nature

Rejecting the aspiration to harmonize with nature marks a second rupture with traditional environmentalism. Ecomodernists are by no means the first to propose that tensions between development and environment can be resolved via innovation. Indeed the 1987 'Brundtland Report', although best remembered for popularizing the concept of 'sustainable development', also argued that there were no 'absolute limits' to growth because progress in 'technology and social organization' could make continuing growth sustainable if states' 'capacity for technological innovation [was] greatly enhanced' (Brundtland 1987, p. 6). The Brundtland Report had been commissioned by the United Nations General Assembly with the express purpose of recommending 'ways in which concern for the environment may be translated into greater co-operation among developing countries and between countries at different stages of economic and social development' (UN General Assembly 1983). In short, the commission's task was to bridge the gulf between the demands of newly decolonized countries for accelerated economic development, and Western environmentalists' insistence on limits to growth. Brundtland's advocacy for state-directed innovation foreshadowed ecomodernism's central argument.

However, ecomodernists go further and identify a distinctive purpose for state-driven innovation: to minimize environmental impacts by decoupling human activity from natural processes. Innovation will have a radically different focus depending on whether the path to sustainability lies in adjectives like synthetic, efficient and capital-intensive, or in adjectives like organic, local and artisanal. The Green movement's ideal citizen grows much of her own food in a suburban yard, buys from local producers, never travels by air and uses rooftop solar panels and batteries to defect from the centralized grid (perhaps exchanging power with neighbours in a local smart grid). In contrast, the ideal ecomodernist citizen lives in a high-rise apartment, eats synthetic/in-vitro/intensively-farmed food, travels via public transport, flies using zero-carbon (nuclear or solar-derived) jet fuel, and connects to a centralized electricity grid powered by zero-carbon nuclear and solar power. While implementing either model would require both social reform and innovation, each presents very different technological challenges.

As the human population approaches eight billion and the global climate becomes more challenging for agriculture, ecomodernists argue that the world will need continued technological innovation if production is to keep pace with demand. Moreover, they insist that the climate predicament is so severe that the potential of *all* mitigation options should be assessed, rather than automatically rejecting any on ideological grounds. In the 230 years since Malthus's essay on population was published, humanity's numbers have increased from approximately 950 million, to over 7.6 billion, yet the average caloric supply of food per person is almost certainly greater today than at any time since the dawn of agriculture. As environmental geographer Ruth DeFries argues, these advances have been achieved through a series of crises and technological 'ratchets' that have hacked the planetary energy cycle. Fritz Haber's invention at the beginning of the twentieth century of a catalytic, high-pressure process to synthesize ammonia and to produce artificial fertilizer is perhaps the most important of these ratchets. Defries – who was a co-author of the *Ecomodernist Manifesto* – wryly observes that synthetic fertilizer's development turned excessive abundance rather than resource scarcity into the dominant driver of ecological problems arising from agricultural production (DeFries 2014). However, in the ecomodernist imagination such adverse unintended consequences are not a reason to reject innovation, but to manage it carefully.

Conversely, as food production has risen, so too has human population. As a consequence, human survival is now dependent on the continued utilization of previous technological advances. Today, fully 1% of fossil fuel consumption is utilized in fertilizer production and terminating use of this synthetic fertilizer through a switch to organic agriculture would reduce global food output by about 40% (Smil 2017). Would it be possible to adequately feed a global population that is approaching eight billion people with 40% less food (even less if other scientifically enabled yield gains were lost)? Greater equity in international food distribution could stretch a reduced food supply much further by reducing the quantity of grain devoted to producing animal protein and biofuels. However, this would require both radical lifestyle changes for meat-eating communities at a time when meat production is increasing rapidly, as well as significant investments in food distribution and refrigeration in the developing world. While both trends would be desirable neither is politically feasible in the short term. The experience of the 2007–8 world spike in grain prices has illustrated that the more likely consequence of a radical drop in agricultural production would be increased hunger. In the course of disproving Malthus's 'limits to growth 1.0' thesis, human society has made the energy intensive and technology intensive agricultural model of food production a necessity rather than a choice.

Nevertheless, Green movement critics challenge each leg of the ecomodernist case for the intensification of production and separation from dependence on natural ecosystems. Are dense cities really kinder to the environment than suburban or rural life? Does the high-productivity of conventional farming or the creation of wholly synthetic products really 'save space for nature' in comparison to organic or subsistence alternatives? Does nuclear power really benefit biodiversity by avoiding the 'energy sprawl' that would be created by widespread reliance on biofuels, wind and solar power? Each of these claims can be tested empirically and answers may change as new technologies are developed. Although ecomodernists advocate intensification as a general rule of thumb, they also claim to be evidence-guided. For example, early Breakthrough Institute publications supported renewable energy exclusively without mention of nuclear power, but this position shifted to embrace nuclear amid growing awareness that intermittent renewables alone were unlikely to achieve deep decarbonization without dramatic advances in storage (see Sivaram 2018). Ecomodernism's distinctive claim is that the climate crisis is so severe that no technology should be off the table.

Ideological differences concerning centralization, materialism and consumption underpin many of these debates over technology. For example, given their narrow focus on climate change, ecomodernists often critique Germany's *Energiewende* (energy transition) policy for phasing out zero-carbon nuclear power plants while retaining polluting coal and lignite. German Greens have responded that the long-term goal of denuclearization justifies any short-term increase in greenhouse gases. But why is eliminating German nuclear reactors a higher priority than climate mitigation? Although long-standing Green critiques of technology, which gained prominence in Germany following the Chernobyl nuclear meltdown, seemed vindicated by the Fukushima

Daiichi Nuclear Power Plant accident, nuclear proponents have pointed out that nearly all of the health impacts from Fukushima resulted from poorly executed and often unnecessary evacuations, rather than from radiation exposure (Tanigawa et al. 2012). This anti-technology ideology also clashes with an earlier tradition of progressive thought, encompassing Marxist and social democratic thinkers, that recognizes a central role for technology in improving human welfare and that views the satisfaction of material needs as the primary political struggle. Today, the view that *culture* constitutes political life has become so influential that, given ecomodernism's focus on innovation and technology, some people argue ecomodernism can scarcely be called a political project (Hamilton 2015).

It is difficult to trace exactly how this move away from materialist politics occurred. It seems likely that it reflects both the post-war decades' unprecedent material wealth in the West, and a reaction against the catastrophes of the mid twentieth century. For example, Zygmunt Bauman's classic reflection on sociology after the holocaust (first published in 1989) exactly mirrors the Green critique of scale and hubristic interventions:

> [T]he bureaucratic culture which prompts us to view society as an object of administration, as a collection of so many 'problems' to be solved, as 'nature' to be 'controlled', 'mastered' and 'improved' or 'remade', as a legitimate target for 'social engineering' and in general a garden to be designed and kept in the planned shape by force was the very atmosphere in which the idea of the Holocaust could be conceived, slowly yet consistently developed and brought to its conclusion. (Bauman 2000, p. 18)

Bauman goes on to develop a wholesale critique of scale, arguing that:

> [T]he increase in the physical and or psychic distance between the act and its consequences achieves more than the suspension of moral inhibition; it quashes the moral significance

of the act and thereby pre-empts all conflict between personal
standards of moral decency and the immorality of the social
consequences of the act. (Bauman 2000, p. 25)

While some Green scholars have critiqued ecomodernism's
'humanism' (Crist 2015), perhaps Green localists are themselves articulating a rival humanist vision. Humanism is
an ethical perspective that focuses on human dignity and
potential. Whereas nineteenth and twentieth-century socialist thinkers generally advocated the centralized, efficient
provision of universal services as a means to satisfy material
needs, Greens now view decentralized, local production as
a more 'authentic' form of existence. Consequently, many
view climate change as a *moral* rather than a technological
challenge. They reason that if technology, industrialization,
materialism and consumption are the vices that have produced this mess, then we should resist each of these logics.
As a result, the environmental benefits of specific technologies become irrelevant. It doesn't matter that nuclear power
offers reliable zero-carbon electricity, that some GM seed
varieties enable increased carbon sequestration through
reduced tillage, or that the production of synthetic animal
proteins could replace the human domination of animals.
To accept these techno-fixes is to double down on the same
hubristic logic that has created the environmental crisis.

Conclusion

Ecomodernism arose as a heresy within the Green movement
and I think this explains its reception. When heretical groups
form, ritualistic mutual denunciations between defenders
of orthodoxy and deviant insiders are often deployed not
just to attack the other side, but also to allay anxieties
and solidify group-identity within each camp (Kurtz 1983).
While the Breakthrough Institute primarily seeks to articulate a positive agenda, ruminations by ecomodernists on
the failings of mainstream environmentalism probably also

serve a similar psychological function. For example, at the 2016 ecomodernist conference known as the 'Breakthrough Dialogue', Indian economist Samir Saran drew the strongest applause with the declaration that 'our poverty must not be your mitigation strategy'. This statement deftly ascribed moral superiority to an ecomodernist in-group, no doubt reinforcing group solidarity. Ritual denunciations flow both ways, of course. However, Greens may find the ecomodernist heresy especially discomforting because it is grounded in the *shared* belief that climate change is an urgent threat. So urgent, say the ecomodernists, that Greens should reconsider the judgements about zero-carbon technologies like nuclear power and hydroelectricity that they formed before the scale of the climate crisis was understood.

Thinking in terms of heresy also helps to explain why some Greens are hostile towards self-described ecomodernists, but are more accepting of non-environmentalists who share ecomodernist values. President Obama has probably been the most prominent advocate of ecomodernist ideas, although never using the word ecomodernist. As a presidential candidate, Obama promoted nuclear power's contribution to climate mitigation long before Nordhaus or Shellenberger advanced this argument. Throughout his presidency, he promoted state investments in low-carbon innovation and argued for a scientifically informed approach to controversial technologies like genetically modified foods. Obama's inaugural State of the Union Address broached a range of ecomodernist themes, including calls to support 'American innovation [for] continued investment in advanced biofuels and clean-coal technologies' and for 'a new generation of safe, clean nuclear power plants'. His 2015 *Mission Innovation Announcement* pledged to double clean energy R&D expenditure. Obama even boasted of having made the 'largest investment in basic research funding in history' (Obama 2010). Perhaps presidents are always held to different standards than environmental think-tanks, or perhaps many find the label 'ecomodernism' off-putting or even inexplicable. However, it is heartening that many who scorn ecomodernism supported President Obama's broadly ecomodernist agenda. The audience for ecomodernist ideas may be broadest when they are not framed as a critique of Green politics.

This chapter has focused on and drawn out the distinctions between ecomodernists' central beliefs and those typical of the Green movement. Consequently, I have largely failed to consider the commonalities between their views. In any event, the period of greatest acrimony over ecomodernism may already be passing. The need for the response to climate change to include improved innovation policy seems to be increasingly widely understood. In fact, a vision of technological transformation of some kind or other is characteristic of all but the most radical Greens.

Both camps also share a love of nature. While anthropologist Anna Tsing has dismissed ecomodernism, most ecomodernists would embrace Tsing's concern to cultivate 'arts of noticing' and 'curiosity' about human-nature assemblages (Tsing 2015, pp. 5–27). For example, Manuel Arias-Maldonado proposes that we should foster 'a sense of wonder' as well as distance 'toward the natural world' (Arias-Maldonado 2016, p. 56), Jessie Buettel has called for the cultivation of biophilia, possibly by gamifying nature, and Emma Marris (2017) paints a vision of 'interwoven decoupling ... in which the nature thriving by virtue of our efforts to consume less of it is easily accessible and part of our daily lives'.

3

Assessing the Technological Challenge

Many climate activists insist that 'we already have the technologies that we need' to eliminate GHG emissions and that the main barrier to effective mitigation is the political opposition of vested interests (Gore 2007, p. 213; see also Klein 2015, p. 16). Ecomodernists disagree. Instead, they argue that innovation and the diffusion of fundamentally new technologies will be needed to eliminate GHG emissions. Will private sector ingenuity or bottom-up social change do the job? Ecomodernists doubt these responses will be sufficient. Instead, they identify the state as the only actor with both the capacity and mandate to drive the necessary innovation. These debates partly reflect ideological differences, but they are also connected to different understandings of facts. Where do most GHG emissions come from? Is there a tiny elite who are responsible for most emissions? Do we already have technologies that, combined with plausible lifestyle change, would allow us to avoid dangerous warming? Is it still possible to avoid warming in excess of 1.5 or 2°C? Since our answers to these questions will guide our political responses, this chapter seeks to address each topic and then to discuss the lines of disagreement in the most politicized case: electricity.

Alternative Visions

Ted Trainer is a retired academic and seasoned political evangelist who, in the 1980s, established an 'alternative lifestyle education site' named Pigface Point on Sydney's suburban fringe. Pigface Point's mission is to demonstrate that a simple and self-sufficient way of life can be more interesting and rewarding than is possible in an affluent, capitalist consumer society. A visit takes in a home-made windmill, mud-brick making equipment and a permaculture garden as well as decorative bridges and whimsical signs, all intended to show the fun side of what Trainer calls 'The Simpler Way'. You've probably guessed that Trainer is not an ecomodernist. Nevertheless, Trainer, a retired academic, publishes both in influential Green journals like the *Bulletin of the Atomic Scientists* and on the ecomodernist 'Brave New Climate' blog run by Professor Barry Brook. Why? Because Trainer scorns the idea that today's renewable energy technologies can support anything resembling contemporary society (Trainer 2010). Radical reductions in production and consumption will be needed. Trainer identifies two pathways towards a low-carbon energy system: a massive roll-out of nuclear power, or a universal transition towards his proposed 'simpler way'.

On the other side of the planet, in Blacksburg (Virginia, USA), sociologist and yoga teacher Eileen Crist offers a different critique of ecomodernism. Crist describes the *Ecomodernist Manifesto* as a distinctly *humanist* response to the climate crisis and admits that there is something attractive in the Manifesto's emphasis on freedom and on universalizing the benefits of modernity. She even writes that ecomodernism probably describes a 'cleaner and better' form of modernization than the path that we are currently on. However, Crist worries that prioritizing human freedom over the natural world's self-expression degrades 'the dignity of the human that humanism holds so dear'. Thus, she argues that if 'human freedom [is] to coexist alongside nonhuman freedom, many of our modern so-called freedoms are in need of restricting' (Crist 2015, pp. 252–4). Which freedoms? Crist suggests it is impossible to sustainably provide for over seven billion people without unacceptable domination of non-human nature. A radical reduction in human numbers is needed. While I accept most steps in Crist's argument, I can't imagine a non-genocidal process through which to reduce the human population at a pace that is commensurate with the climate challenge. While improvements in female education and equality both have the potential to reduce population growth, even the most optimistic scenarios point towards stabilization rather than rapid population reduction (Samir and Lutz 2017).

Trainer, Crist and the ecomodernists all have very different political visions. However, they share a common understanding of some key facts. In particular, they agree that the climate crisis is very severe, will be difficult to address, and that it calls for collective societal responses rather than (exclusively) individual consumption choices. All of these claims are contested. To begin with, the question of whether climate change is real has, bizarrely, become a major point of political contention in the English-speaking world. Climate scepticism, a perspective that is completely unmoored from scientific opinion, even seems to have become a marker of Republican identity in the United States (Kahan and Corbin 2016). Some Republicans, like the Manhattan Institute's Oren Cass, do accept the reality of climate science but argue that humanity can easily adapt to a changing climate. In this view, mitigation need not be a high priority since the economic cost of climate change is trivial when compared with future economic growth (Cass 2018). Another conservative view holds that if a price is placed on carbon emissions, the market will supply necessary innovations. This diversity of perspectives reflects disagreements over values as well as facts. For example, Cass's analysis of climate costs may well be economically accurate, but only because economic analysis 'discounts' the future, accords little value to impacts on people whose incomes are modest, and does not assign a dollar value to ecological impacts that do not directly impact the economy. Thus, if rising seas drive tens of millions of very poor Bangladeshis from their homes, or if thousands of species that do not contribute to economic production become extinct, these tragic events count for little in economic analysis.

On the progressive side of politics there's a strong consensus that climate change is real. However, progressives are in something of a muddle over how difficult decarbonization will be. Some climate activists argue that climate change can be successfully addressed through individual behaviour changes such as flying less, eating local food and purchasing more durable goods. They argue that these changes will benefit everyone save a tiny extractivist elite (Klein 2015, p. 56). This view implicitly refutes the idea that mitigation is intrinsically difficult. By contrast, eco-modernists think innovation and diffusion of fundamentally new technologies will be needed if the entire global population is to access 'modern lifestyles' at the same time as we reduce GHG emission to zero. Amid competing values and contested facts, public discourse swirls between multiple incompatible themes. News articles outlining the top ten things you should do to reduce your emissions (don't have kids, become a vegan, stop driving etc.) compete with calls for private sector leadership, government regulation, divestment, or blockades. Rival narratives promise a Green jobs boom, that 'de-growth' is the only solution, that 'renewables are already winning the energy race' or that the climate emergency justifies a wartime footing.

In what follows I try to separate some evidence-based facts from value-linked disagreement. Much of the chapter draws from the most authoritative source we have – the Intergovernmental Panel on Climate Change (IPCC). There are credible scientists who argue that the IPCC either overestimates or underestimates climate sensitivity (Peters 2018, p. 378). Moreover, the IPCC is dominated by natural scientists from rich countries and this shapes its knowledge claims. Nevertheless, this international, scientific, consensus-seeking body provides the most carefully reviewed account of climate science that we have. It is thus useful for informing political reflection. As we will see, on many topics IPCC reports do not point conclusively towards any particular focus of political or regulatory action, and the IPCC's analysis is often politically inconvenient for all sides of climate debates. For example, it has suggested that carbon capture and storage is far more important for avoiding dangerous warming than is wind, solar or nuclear power. Moving outside the IPCC literature, I also map how emissions are distributed internationally, consider how a more equal distribution of wealth would impact emissions and briefly review the kinds of innovations that might best enable stringent mitigation.

The chapter reaches three conclusions. First, that stabilizing atmospheric concentrations of greenhouse gases at any level will require significant technological advances. The IPCC makes this point in its finding that development of 'new technologies is crucial for the ability to realistically implement stringent carbon policies' (Somanathan et al. 2014, s15.6.6, p. 1178). The phrase 'realistically implement' recognizes that global convergence on a very low level of energy consumption is, although theoretically possible, politically infeasible. If the majority of the world's population aspires to a moderately prosperous living standard (to borrow the Chinese Communist Party's phrase), the low-energy path is clearly impossible. This point links to a second conclusion: although the global distribution of GHG emissions is radically unequal, blame cannot be placed only on some tiny extractivist elite. Third, warming in excess of 2°C is now almost certain, unless some artificial means of reducing temperature (solar geoengineering) or of capturing carbon from the atmosphere (carbon dioxide removal) is developed and deployed.

Sources of greenhouse gas emissions and the need for technological innovation

Any political response to climate change should be built on an understanding of where emissions come from: which industries, which countries and which people are responsible for what? If we accept that we need to achieve zero emissions within a few decades, then we must eventually identify every significant emissions source and eliminate it, either by developing zero-carbon alternatives or by changing our patterns of consumption.

According to the IPCC's Fifth Assessment Report, four economic sectors dominate global GHG emissions: electricity, industry, agriculture and transport (IPCC 2014b, p. 9). Generation of electricity and heat together account for about 25% of global emissions, most of which is consumed by buildings and industry (buildings are responsible for over 18% of all emissions, and about two thirds of this is from electricity). Coal accounts for the lion's share of electricity sector emissions, even though gas, oil and diesel all play a role. The overwhelming political focus on electricity generation is a bit unbalanced, given that it accounts for less than a quarter of emissions. However, decarbonizing electricity is a high priority because abundant clean electricity would assist decarbonizing many other sectors. 'Electrify everything' is a common catch-cry among decarbonization wonks. For example, many industrial processes might be decarbonized through electrification. Industry, which the IPCC suggests accounts for 21% of direct emissions, includes carbon-intensive processes like the manufacture of steel, aluminium and iron. Metallurgical or 'coking' coal plays a key role here – and its use has expanded roughly in tandem with the global demand for steel.

Transport is responsible for only 14% of global emissions. Despite the attention given to electric cars, a high proportion of transport emissions are from shipping and aviation where, despite continuing improvements in efficiency, there are currently no carbon-neutral alternative technologies. The final giant emissions category (24%) is 'agriculture, forestry and other land uses' (IPCC 2014b, p. 9). In addition to CO_2, agriculture is also the dominant source of methane (CH_4) (which accounts for about 16% of GHG emissions), nitrous oxide (N_2O) and some fluorinated gases (IPCC 2014b, p. 6). Here, the IPCC has identified some significant, cost-effective mitigation possibilities, such as 'cropland management, grazing land management, and restoration of organic soils' that would be possible without technological innovation (IPCC 2014b, p. 24). However, innovation is needed to tackle a wide variety of emissions, such as those associated with fertilizer production, ruminant animals and rice farming. Perhaps agriculture is neglected in public discussion because agricultural emissions are so diverse. Or perhaps the deep cultural significance of national cuisines and agricultural practices has prompted climate activists to show deference. Milk, beef and rice are not as easily demonized as coal.

Before moving on, I should emphasize that there is considerable uncertainty surrounding the climate impacts of many specific activities because of the complexity of human impacts. One slightly bizarre example is shipping which, despite being responsible for about 2% of global GHG emissions, probably has a slight net cooling impact globally. Container ships warm the planet through both CO_2 and black soot emissions. However, they also contribute to global dimming through emissions of sulfur (SO_2) and nitrogen oxides (NO_x). What's more, the iron distributed by their exhaust fertilizes the ocean, encourages plankton growth and thus increases the uptake of carbon from the atmosphere (Ito 2013). I'll mention another 'climate forcing' just because it's a rare bit of unambiguously positive good news: the gradual increase in whale numbers since an international whaling moratorium began to be implemented in 1982 has increased the ocean's removal of atmospheric carbon (Lavery et al. 2010; Pershing et al. 2010). Two processes are at work here. First, whale excrement fertilizes CO_2-absorbing plankton growth. Second, whale carcasses contain carbon which is sequestered when they fall to the ocean floor.

The need for technological innovation

What innovations (or social transformations) would be needed to achieve zero, and then negative emissions? Since the list of necessary innovations is pretty much the flipside of the list of sources of emissions, the diversity of challenges can be bewildering. However, the most difficult to decarbonize energy services have been carefully studied. They include aviation, shipping and long-distance transport, as well as carbon intensive materials like steel and cement (Davis et al. 2017, 2018). As we have seen, reliable electricity could be supplied with mature low-carbon technologies like nuclear power. However reliable electricity supply is often included on the list of necessary innovations, because if electricity generation is to include a high proportion of intermittent renewable energy (wind and solar) and nuclear power is excluded, then development of new dispatchable non-CO_2-emitting generation and storage technologies will be needed. Natural gas with carbon capture and storage, flow-batteries and compressed-air storage are all possibilities.

Zero-carbon energy dense fuels are needed for both transport (aviation and shipping) and industrial applications – but how to produce them? Electricity-to-fuel conversion or solar fuels are possibilities. A wide range of innovations are also needed for the quarter of emissions from industrial processes (e.g. cement and steel manufacture). Agriculture is harder still – some emissions here are near-impossible to eliminate without social change. For example, ruminant animals (cattle, pigs etc.) and rice paddies will always produce methane, although some methane might be captured as occurs in some piggeries. Innovations here might create efficiencies (e.g. higher-yield rice) or alternative products (e.g. synthetic meat).

The International Energy Agency's Innovation Tracking Framework identifies about 100 'innovation gaps' across thirty-eight clean energy technologies (IEA 2018). Many of these innovation gaps – such as zero-carbon processes for producing Ethylene, Propylene and Aromatics – will probably remind those of us who are not trained in chemical engineering how dimly we understand the industrial processes on which our lifestyles depend. Methanol is a chemical industry feedstock as well as a fuel, so zero-carbon methanol is an important goal. There are multiple pathways through which zero-carbon methanol might be produced (e.g. from biomass or from electrolytic hydrogen and CO_2) – but the path to cost-effective commercialization is challenging. Innovations are also needed in carbon capture and utilization (CCU) or storage (CCS). Many environmentalists worry CCS's real purpose is to prolong the use of fossil fuels, and they are right. CCS is often promoted by advocates of coal and natural gas. However, were a low-cost, socially accepted form of carbon capture developed, decarbonization of a whole range of industries – including zero-carbon cement, chemicals, steel and iron – would suddenly become feasible. Carbon-utilization or low-cost carbon storage would also clear the path to 'negative emissions' which will be needed if we wish to keep warming well below 2°C (see IPCC 2018, p. 23).

So how is innovation progressing? The International Energy Agency (IEA) maintains a 'tracking clean energy progress' website (IEA 2018), which assesses the kinds of technological progress that would be needed to implement the 'sustainable development scenario' targets for 2030. Ecomodernists will view the IEA's sustainable development scenario as inadequate, as it assumes continuing inequality in international access to energy, and measures technological progress against 2030 targets rather than against the goal of complete decarbonization. However, even with these inadequate standards the IEA has grim news. It identifies only four technologies – solar, lighting, data centres and electric vehicles – where progress is consistent with 2030 targets.

Electricity and innovation

Most of the public discussion of climate policy concerns electricity, and frequently, the need to transition away from coal-fired power. Weirdly, some of the nastiest fights concerning electricity are between people who all agree that we should rapidly decarbonize electricity generation. Peak nastiness was probably reached in November 2017 when

Mark Jacobson, the pioneering advocate of 100% renewable energy, whose work inspires both Bernie Sanders and Naomi Klein, filed a $10 million defamation suit (subsequently dropped) against his academic critics. Jacobson's complaint concerned a paper published in the *Proceedings of the National Academy of Sciences* by environmental scientist Christopher Clack and twenty co-authors, several of whom have links to the Breakthrough Institute. Clack et al. had reviewed a paper in which Jacobson had claimed to demonstrate the feasibility of a 100% renewable electricity grid for the United States. The authors accused Jacobson of 'modelling errors' and 'implausible' and 'unsubstantiated assumptions' (Clack et al. 2017). In academic language that's some extreme shade. Even so, academic brawls are usually settled in academic journals not law courts.

Debates over renewable energy may be especially heated because they connect to a culture war that's been brewing between some Greens and climate hawks. Strip away all the detail and Jacobson's critics are claiming that climate change is so serious that we must think outside Green ideology. Since opposition to nuclear technologies has been central to the development of modern environmentalism, climate change has created something of a dilemma. While the (near) zero-carbon grids of France, Ontario and Sweden provide a template for successful decarbonization, most environmentalists prefer an as-yet-never-implemented strategy of 100% non-hydro renewables. By contrast, ecomodernists typically emphasize the decarbonizing potential of nuclear power. Here, they have gained the support of many scientists. The most prominent is James Hansen, a former NASA climatologist, who is often dubbed the father of climate awareness because in 1988 he was the first to alert the US Senate to climate dangers. Hansen has branded 'Big Green's opposition to nuclear power' as a major obstacle to solving the climate problem and he regularly advocates nuclear power at international climate negotiations. In response, some Green activists have accused Hansen of a 'new form of climate denialism' (Specter 2015).

Whom should we believe – advocates of 100% renewable energy, or their ecomodernist critics? It is not possible to answer this question definitively as the future of technological change is inherently uncertain. Instead I will outline a few key arguments made by both sides, and observe how well they fit with current trends. Renewable energy advocates commonly argue that wind and solar are already the cheapest form of electricity, so their triumph over fossil fuels is now inevitable. This claim mixes truth with fantasy. First the truth: cost declines in solar and wind power have been extraordinary. In much of the world, wind and solar really can produce electricity more cheaply than any other new-build sources of electricity. As a result, wind and solar will now continue to be deployed at scale, even without subsidies. But if wind and solar are cheapest, why is generation from other sources like coal, gas, hydroelectricity and nuclear power also continuing to grow? The basic reason is that dispatchable (on-demand) sources can command a higher price for the electricity they produce. That is to say, dispatchable sources typically make a more valuable contribution to maintaining a stable electricity supply.

The best thing about solar and wind power is that, after their capital costs have been paid, they generate electricity that is basically free whenever the sun shines or the wind blows. Unfortunately, this is also the biggest weakness of intermittent renewables: the fact that they produce abundant electricity sometimes but nothing at other times undermines the economic value of the electricity they produce. By contrast, hydroelectric dams and natural gas 'peaking plants' tend to be very good at switching on and off in response to changing demand. The capacity to 'load follow', ramping supply up or down to keep production and consumption balanced, increases their value to the grid. This is why the claim that wind and solar will soon dominate most grids is a fantasy. Although wind and solar produce the cheapest electricity, supply does not align with when electricity is needed. As long as wind and solar only provide a modest proportion of a grid's energy, their intermittency isn't a problem. For example, solar energy is usually most abundant during the middle of the day, when electricity demand is fairly high, so quite a large amount of solar power is likely to be valuable on any grid. However, as the share of electricity from intermittent renewables increases, so do the challenges of preserving secure supply in months when there is little sun or wind. Maintaining a stable grid requires that supply and demand must be kept in perfect balance at all times. Intermittent supply makes this balancing job harder.

There are many different ways to manage the problem of 'intermittency' and thus to increase the proportion of electricity that can come from intermittent sources: load-shifting, storage and interconnection are three of the most discussed. 'Load-shifting' or 'demand management' refers to efforts to shift energy use to times when renewable energy is abundant. The idea is that smart grids will switch on air-conditioning units, pool pumps and refrigerators at times when the wind is blowing. Another alternative is storage. Lithium-ion batteries have already dropped in price so far that in situations where 'frequent cycling' is needed to regulate frequency on a minute-to-minute basis, grid scale storage is already competitive. However, storage capable of supplying electricity across days or weeks in which there is limited sun or wind is much more difficult. It is possible that future advances in battery storage, such as sulphur flow-batteries, will solve this problem and provide seasonal storage at a very low cost. However, at present the most cost-effective storage is usually from pumped hydroelectricity. These systems pump water to an upper reservoir when electricity is abundant, and run it downhill through generators when supply is needed. Unfortunately, since pumped hydro takes up a bit of space, and is reasonably expensive, it can be difficult to build at scale. A third solution is to connect grids from all around the world with 'interconnectors'. Since the sun is always shining somewhere, a globally connected electricity grid could resolve the problem of intermittency. However, electricity supply is intensely political, and governments have shown little interest in casting their lot – often with geopolitical foes – in such a global scheme. In fact, electricity supply is so politically fraught that many countries still don't even have unified national grids. A global hyper-grid seems a distant prospect.

Load-shifting, storage and interconnection are already playing increasing roles in integrating an ever-greater share of renewable energy into electricity grids. This trajectory still has a long way further to run. However, at the time of writing no significant economy sources more than about half its electricity from intermittent renewables, and the leaders – Denmark and South Australia – both rely on interconnectors with regional grids to supply electricity when the winds are low. In effect, these renewable-energy leaders use surrounding states as batteries. People with great expertise hold widely divergent views on how fast we might make further progress, so I won't pretend to predict the future. My guess is that in countries like Australia with ample solar energy resources, the pace of progress in storage technology will be the limiting factor that will determine how soon a 100% renewable grid might be possible.

For those places that are not blessed with large reserves of hydroelectric storage, it is clear that the dream of 100% renewable energy is at best many decades away. It's also clear that an all-renewable grid will be much more expensive than, say, a 60% renewable grid that sources 40% of its energy from a zero-carbon source of firm capacity (Sepulveda et al. 2018). One of the most influential researchers working on zero-carbon grids, former Breakthrough Institute staffer Jesse Jenkins, uses the term 'zero-carbon flexible base' to describe the type of energy source that, although likely to be more expensive than wind and solar, will be needed to fill in the gaps in intermittent supply. The list of technologies that might supply a 'zero-carbon flexible base' is currently quite short – it includes nuclear power, hydroelectricity, gas + carbon capture and storage, and potentially solar thermal, even if the actual performance of installed solar thermal plants has so far been disappointing (de Castro and Capellán-Pérez 2018).

While decarbonization of electricity grids using nuclear power is clearly technically possible, political resistance is so high that a nuclear-led path to global decarbonization seems equally implausible. Nuclear's share of global electricity grew rapidly until the 1980s, when growth stalled. This stagnation has continued for so long that the world has lost the skills and expertise needed to build nuclear power at scale. While several countries achieved near zero-emissions grids in the 1980s, this achievement seems less feasible today. Some people hold hopes that advanced non-light-water reactors, or possibly even nuclear fusion, will transform electricity generation. However, deployment of these technologies will also require several more decades at best (Morgan et al. 2018).

Nevertheless, electricity is the one area where it is possible to argue that we really do have the technologies we need. Global electricity demand could theoretically be supplied by a combination of nuclear power, solar, hydroelectricity and wind, and there is no technical reason why a transition to nuclear power (and renewables) could not be completed within two to three decades (Qvist and Brook 2015). However, since hydroelectricity and nuclear face significant political barriers, hydroelectricity is geographical limited, and integration of intermittent renewables involves technological hurdles, the carbon intensity of global electricity production has remained almost stable since 1990 (Ang and Su 2016). That is to say that during the era in which we have understood the dangers of climate change, electricity sector emissions have increased at roughly the same rate as electricity generation. While there are several energy sources – solar and nuclear power are the most obvious – that could theoretically supply the entire planet with zero-carbon electricity, the near-term prospects for rapid mitigation are poor. Nevertheless, evidence suggests that a least-cost zero-carbon grid will usually include large amounts of low-cost intermittent renewable energy alongside more expensive 'flexible base' or 'firm' low-carbon resources (Sepulveda et al. 2018). Thus, decarbonization will be faster and cheaper if we are willing to utilize all zero-carbon energy sources.

Is a tiny elite to blame?

As the IPCC's Fifth Assessment Report was being finalized in April 2014, some media alleged it was being 'censored' (Stern 2014). Three graphs, the first depicting historical emissions by region, the second per capita emissions, and the third emissions embodied in trade, had been deleted from the 'Summary for Policymakers' at the last minute. Although the claims of censorship were a beat-up, the story of the deleted graphs is revealing. Each IPCC report consists of a scientific report, and a separate 'Summary for Policymakers' whose contents must be agreed by state representatives. This process is designed precisely so that inconvenient truths can be airbrushed out of the most politically sensitive summary document. The graphs showed that since the mid 1970s most growth in CO_2 emissions had occurred *outside* the OECD, that developed countries were now responsible for less than half of all historical emissions, that per capita emissions in rich countries remained high, and that a significant proportion of the third world's emissions arose from producing goods that were consumed in the rich world. This data torpedoed the G77's narrative that addressing climate change was primarily a first-world problem, but it also undermined any sense that the rich world was making adequate progress towards decarbonization.

Historically, carbon emissions first began to surge in those places that were first to industrialize and exploit fossil fuels at scale: Europe and then North America. Even today, the 1.4 billion people living in rich countries (the OECD) have average per capita emissions (approximately $12tCO_2e$) that are almost four times greater than the per capita emissions of the six billion people living in the third world. Since human development, wealth, energy use and CO_2 emissions are all tightly correlated, inequality in emissions reflects wider patterns of economic inequality.[14] As countries like China and India have industrialized, their emissions have increased rapidly. Consequently, roughly two thirds of all emissions now originate outside the OECD, while the list of the biggest national emitters (China, US, India) includes countries whose historical emissions have been trivial. Even today, India's per capita emissions (approx. 1.8 tonnes of CO_2 per capita in 2017) remain far below the global average of approximately $6.2tCO_2e$ per year (see Chancel and Piketty 2015, p. 11). As third-world people demand the benefits of access to modern energy – things like better paying jobs, refrigeration, electric cooking, washing machines and computers – this shift in the geography of global emissions will continue. If poorer people's demands for modern energy are to be satisfied, the world must dramatically expand energy access even as it cuts pollution.

Comparing average national emissions underplays the depth of international inequality, as it ignores both growing national inequality and international trade. For example, there are hundreds of millions of people in China and India who have now joined the global middle class. Their emissions and lifestyles resemble those in the OECD. Moreover, as third-world manufacturing industries producing goods for Western consumers have expanded, the emissions that support rich people's consumption have shifted 'south'. Inventories that measure national production-linked emissions offer an increasingly poor guide to carbon-linked inequality as a result of the emissions 'embodied in trade'.

In 2015, Lucas Chancel and Thomas Piketty wrote an important paper analysing inequality in global GHG emissions. They found that, although the global distribution of GHG emissions was not quite as unequal as the

---

[14] There are some countries like Uruguay, France, Sweden and Switzerland where measures of human development appear to have decoupled from CO_2 emissions; while multiple factors are at work here, all have significant nuclear or hydroelectricity supplies.

distribution of income, inequalities were still stark. For example, the world's very richest people (the very richest Americans, Singaporeans, and Saudis etc.) have lifestyles that generate roughly 2,000 times the per capita emissions of the world's very poorest (around $0.1tCO_2e$ per year in Honduras, Rwanda and Malawi). Globally, the activities of the top 10% account for 45% of all emissions. These statistics certainly substantiate claims that an elite group is 'most responsible' for climate change, but they also reveal that this elite group is quite large. Most first-world climate activists who focus their resentment upward towards a profligate polluting elite are themselves members of what, by global standards, is a profligate elite. Virtually everyone who lives in rich countries such as the United States, the UK or Australia is part of the most polluting 10%. I'm a childless vegetarian who has never owned a car, but I'm part of the most polluting 1%. Why? Because I travel by air a few times a year. If you want to know if you're also part of the profligate elite, you might begin by looking at your passport.

Meanwhile, the poorest 50% of humanity are responsible for only 13% of global emissions and so might be viewed as blameless victims of climate harms (Chancel and Piketty 2015, p. 30). Many projections of future energy demand anticipate that present-day patterns of inequality will continue into the distant future. If these predictions are accurate, many lower-income communities will have little need for mitigation policy as poverty will ensure that their emissions remain trivial. However, a mitigation strategy that's built around the expectation that half of humanity will remain in energy poverty is both unjust, and likely to fail. Many climate advocates pretend that there's no tension between emissions and development, as they hope future 'development' will utilize only 'appropriate technologies' such as solar power and permacultural farming. However, emissions and human development remain tightly correlated. With today's technologies, reducing poverty necessarily means increasing emissions (Lamb and Rao 2015). It's possible that the correlation between development, wealth and emissions might weaken over time – but an enormous amount of social and technological innovation would be needed to sever this link. Tragically, in the period Chancel and Picketty studied – 1998 to 2013 – the only group whose emissions actually fell were the very poorest decile. In the same period that some third-world people were joining a global middle class of high emitters, the bottom billion were falling further behind.

Degrowth and unequal consumption

Chancel and Picketty (2015) have illustrated the global distribution of emissions by identifying the kinds of people whose emissions are around 7 tCO_2e per person – just slightly above world average. In this category we find the 'top 1% of earners from Tanzania, the upper middle class in Mongolia and China (7th decile) [so there are a couple of hundred million Chinese whose emissions are higher] as well as poor French and Germans (respectively 2nd and 3rd income deciles)'. Chancel and Picketty find that this 'middle 40%' of the global population are responsible for 42% of all GHG emissions, and given the improving economic fortunes of this group, their emissions are also growing fastest (Chancel and Picketty 2015, pp. 30–2).

If rich people could be persuaded to live more simply, would that create headspace for the poor to consume more? Could we converge on a level of consumption that meets everyone's needs while also respecting ecological limits? It depends on where you set the bar. Some scholars who advocate de-growth and radical reductions in material consumption have sought to quantify the level of human development that is consistent with staying within planetary boundaries (O'Neil et al. 2018). While currently there is no country that meets its citizens' basic needs at a level of resource use consistent with avoiding dangerous climate change, basic physical needs such as nutrition, sanitation, minimal access to electricity and the elimination of extreme poverty could probably be met for all people. However, satisfaction of 'more qualitative goals' such as 'high life satisfaction, healthy life, secondary education, democratic quality, social support' cannot be universally met unless we find much more efficient ways to translate resource use into social outcomes (O'Neil et al. 2018, p. 92). There are two obvious ways in which social provisioning might be improved – enhanced public service delivery (as per the social democratic model) and technological innovation.

Back in 2011, the late Swedish statistician Hans Rosling gave a Ted talk titled 'The Magic Washing Machine' that indirectly proposed a point at which material consumption might converge: access to an electric washing machine. Rosling suggested that we should divide the world population into four income levels, which he labelled 'fire people' (lacking any access to electricity and cooking on open fires), 'bulb people' (with intermittent access to electricity), 'washing machine people' and finally the richest group, the 'air people' who potentially have the means to fly. In 2017 around one billion people lived in extreme poverty on less than $1 per day. Another three billion had incomes between $2 and $8; another two billion earned between $8 and $32. This is the income level at which washing machine access (not necessarily ownership) might become possible. At level four, there are around a billion people who earn in excess of $32 per day – these are the air people (Rosling et al. 2018, p. 33). Rosling points out that while the richest billion consume around half of all global energy, even the washing machine people consume more than an equal share. That is to say – if the whole world were to converge at a level of consumption where people could afford access to washing machines, but not air-travel, global energy demand would increase substantially.

Now keep in mind that global population growth, although slowing, is not likely to stabilize until our numbers equal eight billion people. While most predictions suggest a global population of ten billion is likely, improvements in female education and equality could theoretical produce a peak closer to eight billion (Samir and Lutz 2017). Much of this population growth will result from people living longer. Average world fertility is already approaching the 'replacement rate' so, barring disasters, a population peaking at well over eight billion people is almost inevitable. If you share my hope for an egalitarian world in which everyone reaches at least a 'washing machine' level of comfort, the resulting energy demand is vast. Nine billion 'washing machine' people, would require around one and half times as much energy as was used in 2010, even if none of them ever flies in a plane, uses air conditioning or owns a private car.

Since the prospects of persuading the rich world to slash its energy use this much are remote, it might be more plausible to consider the energy demand if nine billion people were to live like those in today's rich world. In this case, total energy demand would be about five times greater than it is today. Now, let's imagine that with reduced consumption in the rich world, and increasing human development in the third world, consumption instead converged around today's level in Sweden, a highly energy efficient country. In this scenario, global primary energy consumption would be roughly four times greater than today.[15]

Personally, I find the vision of global convergence on a low-energy future quite miserable. For example, I think international travel can be enormously enriching (Chen et al. 2018). In my vision of a good life, any ordinary person might hope to spend a semester studying overseas, perform the hajj, visit family during Golden Week, or attend the World Cup. I am shocked and angered by those 'progressive' climate activists like Naomi Klein who hold up Mark Jacobson's plans for an all-renewable future as evidence that we already have the technologies we need for *everyone* to lead a good life. Let's assume that Jacobson's 100% renewable

---

[15] In 2016, Sweden (population 9.8 million) consumed 52 million tonnes of oil equivalent of primary energy (=2.217 exajoules). See BP (2017, p. 7).

proposals could actually be implemented (Jacobson et al. 2017). What world do the 100% renewable advocates aspire to? In Jacobson's model, global energy use would be so radically unequal that even in 2050, each American would consume more electricity than five Indians.[16] Instead of accepting persisting poverty, I think our goal should be to create technologies that allow everyone everywhere to enjoy enriching energy services without GHG emissions.

Assessing the cost of ambitious mitigation

Economic analysis suggests both that there is a compelling cost-benefit case for ambitious mitigation, and that the costs of decarbonization could be relatively trivial. The Intergovernmental Panel on Climate Change's (IPCC) Fifth Assessment Report summarized economic research into mitigation costs as follows:

> [M]itigation scenarios that reach atmospheric concentra-
> tions of about 450 ppm CO_2eq by 2100 entail losses in
> global consumption – not including benefits of reduced
> climate change as well as co-benefits and adverse side-effects
> of mitigation – of 1% to 4% (median: 1.7%) in 2030, 2%

---

[16] These calculations are rough. However, Jacobson's tables for 2050 identify 996 GW/8,725 TWh of total end-use demand for India and 1,291.\ GW/11,313 TWh for the United States. According to the United Nations' 2017 World Population Prospects report, current US population is 324,459,000 and it is projected to grow to 389,592,000 by 2050, while the respective figures for India are 1,339,180,000 and 1,658,978,000. Using 2017 population ratios (which understate the likely per-capita disparity) this suggests a comparison of 0.744:3.979 kW per capita or 6.51:34.87 MWh per capita (meaning that US citizens would use about 5.3 times as much electricity per capita). From: https://esa.un.org/unpd/wpp/Publications/Files/WPP2017_KeyFindings.pdf; http://web.stanford.edu/group/efmh/jacobson/Articles/I/AllCountries.xlsx

to 6% (median: 3.4%) in 2050, and 3% to 11% (median: 4.8%) in 2100 relative to consumption in baseline scenarios that grows anywhere from 300% to more than 900% over the century. (IPCC 2014b, p. 15)

In other words, if we adopted economically ideal policies, avoiding dangerous climate change would be so cheap as to be virtually unnoticeable.

So, is Naomi Klein right after all? Is resistance from fossil fuel industries the only barrier to avoiding dangerous climate change? If only it were that easy. The IPCC explains the key assumptions that inform the above assessment:

Scenarios in which all countries of the world begin mitigation immediately, there is a single global carbon price, and all key technologies are available, have been used as a cost-effective benchmark for estimating macroeconomic mitigation costs. (IPCC 2014b, p. 15)

Unfortunately, not only do none of these three conditions apply, but there are two more important assumptions built into the IPCC's modelling: that deep inequalities in energy access will continue far into the future; and that investments in low-carbon research and development will increase.

Let us take these assumptions one by one. First, ambitious mitigation is not beginning immediately. The Fifth Assessment Report was published in 2014, and serious mitigation is yet to commence. Second, there has been almost no progress towards a global carbon price. National carbon pricing is certainly valuable, but a global scheme would unlock distinct benefits. Since almost all contemporary emissions growth is occurring outside the OECD, this is also where most least-cost mitigation opportunities are located. Economists and ethicists thus typically agree that it would be desirable to invest first-world resources in constructing zero-carbon infrastructure in the third world. Unfortunately, international emissions trading schemes enjoy virtually no political support, despite their impeccable economic credentials. Climate activists often argue that rich countries have a moral obligation to 'lead by example' and to meet their emissions targets without purchasing international offsets. Meanwhile, conservatives typically oppose policies that seem to surrender economic strength. To date the most significant international pricing scheme has been the Kyoto Protocol's Clean Development Mechanism (CDM) which, while mobilizing many billions of dollars, was widely critiqued for serious design flaws. Unfortunately, although the Paris Agreement makes provision for negotiation of a future scheme, it did not build on the experience of CDM to implement any new form of international emissions pricing.

While there has been almost no progress towards *international* carbon pricing, carbon pricing is increasingly common at a domestic level. In late 2017, the World Bank reported that around 20% of global carbon dioxide emissions would soon be subject to some kind of carbon pricing. However, where a carbon price has been implemented, it is usually set at below US\$10/tCO_2e. This is far below the level that would be consistent with achieving the Paris Agreement's temperature goals, which would be in the range of US\$40–80/tCO_2e. Currently, only around 1% of emissions are priced within that range (World Bank et al. 2017, p. 11). The inadequacy of carbon pricing in part reflects resistance from major polluters. Fossil fuel 'extractivists' have worked hard to undermine effective policy. However, carbon pricing also receives a lukewarm public reception. Australia's brief experiment with emissions pricing in 2012 illustrates this political fragility. Although the Australian scheme was designed to be revenue negative (i.e. voters were compensated by more than the revenue raised), the conservative opposition, campaigning on the slogan 'Axe the tax', won the subsequent election in 2013. As this book goes to press in late 2018, yellow-vested rioters, initially angered by increases in fuel taxes, are roiling French politics.

As David Victor observes, carbon prices have been much better accepted in the (mostly European) countries that already have relatively expensive (and highly taxed) energy than they have been in places where energy costs are lower.

Victor attributes this to the human tendency to be loss-averse and to ground expectations in past experience. Voting publics have frequently rejected policies that create a significant proportional increase in energy costs (Victor 2011, pp. 124–5). Meanwhile, jurisdictions as diverse as China, California and the European Union have faced similar problems when implementing carbon-pricing: over-allocation of initial permits has undermined carbon prices, and undermined their effectiveness and ambition (Ball 2018).

The IPCC's economic estimates also stipulate a third condition: the availability of 'all key technologies'. In the IPCC's models, the two technologies considered most valuable for global decarbonization are carbon capture and storage (CCS) and bioenergy. This may seem odd since CCS is currently virtually non-existent and bioenergy supplies only a trivial proportion of global energy. However, CCS will be valuable for decarbonizing many industrial sectors, such as steel making, and CCS combined with bioenergy plays a major role in many of the 'scenarios' that identify how dangerous warming might be avoided, as it is imagined that this combination of technologies might achieve 'negative emissions' (Maher 2018, pp. 102–6). In other words, since it now seems certain that global emissions will exceed a safe carbon budget, CCS combined with bioenergy or potentially direct-air capture, will be called on to clean up the mess.

While the IPCC recognizes that nuclear, wind and solar are all valuable, it places a much higher economic value on CCS and bioenergy (IPCC 2014b, p. 15). The IPCC's analysis here may be fallible. However, the fact that there is virtually no political support for the three technologies (CCS, bioenergy and nuclear power) that the IPCC judges are most valuable to climate mitigation is another reason to believe that mitigation is likely to be considerably more expensive than 'least-cost estimates' suggest. Indeed, given the high levels of political support for renewable energy it seems likely that this more difficult and expensive path will remain central to mitigation efforts. However, if intermittent energy sources are to drive emissions cuts, innovations in storage, associated grid services and development of solar fuels will be needed.

This brings us to assumptions concerning innovation policies in economic estimates of the cost of mitigation. Most major economic studies of least-cost mitigation assume investments in low-carbon innovation will increase to between three and ten times today's levels (Stern 2006; Garnaut 2008, pp. 219–23). The need for increased investment in innovation to correct the 'market failure' that generates inadequate investment in public goods is well established in the economic literature. It is unfortunate then, that these same studies are frequently used to support the claim that mitigation can be cheap and that 'we have all the technologies we need' (Gore 2007, p. 213; see also Klein 2015, p. 16). Instead, economic studies demonstrate that efficient policy would require a suite of policy measures that are almost entirely absent from the public discussion of climate policy: a global carbon price, technology neutral policies, and increased investment in innovation. Arguably, this suggests it might be valuable for climate activism to focus less narrowly on the promotion of renewable energy.

Why warming of 2°C is now all but inevitable

Why do I think 2°C of warming is inevitable? One way to understand the depth of our climate predicament is by considering the pace at which concentrations of greenhouse gases in the atmosphere are increasing, and the levels of warming consistent with different concentrations. Since human activities both warm and cool the planet, and since there are many different 'forcing agents' (pollutants with a warming or cooling impact) such estimates are complex. However, the IPCC creates a standard measure of most human impacts expressed as the atmospheric CO_2-equivalent concentration (CO_2-eq). This number – which the IPCC has estimated was at 430 parts per million (ppm) in 2011 as against a CO_2 concentration of 392 ppm (IPCC 2014b,

p. 8)[17] – provides a measure of the 'concentration of carbon dioxide (CO_2) that would cause the same radiative forcing as a given mixture of CO_2 and other forcing components' (IPCC 2014c, p. 121).[18] In 2018, atmospheric CO_2 concentrations passed 410 ppm for the first time and the CO_2-eq concentration was probably well over 440 ppm. Atmospheric concentrations are continuing to increase at over 2 ppm each year – the increase of almost 3 ppm in 2015 was elevated by the El Nino weather pattern.

What do these numbers mean for future warming? Predictions concerning future warming are confounded by uncertainty about future emissions and uncertainty about how 'sensitive' the climate system will be to elevated concentrations of greenhouse gases. To sort through this complexity, the IPCC develops hundreds of scenarios that map different trajectories of emissions; these scenarios are then fed into models of the climate system. Scenarios where likely temperature increases by 2100 are between 1.5°C and 1.7°C require that atmospheric concentrations be in the range of 430–480 ppm CO_2-eq by the end of the century (IPCC 2014b, Table SPM.1 p. 12). Today's atmospheric concentrations of over 440 ppm CO_2-eq place us in this 1.5°C danger zone, and emissions are rising fast. Thus, 1.5 °C scenarios typically allow for a period of 'overshoot' that is subsequently corrected by negative emissions. A target of 2°C creates a little more breathing room – atmospheric concentrations need only to stabilize at about 500 ppm

---

[17] The inclusion of all forcing agents introduces a high level of uncertainty, so the IPCC is only confident that the figure falls in the range 340 to 520 ppm.

[18] The IPCC (2014b, p. 12) explains that its measure of CO_2-equivalence includes the forcing due to all GHGs (including halogenated gases and tropospheric ozone), aerosols (pollutants that generally cool the planet) and albedo changes (changes in the amount of the sun's energy that is absorbed by the earth or reflected into space, through variations in cloudiness, snow, vegetation and land cover changes etc.).

CO_2-eq by 2100 (IPCC 2014b, Table SPM.1 p. 12). However, while this larger budget appears to offer breathing space, achieving it would require global emissions to fall by about 5% each year until we approach zero emissions. Instead, global emissions are continuing to increase.

Will the Paris Agreement solve this problem? To date, it hasn't. Each year the United Nations Environment Programme (UNEP) publishes an 'Emissions Gap Report' that seeks to quantify mitigation progress. As the title suggests, the report highlights a significant gap between current targets and the kind of progress that could avert dangerous warming. UNEP finds that whereas avoiding dangerous warming will require that emissions start falling rapidly, full implementation of the Paris Agreement targets would achieve only about one third of the emissions reductions needed for a least-cost pathway to limiting warming to well below 2°C. In fact, even with full implementation of Paris pledges, global emissions in 2030 will be higher than in 2017, and 80% of the 'emissions budget' consistent with 2°C of warming will have been exhausted (UNEP 2017, pp. xiv–xv). As the IPCC explains, 'halting the global average temperature rise at any level will require net zero global CO_2 emissions at some point in the future' (UNFCCC 2015a, p. 8). Consequently, even limiting warming to 3°C would require 'a fundamental transformation of the energy system and global GHG emission levels towards zero by 2100' (UNFCCC 2015a, p. 10).

Conclusion

What are the political implications of climate change? Many Green political theorists argue that the imperative to preserve a habitable climate demands some limit to individual freedom. However, they often don't specify the extent of these limits, or else they imply that the climate challenge can be managed with just a little more deployment of existing renewable energy and through beneficial lifestyle changes

– more cycling, meatless Mondays and low-energy light bulbs, for instance. This individualism is probably intended to be empowering, but it contributes to collective inaction.

This chapter has sought to explain why innovation must be at the heart of our climate policies. Since the technological metabolism of contemporary civilization is ecocidal, we need an entirely new set of technologies for food production, transport, industry and electricity. Such rapid technological change will only happen if low-carbon innovation becomes a political priority.

A proper understanding of the climate crisis's dimensions is also necessary to understand our limited freedom of choice. Dangerous climate change can only be averted through some combination of three strategies: (1) *innovation of new technologies* that might transform our energy systems and physical environment; (2) *extreme constraints on human freedom* that could ration electricity use, transport and consumption and reproductive freedom; (3) *geoengineering measures* that might intervene in climate systems to avert the most harmful impacts of warming. The next three chapters reflect on the wider politics of these different paths.

4

The Politics of Low-Carbon Innovation

Ecomodernists argue that states are the only actors with both the legitimacy and capacity to develop and deploy new zero-carbon technologies at speed and scale. But what kind of politics and policies can efficiently mobilize the state's capacities for entrepreneurialism and innovation? Gentle reader, stifle your yawns. Yes, 'innovation policy' is abstract and wonky. This is precisely our problem: so much depends on optimizing a set of policies most of us find impossibly dull. In the decades after the Second World War, there emerged a lasting political consensus in the US that the state should fund basic scientific research (see Bush 1945). In the post-war decades, as the US state made technological leadership central to its national security strategy, it developed a 'vast state machinery geared towards perpetual innovation' and commercialization of new technologies (Weiss 2014, p. 2). Albeit in a weakened form, this innovation-machinery continues to function. Yet, it has not been focused on the challenges of low-carbon. Moreover, since the 1970s the idea of an active, innovative state has come under sustained attack. To be sure, innovation has many half-hearted champions, but outside a few sectors – primarily defence, health and agriculture – where significant government investments are the norm, support for innovation lacks passion. Green culture celebrates activism where individuals put their bodies on the line – picketers blocking the Dakota Pipeline, sea-shepherds harassing whalers, or Pacific Climate Warriors' forming a flotilla-blockade of the Newcastle coal mine. Consequently, the climate movement's intellectual leaders such as Al Gore, Bill McKibbon and Naomi Klein, never urge us to take to the streets demanding state-investments in low-carbon innovation. Of course, individual innovations can be exciting. My initial encounter with a friend's iphone is seared in my memory. But innovation *policy* interests only boffins. Meanwhile, the long time-frames required for low-carbon innovation defy the short horizons of both financial and political capital.

This book's introduction began with a rare exception, the story of how activist group ACT UP targeted government funding and reform of HIV research. Why was ACT UP so different? For one thing, the terror of plague made the benefits of innovation obvious. For a time, an HIV diagnosis was a death sentence that could be commuted only by medical breakthroughs. Some of those diagnosed were sufficiently powerful that they could credibly imagine actually shifting research agendas. For example, Donald Trump's late mentor, New York lawyer Roy Cohn, was one of the earliest beneficiaries of the anti-retroviral drug AZT (we can be confident that Cohn, who denied both his sexuality and his diagnosis, was not a supporter of ACT UP). Second, AIDS struck a politicized community who saw the new gay culture that had emerged in the 1970s as precious and worth defending. Activists were anxious to put HIV behind them and to 'get on with gay liberation' (Berkowitz et al. 1983, p. 37). If the enlightenment idea of progress can be understood as demystification and exposure of ungrounded tradition to the light of reason (Bronner 2006, pp. 19–20), then the gay liberation movement was enlightenment's sequined Pretorian guard.

Yet, none of the factors that motivated ACT UP to focus on innovation appear to hold much appeal for climate activists. Whereas HIV research promised benefits that were personal and (potentially) immediate, investments in zero-carbon innovation yield highly diffuse, global, long-term gains. Second, whereas most HIV activists saw gay culture, including sexual culture, as valuable and worthy of protection, Greens commonly bemoan the consumerism of contemporary society. If innovation allows first-world lifestyles to continue apace, or for third-world people to also become prolific energy consumers, many people will be disappointed. Third, advocates of low-carbon innovation – from George Bush to Björn Lomborg – have often seemed disingenuous. Consequently, some people see the intellectual case for innovation as a pretext for conservatism and inaction. It is little wonder then that the climate movement has not made innovation a priority. With no vocal advocates, public spending on energy related research and development has fallen throughout almost the entire period in which climate change has been an issue of public concern. The IPCC blew the whistle on this neglect in its Fifth Assessment Report of 2014. It noted that among IEA member-states – a group of rich countries who until recently have dominated global research and development – energy's share of state research expenditure had more than halved since 1980 from 11% of total expenditure to just 5%. After 2009, expenditure even declined in absolute terms (IPCC 2014b, 7.12.4). Meanwhile, many economists have argued that carbon pricing, not innovation policy, would provide a more efficient climate response. Unfortunately, where carbon prices have been implemented, they have generally been too low to drive significant innovation.

Ecomodernism's advocacy of state-initiated, 'mission-oriented' innovation might be distilled into six propositions. Since (1) climate change is a serious threat, (2) mitigation should be a goal of public policy, however, (3) aggressive mitigation is proving politically impossible with existing technologies so, (4) dramatically more attractive low-carbon technologies are needed; (5) historical evidence suggests that accelerated technological innovation primarily occurs through deliberate state intervention, consequently (6) climate activists should make demands for greater state involvement in low-carbon innovation central to their politics. The first two of these claims are opposed by many conservatives, and the fourth is rejected by many Greens.

My concern here is to examine the final two propositions: is the project of utilizing state power to accelerate the pace of low-carbon innovation politically plausible? This chapter argues that it would be valuable for climate activism to focus on precisely this goal. While this argument implicitly critiques the climate movement for its failure to promote innovation, I should be clear that Green ambivalence has not been the primary barrier to low-carbon innovation or industry policy; instead, the limiting factor has been the ambiguous place of state-directed innovation in the wider political culture. I review this wider politics of innovation and suggest that the ecomodernist vision of mission-oriented innovation combines two ideas that push back against the passivity of a neoliberal economic model. The first is that the state's economic role should be enlarged so it becomes a significant entrepreneur and instigator of innovation. The second is to suggest that the trajectory of technological innovation should not be left to the free market or military imperatives, but should instead be brought under deliberate, ecologically minded political control. A version of this idea – that the technological constitution of society should be the subject of political deliberation – has long been articulated by Green scholars of society and technology such as Langdon Winner. However, whereas Winner focuses on technology's impact on our everyday lives and democratic politics, ecomodernists suggest technological choices must be framed by the urgent need to mitigate climate change. As against those environmentalists who view the state as intrinsically coercive and ecologically destructive, ecomodernists see governments as the only actors that can initiate the necessary technological change,

If the entrepreneurial state is opposed by both the Green left and the neoliberal right, is a radical innovation agenda politically doomed? Not at all. Activist governments' successes in cultivating wind and solar power so that they are now genuinely competitive technologies should give us hope. If political stars align, we may be able to replicate this success elsewhere. In fact, the constellations may already be shifting. One change is driven by great power politics. China's rise and America's rejection of a globally integrated liberal economic order are making the world a more dangerous place. Ironically, this return to a more competitive 'multipolar' world might enhance the state's interest in innovation since state interest in technology is often prompted by threat. The intellectual climate is also changing. The chapter ends by discussing the Obama Administration's Mission Innovation initiative – a multilateral pledge to double expenditure on clean energy R&D. Mission Innovation's survival despite the loss of US leadership suggests elite awareness of the need for low-carbon innovation is growing (see Trembath 2015). However, this new climate-innovation agenda will only flourish if it gains wider public support.

Mariana Mazzucato, Fred Block and 'Mission-Oriented' Innovation

Ecomodernists draw on the language of 'mission-oriented innovation' and 'directed technological change', and many of their arguments concerning the state's role in innovation derive from a group of scholars among whom Mariana Mazzucato (2015) and Fred Block (2011, 2018) are most prominent (see also Acemoglu 2002; Mazzucato 2015; Weiss 2014; Mazzucato and Semieniuk 2017). As against those on the left who are primarily concerned with questions of distribution, both Mazzucato and Block believe progressive governments should also seek to accelerate growth. They think it is easier to achieve a fairer distribution of income and wealth in a fast-growing economy. Block argues that 'when growth comes more slowly, efforts to redistribute are bound to be met with fiercer resistance', and that this dynamic of 'rich reactionaries successfully fighting for an ever-larger share of the slowly growing economic pie' has characterized US politics over the past forty years (Block 2018, pp. 65–76). Block observes that his pro-growth progressive agenda is subtly different from that of the guaranteed-minimum income or job-centred left, and radically different from Green visions of de-growth or of a 'stable-state' economy.

Although Mazzucato and Block's work has shaped eco-modernism's climate response, neither of these scholars' primary concern is environmental. Instead, they are responding to the growing inequality, sluggish economic growth and declining living standards that are corroding political life across much of the developed world. Mazzucato argues that arresting this 'drift into secular stagnation requires policies that aim at *smart*, innovation-led growth and *inclusive* growth at the same time. It requires the State to think big' (Mazzucato 2015, p. 14). However, she thinks it has become increasingly difficult for governments to openly take on this ambitious role. While the idea that the state should be a 'mere facilitator, administrator and regulator' gained economic ascendance in the 1970s, Mazzucato argues that this stripped-back vision of the state has become even more deeply entrenched since the global financial crisis of 2008. This argument perhaps overlooks the fact that investments in innovation and deployment of Green technologies – sometimes dubbed Green Keynsianism – actually formed part of the response to the financial crisis in the United States and China. In fact, Mazzucato recognizes that despite their adherence to small-state rhetoric, governments have continued to support innovation. However, they have usually done so through concessional loans and investments in basic research – policies that have allowed the private sector to appropriate profits. Mazzucato's political goal is to push back against this reigning ideology. The first step is to acknowledge the state's actual role in innovation. The second is to redouble these efforts and focus them on advancing shared public interests.

How to achieve inclusive, innovation-led growth? Mazzucato believes that an economy's performance can be optimized if we reconceptualize government as a risk-taking *entrepreneur*. In classical liberal economics there is a role for state interventions to correct 'market failures'. One widely recognized failure arises when an innovation creates 'positive externalities', whose value will not be easily captured by the innovator. For example, although a new production process that reduces air pollution may eventually benefit an entire community, the private sector may have little motivation to pursue such an innovation. This much is widely accepted. However, Mazzucato points to a variety of ways beyond narrow market failures in which the private sector's near-term investment horizons and low risk-appetites limit innovation. If an entrepreneurial state captures these opportunities, it can increase the entire economy's growth. However, achieving this will require both public investments in high-risk innovations, and public provision of patient, risk-tolerant finance.

Sceptics of state intervention will worry that graft, rent-seeking and other forms of government failure will burn more resources than are generated. Mazzucato seeks to head off this critique by grounding her claims in historical analysis. She shows that governments, usually motivated by security concerns, have long been central players in the process of innovation. In addition to funding basic research (which most economists endorse), governments also routinely support applied research, provide early stage finance, and utilize procurement policies and demand policies to nurture new markets and promote technological diffusion (Mazzucato and Semieniuk 2017; see also Edler and Georghiou 2007; Weiss 2014). While the US state's role instigating most major advances in computing, information technology and smart phones in the last half century is fairly widely recognized, Breakthrough Institute research has outlined how the US government has nurtured a series of technologies, including railroads, new crop varieties, nuclear power, biotechnology and fracking (Jenkins et al. 2010). Many of these government-backed innovations – including nuclear power, hydroelectricity, and the shale gas revolution through a coal-to-gas transition – have played a role in reducing US greenhouse gas emissions. So too has development of wind and solar power, which has primarily been developed by Denmark, Germany and China.

What impact does state-supported innovation have on inequality? Might the private sector capture the benefits of publicly funded research? For example, it is investors in companies like Apple and Marcellus (shale gas), rather than the community as a whole, that have reaped the biggest gains from the US governments' recent investments in innovation. However, Mazzucato argues that flawed policies have been responsible. If the 'distribution of financial reward from the innovation process reflects the distribution of contributions', innovation can reduce inequality (Mazzucato 2015, p. 201). To put this another way, state-directed innovation can reduce inequalities if economic benefits flow both to the state that underwrites innovation, and to the entire workforce that contributes to it. What is required, suggests Mazzucato, is for states to gain a fair return for society by taking an equity stake in businesses that commercialize state-financed innovation.

Why have states failed to take this approach? Mazzucato argues that the private beneficiaries of publicly financed innovation have been able to propagate ideologies – such as the mythology of the individual entrepreneur-innovator – that justify their own enrichment. There is no question that private sector innovators perform much important work. Yet since the private sector's primary task has been to commercialize state-funded technological advances, the underlying economic structure is parasitic. The result has been populist resentment of educated elites and growing public suspicion of innovation in general. Innovation thus faces a triple-threat: Green advocates of appropriate technologies, left-wing defenders of equality, and the advocates of a stripped-back state all inadvertently work together to undermine any renewal of a developmentalist project.

Mazzucato is about as close to a celebrity as an academic economist can get. Her ideas have found a wide audience and have been particularly influential within the UK Labour Party. For example, shadow chancellor John McDonnell has described the party's industry policy as built around 'national missions, closely following the approach suggested by the work of Mariana Mazzucato' (McDonnell 2017). Yet, acclaim among progressive politicians does not mean that there is a scholarly consensus concerning optimal innovation policies. While there are plenty of examples where entrepreneurial states really have picked winners (e.g. Japan, Taiwan and South Korea), there are also examples where rapid innovation has occurred without interventionist industry policy. The Israeli government, for instance, has funded basic research and the private sector has dominated innovation. While successful innovation seems to depend on state policies that address basic market failure and network problems by connecting scientists to businesses capable of utilizing their ideas, etc., other scholars point to a wide variety of policy combinations that can achieve this goal (Taylor 2012, p. 118). Critics are also correct to note that Mazzucato offers cherry-picked positive examples, and that a more systematic analysis of innovation policies might reveal instances of inefficiency or graft (Mingardi 2015, p. 603).

If our interest is in accelerating the pace of low-carbon innovation, debate over the inefficiency of government is of only limited relevance. Even if the neoclassical economists are correct in saying that national innovation rates and economic growth will increase when governments fund basic research but leave innovation to the private sector, this tells us nothing about how to maximize the pace of *zero-carbon* innovation. Profit-oriented companies have minimal incentives to develop low-carbon technologies so unregulated free markets, no matter how innovative, are unlikely to take on this task. Policy-makers seeking to accelerate the pace of specifically low-carbon innovation thus have two broad policy levers: pricing emissions or state intervention to promote zero-carbon innovation. Many economists argue both approaches are needed. For example, national climate policy reviews commissioned by governments in the UK (Stern 2006) and Australia (the Garnaut Report 2008) have argued for both carbon pricing and innovation policies. However, to date, innovation and industry policy has focused on the narrow goal of promoting renewable energy, rather than on the wider decarbonization agenda. Carbon prices, where they are implemented, have also been set too low to drive change.

Let's imagine that governments do invest heavily in low-carbon innovation. Would they be successful? One critique suggests that states are not very good at setting and achieving specific technological goals. Consider the internet and the smart phone. Although both were products of US government research, policy-makers never intentionally set about trying to develop an interconnected global computing network or a phone that could produce Instagram-worthy selfies. Nevertheless, the history of military innovation and, for that matter, the development of nuclear power and modern renewables, suggests that the state does sometimes achieve specific technological missions. Especially when conflict seems immanent, governments have repeatedly demonstrated their capacity to turn scientific knowledge into deployable innovations. As Fred Block (2018, p. 73) reminds us: 'World War I drove significant advances in airplane and radio technology, and World War II gave us atomic power, radar, the first electronic computers, and antibiotics.' In the case of zero-carbon innovation, state-initiated technological missions may be our only option. If so, instances of failure and inefficiency may be a necessary cost that can be managed, but not completely eliminated. The real question will concern what mix of policies are best suited to the different innovation tasks at hand.

To illustrate this point, consider the world's five largest sources of near zero-carbon energy: hydroelectricity, nuclear power, wind power, bio-power and photovoltaic power. Development of each has proceeded via a baton-race between the state and the private sector, although in each case, it has been deliberate state action that has enabled development and deployment at scale. For example, although much of the early development of hydroelectricity was driven by the private sector, the scale and physical requirements of hydroelectricity meant that construction of large-scale projects has usually been orchestrated by the state. The world's first large-scale hydroelectricity project, the 2,000MW Hoover Dam, for instance, was initiated by the US Congress, which, in 1928, allocated $165 million to the project under the Boulder Canyon Project Act – at the time the largest ever single appropriation (Hiltzik 2010, p. 120). On the other hand, the development of nuclear technology began almost exclusively as a competitive state-driven project. A civilian nuclear power industry became possible as a consequence of the race to develop the atomic bomb, which, between 1939 and 1945, drove a rapid acceleration in atomic science. Light-water reactors came to dominate civilian power as a consequence of another military project, the development of nuclear-propelled submarines (Cowan 1990). Although private companies eventually constructed civilian nuclear power plants in the United States, this industry was another product of state research.

Wind and solar power have developed into mature technologies through successive waves of state support in the United States, Japan, Europe and China. Michaël Aklin and Johannes Urpelainen have mapped this story in their 2018 book *Renewables: The Politics of a Global Energy Transition*. Both wind and solar have long histories. For example, the first solar engine was demonstrated (driving a printing press) by French mathematician Augustin Mouchot in 1874, and the first silicon solar PV cell was produced in 1953 (Sivaram 2018, pp. 30–3). However, it was only following the oil crisis of the 1970s, which spurred a significant increase in government support for all types of energy research and development activity, that modern renewables began to progress. The United States and Germany initiated significant solar research programmes (Aklin and Urpelainen 2018, p. 114). Meanwhile, in Denmark, tax credits, investment subsidies and other regulatory measures prompted private-sector wind development and deployment, primarily within agricultural cooperatives. US support waned under the Reagan Administration, but the baton was taken up by European and later Chinese state investments. The result has been rapid technological advances and cost declines.

Aklin and Urpelainen note that patterns of renewable deployment seem puzzling, as they do not correspond at all closely with natural resource endowments. Renewable energy makes only a limited contribution in the UK despite that country having excellent wind resources, while Germany has deployed wind and solar at scale despite unfavorable environmental conditions. Aklin and Urpelainen argue patterns of deployment reflect 'factors such as public opinion, partisan ideology in the government, and the political-economic clout of various industries' rather than efficiency (Aklin and Urpelainen 2018, pp. 4–14). Elevated public concerns about nuclear power are one important factor explaining why the renewable energy advocacy coalition was particularly powerful in Germany and Denmark. In both of these countries a 'renewable energy lock-in' has now replaced the fossil-fuel lock-in that remains typical across most of the world. Meanwhile, the choice of R&D policies or incentive schemes adopted in different jurisdictions primarily reflects the prominence of particular policy ideas in the national 'policy soup'. That is to say, the ideas accepted by governing elites at a particular juncture tend to shape the specific policy mechanisms utilized.

Since Aklin and Urpelainen's primary interest is in the political economy of renewable energy rather than climate policy, they do not dwell on Germany's stubbornly high greenhouse gas emissions. Nevertheless, they are correct to note that as the cost of renewable energy has fallen this, combined with the availability of proven policy models and renewables' positive image, has made renewable energy programmes attractive to a wide variety of governments. In the developing world, solar power has become particularly useful as a way of extending household energy access to remote locations outside the grid. Wind and solar have gone from supplying a negligible share of global electricity in 2000 to supplying 4% in 2017. Their current growth rate far exceeds that of any other energy source and their deployment would now continue even in the absence of government subsidies.

Yet, renewables have only reached this point because an environmentally motivated advocacy coalition has pushed for industry and innovation policies. This raises the question of whether renewables' development provides a template for other low-carbon technologies that will be needed for rapid decarbonization. The role that first-world public opinion has played in driving research priorities (so developing world illnesses are largely ignored), or in national battles over renewable energy, creates some reason for concern. It seems likely that direct-air capture, or carbon capture and storage will prove less politically attractive than renewable energy. Perhaps the public will offer greater support for research into advanced storage, solar fuel, hydrogen-based technologies or even nuclear fusion. What the renewables story does establish is that pro-innovation political activism and government investments in mission-oriented research have the potential to drive technological change.

Neoliberal and Populist Progressive Opposition

Aklin and Urpelainen's argument that elite ideologies help to promote or block technological innovation tells us that success is possible. However, it is also troubling, because

– with the exception of wind and solar power – neither progressive nor conservative elites have embraced state-backed innovation as a favoured climate response. The idea that the state should play an active role in driving innovation, or that the trajectory of technological innovation should be shaped by political rather than market forces is anathema to orthodox neoclassical economic theory. Consequently, during the Thatcher era, state involvement in even basic scientific research came under direct ideological assault (Kealey and Nelson 1996). Today, while state investments in defence, agriculture and medical research remain common, these are justified as exceptions. Thus, the first barrier to mission-oriented innovation is that – outside of research that meets the needs of the national security state – it runs counter to the economic zeitgeist.

The admonition for governments to 'get out of the way' of innovation while still funding research and development, is doubly toxic because it allows the private sector to capture the profits of innovation. Governments know that a high proportion of innovative ventures will fail and that the failure of any single government backed business creates an opportunity for political opponents to allege bungling and profligacy. Thanks to the ideological consensus that governments have no business in innovation, such allegations usually stick. An example of this occurred when Solyndra, a start-up solar panel manufacturer, failed with unpaid debts to the US Energy Department Loan Programs Office. Republicans relentlessly alleged that Solyndra's failure reflected the Obama Administration's incompetence. It didn't matter that the Loans Program Office's wider investment portfolio was a success. The likelihood that politicians will be judged against harsher standards than fund managers ensures that when governments do invest in innovation they will usually take political insurance by creating some distance from their investments.

Now let's consider how innovation is viewed by progressive populists. In his 2017 book, *Listen, Liberal*, American journalist and historian Thomas Frank took aim at the fable of 'inno' on which he blamed the impoverishment of the American middle and working classes. Frank argues that:

> Technological innovation is not what is hammering down working people's share of what the country earns; techno-logical innovation is the excuse for this development. Inno is a fable that persuades us to accept economic arrangements we would otherwise regard as unpleasant or intolerable – that convinces us that the very particular configuration of economic power we inhabit is in fact a neutral matter of science, of nature, of the way God wants things to be ... We have been hearing some version of all this inno-talk since the 1970s – a snarling Republican iteration, which demands our submission before the almighty entrepreneur; and a friendly and caring Democratic one, which promises to patch us up with job training and student loans. (Frank 2016, pp. 215–16)

Frank's discussion strikes me as somewhat shallow as he focuses on apps like Uber and Task-rabbit that simply create new ways of connecting workers to customers (albeit poten-tially new ways of undermining labour standards) rather than on technological innovations that have unambiguous societal benefits like the development of low-cost solar cells, a more effective malaria treatment or synthetic fuels. However, Frank's scorn illustrates the political challenge facing an innovation-led climate response. Frank's real concern is economic equality, and, perversely, I think he underplays the social costs that are inherent to any suc-cessful innovation. Far from being a fable, innovation has direct distributional consequences. Innovation may benefit society in general, but as it does so it 'hammers down' on specific groups of working people. For example, innova-tions in renewable energy and natural gas extraction have reduced America's dependence on coal, at the same time that the increasing automation of mines has hammered down on mining communities. According to the US Bureau of Labor Statistics, between 1985 and 2018 the number of coal miners in the United States fell from over 170,000 to about 52,000.

The same pattern has played out across other industries. My first permanent job – in a call centre for a bank – provides just one example of the dynamics of innovation and redundancy. To begin with, my workplace grew rapidly. Sales and customer service jobs shifted from branches to call centres where service and training were more easily standardized and efficiencies were pursued. Next came rounds of redundancies as call centre work relocated to low-wage countries like India and the Philippines. Today, AI-assisted chat threatens even these jobs. Each of these shifts was enabled by the same computing and communications revolutions Mazzucato celebrates. Very probably the new AI-programming jobs are higher-skilled, better paid and hopefully more rewarding than the jobs they replaced. Eliminating a vast workforce has also lifted the economic productivity of the entire economy. However, these abstract benefits don't help redundant workers or their communities. Some innovations are more unambiguously positive. Improvements to drinking water, sanitation, vaccine access and public health have produced rapid gains in life expectancy and health in even the poorest countries. Yet, although the benefits of reduced child mortality are readily apparent, even these life-preserving innovations face some resistance from groups such as practitioners of traditional medicine and opponents of vaccination. Innovations always create inequalities and destroy established ways of life. Unless the process is stage-managed by a progressive government or by powerful trade unions, it will almost inevitably generate political resistance. Whereas neoclassical liberal economics welcomes innovation but doesn't think the state should be involved, many progressives are suspicious of innovation and want governments to control and limit it. The constituency for an entrepreneurial state may be narrow.

How Should the Climate Movement Think about Technology and the State?

The Green movement has often been both sceptical of both the state and of advanced, 'hubristic' technologies. How well do these instincts serve climate activism? Although ecomodernist arguments for state intervention and for increasing technological complexity seem to defy Green wisdom, in another sense they have roots within the Green movement. First, let's consider ecomodernism's overarching argument that human societies should seek a self-conscious, democratically governed, transformation of their own technological foundations. Here, ecomodernism follows directly in the footsteps of Langdon Winner whose classic study of the politics of technology, *The Whale and the Reactor*, responded to the failure of modern political thought to undertake 'the critical evaluation and control of our society's technical constitution' (Winner 1986, p. 57). Winner's primary concern was with technology's impact on everyday life, including on 'individual habits, perceptions, concepts of self, ideas of space and time, social relationships, and moral and political boundaries' (1986, p. 58). Winner offered prescient reflections on the potential for the 'computer revolution' to undermine sociability and democracy (1986, pp. 99–102), and argued for political deliberation on the 'ways, both obvious and subtle, in which everyday life is transformed by the mediating role of technical devices' (1986, p. 9). His call for political deliberation on technology's impacts on everyday life seems even more vital today as our attention-spans atrophy under assault from intentionally addictive apps, and as advertising algorithms destroy shared spaces of political deliberation by dividing our newsfeeds into isolated echo-chambers.

However, *The Whale and the Reactor* was published in 1986 at a time when climate change was not widely recognized as a threat. Important as technology's social impacts may be, how should they weigh against climate concerns in our technological choices? Some people believe that the same soft, 'appropriate' technologies that the Green movement advocated in the 1970s also offer the best responses to climate change. Ecomodernists disagree. They insist that the severity of the climate crisis should compel us to look at technological choices with fresh eyes. Winner's paradigmatic case of inappropriate technology – the nuclear reactor – has become a cause célèbre for ecomodernists, as nuclear power is a source of the dispatchable (on demand) zero-carbon electricity that ecomodernists argue is essential for a zero-carbon grid. In fact, the very same nuclear reactor at Diablo Canyon California that inspired the title of Winner's book, has been a particular focus of ecomodernist activism. In June 2016 when it was announced that Diablo Canyon would close, a group of ecomodernists including Michael Shellenberger, film-maker Robert Stone, and writer Gwyn Cravens, joined a group of protesters who locked down the entrance to Greenpeace's San Francisco headquarters in protest (Barmann 2016). Since the reactor supplied 7% of San Francisco's electricity with near zero-carbon emissions, these ecomodernists denounced Greenpeace's campaign to close it as ecocidal.

Langdon Winner's central argument is that 'we should try to build technical regimes compatible with freedom, social justice, and other key political ends' (1986, p. 55). Ecomodernists agree. However, they think climate safety and universal energy access are prerequisites for both freedom and social justice. Winner endorses Ernst Schumacher's claim that 'small is beautiful' because he believes small systems and locally controlled technology are most consistent with participatory democracy; thus, he rejects even industrial scale renewables, worrying that they will elude local democratic control (1986, p. 32). By contrast, ecomodernists ask what technologies could provide zero-carbon energy on a scale that might allow a global population of seven to ten billion people to access modern lifestyles. If we hope to bring global emissions to zero, then scale will be more valuable than beauty as vast 'terawatt scale' zero-carbon energy sources are needed (Smalley 2005). Winner critiques both Liberal and Marxist theory for seeking 'freedom in sheer material plenitude, welcoming whatever technological means (or monstrosities) seemed to produce abundance the fastest' (1986, p. 58) and he would doubtless view ecomodernism through the same lens. Yet, ecomodernism differs from these earlier ideologies in that it is motivated by the urgency of climate mitigation as well as the pursuit of human development. Indeed, ecomodernists believe that the two can only be achieved simultaneously.

Ecomodernism's claim that the state must be the primary driver of ecological change also has a complicated relationship with Green theory. Some leading environmental scholars such as Robyn Eckersley have also argued that since the state has 'overarching political and legal authority within modern plural societies' it is the most promising agent of ecological transformation (Eckersley 2004, p. 12). However, Eckersley observed that in defending states' roles as ecological actors she was 'swimming against a significant tide of Green political theory that is mostly sceptical of, if not entirely hostile toward the nation-state'. Instead, the majority of Green theorists and activists have called for 'alternative forms of political identity, authority and governance' (2004, pp. 4–5). Many argue that it is precisely because states are centralized, bureaucratic and coercive that they are incompatible with Green visions of participatory democracy. As an institution of hierarchical domination, the state will inevitably buttress and enable multiple other forms of domination including patriarchal domination of women and of nature (Torgeson 1999; Eckersley 2004, p. 86).

Eckersley has reviewed these critiques and responded with an appeal to moral consequentialism:

> Given the seriousness and urgency of many ecological problems (e.g. global warming), building on the state governance structure that already exists seems to be a more fruitful path to take than any attempt to move beyond or around state in the quest for environmental sustainability. (Eckersley 2004, p. 91)

Eckersley noted that the problems of violence, domination and ecological degradation pre-dated the modern state system, and that there was no reason to assume that future alternatives would be less burdened by these problems. Much like the ecomodernists, Eckersley has argued that addressing environmental challenges is too urgent to delay until ideal political (and economic) systems are designed. In fact, while Eckersley's support for the 'Green state' may be rare among Green political theorists, the vast majority of climate activists have taken a similarly pragmatic view. Calls for carbon taxes, feed-in tariffs for roof-top solar power, renewable energy mandates and vehicle efficiency standards all focus on utilizing state power to pursue environmental ends.

As we have seen, state investments have also driven recent advances in low-carbon technologies such as wind and solar photovoltaic efficiency and current development of perovskite solar cells etc. (see Lachapelle et al. 2017; Mazzucato 2015; Sivaram 2018). Does this mean that ecomodernism's vision of an 'entrepreneurial state' simply describes policies that have already been implemented? It would be more accurate to say that ecomodernists argue that the policies that have successfully nurtured renewable energy to technological maturity should now be applied, urgently, across the full range of low-carbon technologies. The list of research targets should now include negative emissions technologies, synthetic/solar fuels, flow-batteries, zero-carbon industrial processes, in-vitro meat and dairy products, and advanced nuclear and next-generation solar technologies.

What Determines National Innovation Rates?

If the story I have told so far is accurate then the most influential advocates of innovation will probably be firms that stand to profit from new technologies, often by appropriating the value generated by public investments. Meanwhile, innovation will normally be resisted by business owners and workers in entrenched industries who face disruption. Public opinion and national security concerns may tip a government's hand in specific disputes, and states may routinely back innovation in a few politically propitious sectors such as agriculture, health and defence. This narrative is consistent with the role that public opinion has played in driving early state investments in the research and deployment of wind and solar power. This raises the question of what determines the state's role in the wider conflict between innovation and its opponents? In order to explain why I think the entrepreneurial state's prospects might be about to brighten, I will draw on a *theory of innovation rates* that Mark Taylor has propounded in the field of security studies (2012, pp. 113–52).

Taylor begins by recognizing that technological innovation has distributive effects. Some of those who lose out – such as established industries or large concentrated workforces – wield considerable political influence. If these vested interests are sufficiently organized and powerful, they may successfully pressure governments to slow the pace of change through such things as regulatory measures, taxes and subsidies. Examples include the German auto-industry's success in persuading Angela Merkel's government to water down the EU's emission standards (Mazur et al. 2015, p. 96), the Trump Administration's steel tariffs, and the Trump Administration's efforts to support 'fuel-secure' coal-fired power stations. However, Taylor argues that external threats create political pressure in the opposite direction. If a country faces significant international threats, and if elites believe innovation will enhance national military or economic security, systemic forces will push governments to resist lobbying by incumbent industries. This concern doesn't simply promote investments in security linked technologies. Economic strength gives governments various means with which to bolster alliances and manage threats and is indirectly a source of military strength. When external threats are economic rather than military, this may also promote internal innovation. Of course, this is not a hard rule. Sometimes, as is arguably occurring in Trump's America, governments may respond to perceived international threats with protectionism. Nevertheless, Taylor argues that international threats typically nudge national elites towards embracing innovation.

However, elites are not only concerned with international threats. While Taylor argues that national innovation rates reflect a balance between domestic tensions (which usually militate against technological change) and external threats (which may prompt elites to prioritize innovation), a second rule of thumb suggests that innovation will tend to be harder to manage in more divided communities. Since innovation has distributional effects, it is likely to amplify societal divisions and may create discontent which may prompt governments to constrain technological change. By contrast, more cohesive communities that have efficient mechanisms for socializing costs and benefits may find innovation less politically disruptive. For example, the generous social welfare systems typical of Nordic countries may enable forms of collective risk-taking. Once again, these tendencies are not definitive rules. The government of a divided community may represent the beneficiaries of innovation, or else elites may have sufficient power to suppress resistance and capture benefits for themselves.

Taylor reviews a wide spectrum of academic research and shows that this model explains cases such as the rapid technological progress achieved by Japan, South Korea, Taiwan, Finland, Israel, Ireland, India and China (Taylor 2012, pp. 123–7). Looking further back, the same theory might account for how external threats prompted Japan's Meji restoration, the development of computing at Bletchley Park during the Second World War, and the Soviet–US space race. Obviously, I've just cherry-picked a list of successful examples straight from the History Channel, and a methodical review of wartime research efforts would no doubt find that many have proven fruitless. Nevertheless, the theory that tensions promote innovation makes a certain intuitive sense. Since we appear to be entering an era of increasing great power rivalry, the hope that an improved climate for innovation will be a silver-lining of increasing geopolitical risk might provide some consolation. Will security oriented innovation spur low-climate innovation, though? There is certainly a risk that innovation focused on military security might lock in existing, carbon-intensive economic models.

There is also reason to hope that increased expenditure on research and development, even if it is narrowly focused on national security and prestige, will benefit mitigation. For example, China currently appears to be pursuing a 'techno-nationalist' goal of achieving technological leadership and export dominance in clean energy technologies such as solar and nuclear power (Kennedy 2015). Many low-carbon technologies also have direct military applications. For example, the US military researches both ultra-efficient solar panels for supplying energy in remote locations, and carbon-capture technology that would synthesize jet-fuel in remote locations (Parry 2017). More generally, development of technologies such as nuclear fusion could have such significant national benefits that rivalrous states may be motivated to pursue them. Interventions to prevent climate impacts may also emerge from inter-state rivalry. For example, it is possible that involvement in a benevolent solar geoengineering programme might plausibly boost China's international prestige as well as provide a pretext for a rising power such as China to deploy its air force to offshore bases.[19]

As we move deeper into the Anthropocene, looking to the state for leadership in low-carbon innovation may seem anachronistic. Our planet's organization into rivalrous states is often viewed as a fundamental obstacle to environmental progress. Thus, some people have insisted that fundamental reform of international politics or the overthrow of

---

[19] I thank my colleague Adam Lockyer for this observation.

capitalism are necessary precursors to climate action. Whatever the intrinsic merits of such reforms might be, they seem unlikely to be achieved in a timeframe that is commensurate with the urgency of climate action. Almost four decades ago, Hedley Bull wrote that:

> It is the system of states that is at present the only political expression of the unity of mankind, and it is to cooperation among states, in the United Nations and elsewhere, that we have chiefly to look if we are to preserve such sense of common human interests as there may be, to extend it, and to translate it into concrete actions. (Bull 1979, p. 120)

As the European Union's hesitant development and phases of retrenchment suggest, institutional innovation in world politics occurs only slowly. Even scholars who believe that a 'world state is inevitable', argue that greater global integration will take many decades or centuries (Wendt 2003, p. 506). It will certainly occur at too glacial a pace to assist climate mitigation.

Rather than reaching above the state to supranational institutions, others look to non-state actors for an ecological vanguard (Ostrom 2015). Non-state actors do play an ever-increasing role in climate politics, and across much of the world it is private companies that are deploying low-carbon technologies. While ecomodernists emphasize state-led innovation, they also see a significant role for the private sector in bringing innovations to market. Some of this private sector innovation may even be oriented by the pursuit of public goods as well as the profit motive. For example, on the first day of the 2015 Paris Climate conference, Bill Gates launched the Breakthrough Energy Coalition – a group of investors who promise to be 'truly patient, flexible' and to be motivated as much by the 'criticality of energy transition' as by the hope of outsized profits (Breakthrough Energy Coalition 2018). The coalition has announced that its early investments will focus on grid-scale storage, liquid fuels, micro-grids for Africa/India, alternative building materials and geothermal energy. To my way of thinking, looking to benevolent billionaires to avert climate disaster reflects a deeply flawed political and economic order. Even Bill Gates has argued that only governments have the capacity to fund the necessary basic and applied research. The coalition's website promises both to '[m]atch cutting-edge science from government research labs with investors willing to help scientists guide those innovations from the lab to the market' and to '[e]ngage with governments to ensure that policy and regulation are encouraging the pipeline of potentially transformative ideas, projects and start-ups', so it is at least intending to focus political attention on the challenges of low-carbon innovation. Nevertheless, some might accuse Gates's coalition of perpetuating the parasitic model in which venture capitalists swoop in and appropriate the profits of publicly funded research.

The Breakthrough Energy Coalition was launched alongside a more important multilateral initiative: Mission Innovation (MI), which was the brainchild of President Obama and Bill Gates. Countries that join MI – initially there were 21 – promised to double state expenditure on low-carbon innovation between 2016 and 2021. From a baseline of $15 billion in research support, this pledge suggested a steady increase to $30 billion of annual funding. However, MI's membership seems to have been cobbled together by the Obama Administration rather than reflecting a deep international commitment. For example, when I spoke with Australian climate officials just two weeks before Australia's participation in Mission Innovation was announced, they seemed completely unaware that any international research agreement was in prospect.

Given this shallow international support, I anticipated that under the Trump Administration, MI would quickly fold. When the Trump Administration's first budget proposals promised to slash energy research budgets and eliminate all support for Mission Innovation, my pessimism deepened. However, a funny thing happened on the way to this Trumpian climate policy fiasco. The international community stepped in and breathed new life into Obama's initiative. New members joined MI including the European Union; the EU Commission and the United Kingdom took over administrative leadership from the US; agreement was reached on a range of measures including information sharing, joint research and capacity building, and business and investor engagement; and seven priority innovation challenges were identified – smart grids, off-grid access, carbon capture, biofuels, solar fuels, clean energy materials, and affordable low-carbon heating and cooling. Meanwhile, the Trump Administration's budget proposal to slash research spending was rejected by a Republican-dominated Congress, and most innovation budgets were preserved. Although the United States is no longer leading, it has continued to attend Mission Innovation meetings.

I don't want to overstate Mission Innovation's success. At the time of writing we are half-way to 2021, and innovation budgets across member states have only increased slowly or have decreased slightly in some countries. Nevertheless, Mission Innovation claims an aggregate increase of $2billion, and real progress seems to be occurring towards some innovation challenges (e.g. smart grids and materials research). It is also unclear what new contribution Mission Innovation can make to international R&D governance given that the International Energy Agency has been promoting just such a cooperative approach since its establishment in 1975, and now oversees thirty-nine Technology Collaboration Programmes (TCP) (Yan et al. 2018, pp. 10–11; IEA 2013). The very limited media coverage of Mission Innovation's activities also suggests that the agreement has almost zero public engagement. As 2021 draws closer, and the target of doubling low-carbon R&D is missed, it is probable that Mission Innovation will fade into obscurity. Yet, at least for now, Mission Innovation inches forward, and its programme of ministerial meetings and national reporting requirements continues to nudge governments towards supporting low-carbon innovation.

Mission Innovation's survival suggests a growing elite awareness concerning the value of state investments in climate-related innovation. Elite awareness alone will not secure a successful innovation agenda. Yet, as Aklin and Urpelainen's research into renewable energy has demonstrated, R&D programmes emerge where public opinion and elite attitudes converge at opportune moments. National budgets are always tight. Governments juggle many priorities and without a strong advocacy coalition behind it, low-carbon innovation will remain a low priority. Yet, were climate activists to turn low-carbon innovation into a key political demand, there is every reason to believe they could make progress.

Conclusion

When climate activists like Al Gore and Naomi Klein claim 'we have the technologies we need', I suspect they are motivated by a well-intentioned desire to motivate political action with a positive message. Just like the ecomodernists' promise of a 'great Anthropocene', they anticipate that positivity is essential for action. Perhaps they also believe that we should deploy the low-carbon technologies we do have before worrying about difficult to decarbonize sectors. Unfortunately, the results have been disappointing. Greenhouse gas emissions increase steadily, and research and development budgets stagnate. Mission Innovation's target – to double low-carbon research and development spending to $30 billion annually – is both politically ambitious and also inadequate. Economic analyses have suggested much greater investments, perhaps around $100 billion annually, would be needed to provide economically efficient mitigation if we hope to limit warming to 2°C above preindustrial levels (Garnaut 2008, pp. 219–23).

Ecomodernism's vision of state-led zero-carbon developmentalism is out of step with dominant economic thought and with Green activism. Yet, for much of the twentieth century, state-led developmentalism was the norm. It has been embraced by European social democracies, the newly decolonized states that advanced the Third World Project' in the 1960s and 1970s, and more recently by the East Asian state developmentalist model. However, since the 1970s, mainstream economic thinking has insisted that the state should be scaled back. Meanwhile, some of those who resist the 'neoliberal' agenda most energetically from the Green-left side of politics often hesitate to advocate state involvement in low-carbon innovation. Many of their concerns are well grounded. Yet, since the ambition of global climate action will be limited by the pace of technological change, I think the climate movement should make low-carbon innovation a priority. And I think there's some reason to hope this strategy could find success.

5

Human Flourishing amid Climate Harms

In February 2003, tens of millions of people around the world marched against the invasion of Iraq. In my home town of Melbourne, Australia, I joined a crowd of over 200,000 people who took to the streets denouncing neo-colonial intervention. These protestors were not swayed by the invaders' lofty promises to 'tear down the apparatus of terror', to banish the 'torture chambers and rape rooms' and to 'build a new Iraq that is prosperous and free' (Bush 2003). One of the more controversial arguments associated with ecomodernism is the idea that some arguments advanced by Western Greens might be similarly self-serving. In this chapter, I want to consider how the same habits of respect for self-determination and scepticism towards self-serving humanitarianism that inspired the anti-war protests might apply in respect of what I'll call *Green conditionality* – efforts to shape other countries' environmental policies by imposing conditions on aid, finance or trade.

These questions are vexed and the distinction between 'international solidarity' and 'neocolonial influence', much like that between terrorist and freedom fighter, is frequently in the eye of the beholder. When the World Bank announces a ban on financing developing world oil and gas developments

(Kim 2017), when the EU pressures its trading partners to reject genetically modified (GM) food, or when Greenpeace-allied activists destroy GM test crops in the Philippines, ecomodernists see forms of conditionality and neo-colonial influence. Meanwhile, many Greens make the same accusations concerning the Gates Foundation's crop research, American distribution of GM produce as food aid or ecomodernism's advocacy for urbanization and high-density cities (Monbiot 2015).

Debates over Green conditionality are complicated because climate change is connecting the world's communities in new ways. First, since the greenhouse gas emissions of affluent communities are already harming the world's most vulnerable people, the moral case for compensation is strong. Reflecting the sense that a 'climate debt' might be owed, the Paris Agreement promised $100 billion in annual assistance for adaptation and mitigation. Yet, as the mixed record of international aid reveals, promises of international assistance are rarely honoured, and when assistance is offered it frequently does not reach the most vulnerable people. This raises questions concerning what form of international engagement might best respond to climate-linked injustices.

A second challenge arises because development choices now have global climate impacts. As a result, many people think it might be appropriate for rich states and international institutions to use their power to promote lower-carbon forms of development. Some question whether third-world people should be permitted to pursue first-world development patterns or to embark on fossil fuelled development (Klein 2015, p. 417). While I argue that Western power should not be used to deny poorer nations self-determination, I do not pretend that these questions are easy.

In order to examine how ecomodernism might better address climate-change linked injustices, in this chapter and the next I will return to my observation that ecomodernism is essentially a social democratic philosophy, and begin to piece together an explicitly social democratic response to global challenges. Here, I am guided by Sheri Berman's advice that any social democratic response must (a) emphasize 'a belief in the primacy of politics and a commitment to using democratically acquired power to direct economic forces in the service of the collective good', (b) 'manoeuvre between the globophilia of neoliberalism and the globaphobia of many current leftists' by supervising and containing markets, and (c) rediscover the value of communitarianism (2006, p. 211–12). To date, ecomodernists have tended to approach the dilemmas of climate-linked injustice by rejecting Green conditionality and supporting developing states' self-determination. Believing that state-led development can address poverty and build climate resilience, ecomodernists have sought to maximize the space in which national communities can make their own choices. This much I agree with, and I seek to show how divergent perceptions of *risk* in the rich and poor world, can make Green conditionality especially harmful. However, respecting pluralism and rejecting Green conditionality, although important, is an insufficient response to climate harms. A social democratic climate response must simultaneously defend the primacy of politics within national communities while also working to promote the development of social democracy beyond national borders.

The chapter begins by revisiting the Third World Project's campaign for a 'New International Economic Order', as I believe this earlier effort to achieve universal human flourishing through the 'integrated development of the globe' contains lessons for ecomodernism (Bedjaoui 1979, p. 24). Despite its very different origins, the Third World Project parallels ecomodernism, in that it was a developmentalist movement that critiqued an inequitable international order, free-market economics and Green Malthusianism. Of course, the Third World Coalition was defeated, and progressive scholars have tended to identify Western political interference and economic conditionality as being at least partially responsible for its demise. I argue that this story has continuing relevance today. Although debates over international influence are complex, we can cut through them by adopting a position that was repeatedly articulated by the Third World Coalition: that international interference and conditionality are inherently unjust. Instead, 'each community' should ideally 'find its own solutions' (Strong 1971, s 3.1). This principle will be especially important as the planet warms, because affluent people are poorly placed to assess risks from the perspective of the poor.

The chapter's second section applies this framework to contemporary debates over energy and agriculture. I conclude by proposing the idea of 'global social democracy' as a guiding metaphor, much like the ecomodernist metaphors of 'innovation', 'intensification' and 'decoupling'. Were ecomodernists to explicitly advocate global social democracy, including both the universal provision of basic services and democratic control of earth systems governance, they would become utopian in a way that might appeal to radical progressives. However, such radicalism would also create new challenges, the most significant is how to nurture forms of political identification that could ground these universal commitments. Admittedly, implementation of global social democracy seems like a distant prospect. However, during the era of worsening climate harms, ecomodernism's vision of 'universal human flourishing' is unlikely to be achieved unless the passivity of laissez faire economics is countered globally by bold investments in human development.

'Third Worldism' and the 'New International Economic Order'

Historian Vijay Prashad opened his history of *The Darker Nations* (2008, p. 1) by explaining that:

> The Third World was not a place. It was a project. During the seemingly interminable battles against colonialism, the peoples of Africa, Asia, and Latin America dreamed of a

new world. They longed for dignity above all else, but also the basic necessities of life.

My interest in the Third World Project arises because, historically, it was the most significant political movement to engage 'limits to growth' arguments by advocating egalitarian global development. Not only was the Third World Project a precursor to ecomodernism, but if ecomodernism ever finds a significant international support base I think it will be by drawing on the same ideals of egalitarian human development.

The term 'third world' seems to have been first used in 1952 by demographer Alfred Suavy to suggest a parallel between the role that newly decolonized states might play internationally, and the contribution that the progressive third estate (*tiers état*) made in the French Revolution (Bedjaoui 1979, p. 25). In 1955, twenty-nine new nations and decolonization movements met in the Indonesian city of Bandung to develop a political strategy and vision that would reflect the aspirations of the formerly colonized peoples of Africa and Asia. Prashad (2007) described the Third World Project that emerged from this 'Bandung Conference' as encompassing three principles: peace (including nuclear disarmament), bread (a demand for a New International Economic Order), and justice (including universal social development and an end to racism and hierarchical international politics).

The New International Economic Order (NIEO) was a set of proposals which, although not a single coherent plan, focused on ending the formerly colonized world's economic dependency, especially by improving the terms of trade. Its apogee came in 1974, when the United Nations General Assembly passed a declaration titled 'Declaration on the Establishment of a New International Economic Order'. The declaration's stated objective was to transform the governance of the global economy to redirect more of the benefits of transnational integration towards 'the developing nations'. It called for this new order to be 'based on equity, sovereign equality, interdependence, common interest and cooperation...which shall correct inequalities and redress existing injustices' (UN General Assembly 1974).

Certainly, the NIEO reflected a radical economic agenda that ecomodernism generally lacks (Prebisch 1962). For example, the NIEO's programme of action included restitution for colonialism, stabilization of prices of raw materials, removal of tariffs on developing state exports, stabilization of exchange rates, a code of conduct for multi-national companies (MNCs) and specific targets for economic assistance. Yet, the NIEO shared ecomodernism's basic goal of achieving a universal modernity. It may seem astonishing that, only a few decades ago, a majority of the world's states made such radical demands. However, there was a moment following the OPEC oil embargo of 1973 and the breakdown of the Bretton Woods fixed exchange rate regime (1968–73) when it appeared that third-world solidarity might reshape global economic structures (Gilman 2015, p. 3). Today it again seems clear that some similar form of radical economic redistribution would be necessary to achieve either 'climate justice' or 'universal human flourishing'. Yet, despite the humanitarian intentions signalled by initiatives such as the UN's 2030 Sustainable Development Goals, the prospects for a more radical agenda seem remote.

The Third World Project's emphasis on equality encompassed both political and material equality, and so it generally articulated an unapologetically materialist vision of universal human development. For example, Algerian jurist Mohammed Bedjaoui described the proposed NIEO as involving 'a theory of accumulation on a world scale, operating...through reciprocal relations established as part of an *integrated development of the globe*' (Bedjaoui 1979, p. 24, emphasis added). More recently, postcolonial theorists have tended to critique such concepts of industrialization and modernity as involving a continuing process of 'accumulation by dispossession' (Harvey 2003). However, while some of those associated with the NIEO sought to defend peasant life against urbanization, most viewed economic development and industrialization as central to an *anti-colonial* agenda. For example, Bedjaoui condemned the inequality that meant that in 1975 Sweden's 10 million people consumed more electricity than India's 600 million. Bedjaoui (1979, p. 27) observed that 'to attain a level of production and consumption equal to that of Sweden, the government of New Delhi would have to construct 10,000 nuclear power stations with a capacity of 500 megawatts each'. It is true that the model of export-led industrialization that has since transformed much of East Asia has generated new forms of national inequality and has often involved the suppression of workers' movements and the dispossession of traditional land-owners. However, many developing countries have gained sufficient economic strength that they are now restructuring the capitalist world order from within (Golub 2013). These achievements include declining levels of poverty, the consolidation of transnational South–South trade and investment flows and the re-emergence of Asia and the Pacific as centres of world economic power (Golub 2013). Ironically, the Third World Project's aspiration to end Western domination may be achieved even as its egalitarian promise remains unfulfilled.

Although alive to environmental concerns, advocates of the NIEO were generally enraged by the 1960s' environmental movement's embrace of Malthusian population policies. At the very moment when the formerly colonized world had won independence and was demanding national control over the extraction of natural resources, Western environmentalists were insisting there must be 'limits to growth'. Responding to growing North–South tensions, the UN commissioned a report to summarize third-world perspectives ahead of the 1972 Stockholm Conference on the Human Environment. The resulting 'Founex Report' opened by emphasizing the 'compelling urgency of the development objective' and observing that 'the current concern with the Human Environment has arisen at a time when the energies and efforts of the developing countries are being increasingly devoted to the goal of development'

(Strong 1971, s 1.4). While recognizing a need to avoid the 'mistakes and distortions' of Western industrialization, the report observed that 'the major environmental problems of developing countries ... reflect the poverty and very lack of development of their societies' such that 'life itself is endangered by poor water, housing, sanitation and nutrition, by sickness and disease and by natural disasters'. It was these problems, rather than industrial pollution, that were the primary challenges for 'the greater mass of mankind' (Strong 1971, s 1.4).

The Founex Report both defended national sovereignty and also proposed a reflective, egalitarian form of developmentalism. Rapid economic growth was identified as 'necessary and essential' but insufficient to 'guarantee the easing of urgent social and human problems' given the risks of continuing unemployment and income inequalities. While the Founex Report emphasized the value of modern agriculture and of 'chemical fertilizers and pesticides, high yielding varieties of seeds and irrigation works, and a degree of mechanization', it also acknowledged that these advances created 'side effects' that had to be managed by 'planning the use of these inputs to expand agricultural production' (Strong 1971, s 2.12). Increased urbanization seemed inevitable since 'modern social, cultural, and economic activities capable of attracting educated youth may not exist in the rural areas', yet any planning process should also promote rural development and manage the process of transition. For example, the report suggested that developing world cities should generally be built around mass transportation systems rather than owner-operated vehicles. Above all, however, the third-world countries emphasized the need for national self-determination: '[e]ach country must find its own solutions in the light of its own problems and within the framework of its own political, social and cultural values' (Strong 1971, s 3.1).

This principle of self-determination was not respected. When Prashad took on the sobering task of tracing the Third World Project's demise, his narrative described the widely recognized 'pitfalls' of authoritarianism, corruption, economic ineptitude, militarism, nationalism, elite predation, military coups, post-Mao China's integration into global capitalism and internal divisions such as those between oil producers and consumers. His overarching claim, however, was that the Third World Project had been 'assassinated'. The West, and particularly the United States, had worked to undermine it from the beginning, for example by interfering in internal affairs to bring US-allied governments to power. However, it was the debt crisis of the early 1980s and the international financial institutions' subsequent enforcement of radical free-market economic policies that finally defeated third worldism. In the process, as Prashad observed, it liberated national elites to pursue more narrowly self-interested projects and created space for the emergence of cultural nationalism, fundamentalist religion and other atavisms (2008, p. xviii).

Conditionality

In her 2007 book, *Shock Doctrine*, Naomi Klein offered a withering critique of how Western-dominated international organizations have deployed 'conditionality' against the developing world. Klein focused on Chicago School economist Milton Friedman and his argument that radical economic liberalization could only be achieved at moments where crises broke the 'tyranny of the status quo'. Friedman first achieved political success as an economic adviser to the Chilean dictator Augusto Pinochet, and Klein described how, in the months after taking power in a coup in 1973 and under the guidance of Friedman, Pinochet implemented a radical economic programme of cuts to social services, privatization (even of schools), tax cuts and free trade, quashing opposition through a brutal regime of torture and repression.

Building on his successes with Pinochet, Friedman's next challenge was how to achieve a similar economic revolution outside of Chile. Chicago School economists soon found the perfect agents of influence in the International Monetary Fund (IMF) and the World Bank. Although the IMF had been established with the goal of maintaining international financial and monetary stability, the radical new economic doctrines of the Chicago School corrupted its mission. From the 1980s onward, IMF assistance became conditional upon recipient states implementing a raft of radical free market reforms, including privatization, opening economies to trade and foreign investment, fiscal discipline and the reduction of many social support programmes. This programme came to be known as the 'Washington Consensus'. Klein wrote that these policies were frequently spoken of as a 'second colonial pillage ... in the first pillage, the riches were seized from the land, and in the second they were stripped from the state' (2007, p. 245).

Chicago School economists were by no means the first to attach conditions to finance or international aid. Most famously, the US imposed currency convertibility and free trade on countries that participated in the Marshall Plan for the post-war reconstruction of Europe. However, the economic policies the IMF imposed became increasingly radical. Washington Consensus policies required opening capital markets and reducing the state's economic role without reference to its level of economic development. In the wake of the Asian financial crisis, some states, such as Malaysia, sought to avoid the IMF's policy prescriptions in order to preserve a developmental state model (Lai 2012). Meanwhile, states such as Indonesia that had adopted IMF prescriptions were destabilized by destructive riots as social protections were stripped away. The economic impacts of Washington Consensus policies also turned out to be very mixed. Even where liberal reforms brought economic progress they often increased inequality and harmed the poor through reduced state spending on health, education, and income support. All up, conditionality undermined the IMF's prestige.

Critique of structural adjustment and the Washington Consensus is now pervasive and even the IMF has acknowledged mistakes (Stiglitz 2002). But was the problem the specific details of the Washington Consensus, or with the idea of conditionality more generally? Intuitively, conditionality seems less troubling if it is used to promote democratic governance, gender equality or raised environmental standards than if international institutions demand cuts to health, education and social security budgets. But how can we distinguish between harmful and benevolent conditionality? While everyone seems to agree that the IMF's policies were flawed, there is less consensus about the conditions in which conditionality might be justified. In her book on the ethics of incentives, *Strings Attached*, political scientist Ruth Grant argues that the basic problem with IMF conditionality was that it exploited developing states' weaknesses to impose policies that should properly have been determined by domestic political processes. Grant argues that conditionality can only be legitimate if it passes both procedural (conditions should be voluntarily and democratically accepted) and substantive tests (conditions must benefit the recipient) (Grant 2011, pp. 110–11). I think political progressives should probably apply these same tests to the forms of conditionality that we favour.

Consider the example of population policies. In the same era that the IMF was imposing 'structural adjustment packages', World Bank loans as well as Swedish and US aid were also frequently conditional on adoption of coercive population policies. In the 1970s and 1980s, tens of millions of third-world people were sterilized, frequently involuntarily, under such programmes. Strangely, these forms of conditionality have attracted much less sustained academic critique. To be sure, many of those who promoted coercive population policies believed that they were essential to avoid famine, but so too did many advocates of Washington Consensus policies believe that their economic model offered a proven path to improved economic performance and human welfare. Eugenicist policies, including efforts to control developing world populations, have always reflected an odd mix of utilitarian, colonial and racist logics. However, in the 1970s, the new environmental critique of overpopulation seemed to burnish these impulses with an ostensibly post-racial logic. For example, Paul Ehrlich's promotion of sterilization targets was grounded in a Malthusian analysis of limits to food supply and a coming era of hunger (see Hardin 1968, 1974 and Cullather 2014). In his 1968 book, *The Population Bomb*, Ehrlich's (pp. 165–6) enthusiasm for coercive population measures was uncompromising:

> When he [Dr S. Chandrasekhar] suggested sterilizing all Indian males with three or more children, we [the United States government] should have applied pressure on the Indian government to go ahead with the plan. We should have volunteered logistic support in the form of helicopters, vehicles, and surgical instruments. We should have sent doctors to aid in the program by setting up centers for training para-medical personnel to do vasectomies. Coercion? Perhaps, but coercion in a good cause. I am sometimes astounded at the attitudes of Americans who are horrified at the prospect of our government insisting on population control as the price of food aid.

Coercive population control policies rarely gained the support of those countries that were their targets. At the Bucharest UN World Population Conference of 1974, the Third World Coalition mounted a cogent attack on Western states' eugenicist arguments, arguing that overpopulation was a product of colonial exploitation and deliberate underdevelopment (Hartmann 1997). Reversing the Malthusian logic, they argued that the third world was 'prolific because underdeveloped, not underdeveloped because prolific' (Bedjaoui 1979). According to Prashad, third-world thinkers believed Paul Ehrlich's *The Population Bomb* 'received such tremendous acclaim in the First World because its neo-Malthusian ideas had already become commonplace: that the reason for hunger in the world had more to do with overpopulation than with imperialism' (2008, p. 8).

Although most third-world thinkers tended to believe that universal human development would create a path to environmental protection rather than the reverse, some developing world elites were persuaded by the risks of overpopulation and embraced policies that included family planning, promotion of contraceptives, abortion and sterilization. In 1978, a Chinese missile scientist, Song Jian, heard about the Club of Rome's report on limits to growth while attending a conference in Helsinki. Song assembled a research team to prepare a similar report for China. He found that with elevated birth rates, China's population might reach four billion by 2080. By 1980, Song's work had inspired the Chinese Communist Party (CCP) to adopt its one-child policy (Mann 2018, ch. 6). In the decades that the one-child policy remained in force, widespread coerced abortions and other violations of reproductive freedoms were practised across China (Hesketh et al. 2015).

While these rights violations are distressing, I think there's an important ethical distinction between situations where coercive population policies are adopted by a national political process (as in China), and situations where they are externally imposed (as in India).[20] Many of the impulses that have led Western states to promote interventionist population policies were admirable. Family planning initiatives that expand sexual freedom and reproductive choice can achieve social and environmental benefits. However, the use of aid conditionality to promote coercive population control policies such as involuntary sterilization, can readily be understood as a form of neo-colonial structural violence. The fact that these policies were promoted by much of the Western Green-left (Ehrlich 1968) should give us pause. Is it possible that there are contemporary progressive agendas that are similarly harmful? In the next section I highlight two debates – over energy and genetic technologies in agriculture – where ecomodernists suggest that

---

[20] Although China's one-child policy received international support – including a significant amount of Japanese funding funnelled through the United Nations Fund for Population Activities (as it was then called) – it was primarily a CCP initiative.

Western power is again being used to constrain developing world choices. While I think there are genuine complexities in both cases, I endorse Grant's argument that it is illegitimate for any actor to utilize power differentials to impose specific policies. It is impossible for a powerful outsider, no matter how well meaning, to understand specific policies' local meaning and impacts or to make a valid assessment of risks. Wariness concerning conditionality seems to provide a useful guide.

Contemporary Conditionality – Biotechnology and Energy

In this section I review two contemporary debates where some ecomodernists allege Green conditionality is undermining the self-determination of third-world communities – the debate over the application of biotechnology in agriculture, and the debate over the construction of energy infrastructure. The relevance of biotechnology to climate change may be unclear. However, as the climate warms, many regions will become less hospitable to agriculture. Enhancing food security on a warming planet will probably require the development of crop varieties that have greater heat, drought and pest resistance. Ecomodernists point to the yield gains made possible by advanced agriculture and welcome the possibility that more productive farming techniques might allow more land to be spared for nature. While the yield gains from genetic modification have to date been somewhat disappointing, advances in biotechnology such as CRISPR are rapidly reducing the cost and improving the accuracy of gene editing, opening up the possibility that a wide variety of improved crops might be developed and widely distributed. In energy, the debates are slightly different. International assistance for wind, solar power and micro-grids is currently growing rapidly, but finance is increasingly limited for many other energy sources such as coal and hydroelectricity. Although welcoming the increasing availability of renewable energy, ecomodernists tend to argue it is unjust to deny the third world access to the sources of dispatchable energy on which affluent countries continue to rely.

Genetically modified food

Contemporary debates over genetically modified food involve contending morally charged narratives. In the eyes of anti-GM campaigners, genetically modified seeds have contributed to a corporatization of agriculture that is impoverishing subsistence farmers, reducing biodiversity, harming the environment, destroying traditional practices and enriching giant multinational corporations. While concerns about corporatized agriculture deserve to be taken seriously, some Green critics of GMOs also promote entirely unscientific claims concerning health risks and 'terminator genes' which allegedly make it impossible for farmers to save and plant their own seeds. These last two claims have no more scientific credibility than does climate-change denial. There is a deep scientific consensus supporting the safety of consuming those GM crops that have been commercialized to date (DeFrancesco 2013) and no terminator gene has ever been deployed in agriculture. The only deployment of what might plausibly be labelled a terminator gene has been the company Oxitec's trial of 'self-limiting genetic technology' to control Zika-virus transmitting mosquitos (Carvalho et al. 2015).

The anti-GM case, which is grounded in ideas of safety, tradition and community, can be coherent without false safety claims. For example, Greenpeace's website describes its food campaign as:

[H]ere to support the global food movement based on 'ecological farming' – where most of our food is grown ecologically, and farmers together with consumers reject toxic pesticides, chemical fertilizers and GMO seeds. It's a future where people from all walks of life work together to build a system that is best for their families, farmers, and for the planet. (Greenpeace International 2015)

This discourse mobilizes imagery of communities uniting against corporate domination of agriculture that would be powerful even without the misleading implication that GM food is necessarily connected to increasing chemical use.

By contrast, in the pro-GMO narrative, biotechnology is a powerful tool that could be used to make farming more sustainable. GM crops typically reduce the use of pesticides, increase yields, and are thus invaluable for addressing poverty and malnutrition. In this view, the poor world has been deprived of potential benefits by well-intended, but misguided Western intervention. Green campaigners' success in persuading the European Union to reject biotechnology has had tragic global consequences. Already affluent and well nourished, Europeans could afford to protect themselves against imagined risks. However, the subsequent international campaign against biotechnology has pitted the power of European states and Western NGOs against small-scale farmers of Asia and Africa and denied them the benefits of disease-resistant crops.

In *Seeds of Science* (2018), Mark Lynas explains his personal conversion from anti-GM activist to ecomodernist gene-tech proponent. The book opens with the story of Lynas narrowly escaping arrest when he joins a group of activists as they destroy a trial GM maize crop 'somewhere in eastern England'. The narrative then follows Lynas's travels in Tanzania and Uganda where he talks with farmers whose cassava and banana crops are blighted by disease, and then with scientists who have developed new, more resilient seed varieties. These scientists work for public or philanthropic-funded agencies rather than for 'big-ag', yet their crops are banned from public release. Lynas describes seeing disease-resistant varieties flourishing behind security fences and biohazard signs only a short distance from places where communities went hungry owing to crop failure. He weaves a morally compelling story in which European-funded

NGOs have persuaded governments to block the release of crops that could enhance nutrition and food security. At one meeting, Lynas witnessed NGO activists telling farmers that children who ate GM-crops would become homosexual (Lynas 2018, p. 140). Later, he uncovered and reported the scientific falsehoods about gene technology that the UK Charity *ActionAid* had been spreading on Ugandan radio advertisements. When the story was covered in the UK press, *ActionAid*'s head office issued a public apology. However, scientifically deceptive activism continues (Lynas 2018, p. 144).

Lynas acknowledges that genetic technology is dominated by large corporations rather than public interest research, and he speculates that Monsanto's decision to make Roundup Ready Soybeans the first GM crop that it commercialized, rather than a pest-resistant variety of seed, may have done more than anything else to blight the technology's reputation (Lynas 2018, pp. 98–9). Most GM crops *reduce* the need for chemical insecticides (and in some cases fertilizers) and thus promote less chemically intensive agriculture. However, Monsanto's Roundup Ready seeds are a partial exception. Roundup Ready crops are resistant to the wide-spectrum herbicide Glyphosate, which was at first sold exclusively by Monsanto under the brand *Roundup* – thus setting up a necessary commercial connection between the seeds a farmer uses and their choice of herbicide. Nevertheless, defenders of genetic technology point out that even Roundup, the most vilified of chemicals, actually has environmental benefits. For example, it enables 'no-till' farming that lowers greenhouse gas emissions and increases the carbon retained in soils (Brookes et al. 2017). Still, Roundup Ready crops seem to best embody the GM-opponent's critique, as they enriched Monsanto by requiring the application of one particular, broad-spectrum herbicide over others.

Since the development of the revolutionary gene-editing technique known as CRISPR, the cost of creating new seed varieties has plummeted. Lynas argues that biotechnology's domination by giant profit-driven corporations rather than public-interest innovation could easily be overcome. Ironically, agribusiness's continuing dominance is a direct consequence of a regulatory environment that has been distorted by environmental activism. Any new crop must first overcome significant regulatory barriers and legal challenges before it can be grown by farmers. These barriers are so great that not-for-profit innovations are usually locked out. Only large and powerful corporations have the resources necessary to bring new crops to market. In some cases, promising public sector innovations have not been commercialized because, without a powerful corporate backer, Green resistance has proven insurmountable.

Where does the truth lie in this debate? Does GM food enrich or impoverish developing world farmers? Although existing generations of GM crops, like the business model that has created them, are highly imperfect, even these flawed crops demonstrate the potential benefits of biotechnology. For example, a meta-analysis of 147 different studies of GM technologies' impacts reached the following findings:

> On average, GM technology adoption has reduced chemical pesticide use by 37%, increased crop yields by 22%, and increased farmer profits by 68%. Yield gains and pesticide reductions are larger for insect-resistant crops than for herbicide-tolerant crops. Yield and profit gains are higher in developing countries than in developed countries. (Klümper and Qaim 2014)

If nothing else, this summary makes clear that GM crops can enable less chemically intensive agriculture and are of potential value to developing world farmers. Unfortunately, many anti-GM campaigners reject academic research for the same reason that climate deniers reject climate research – the belief that science has been corrupted by vested interests.

The speed with which farmers have taken up those GM crops that are approved seems to corroborate the research claiming that GM crops benefit developing world farmers

(Herring and Paarlberg 2016, pp. 402–3). For example, after approval by the Indian Government in 2002, Bt cotton had surpassed 90% of all crops by 2014, with seeds being widely traded on the gray-market; Brazilian GM soybeans captured an 83% crop share eight years after approval; within a decade of GM white maize being approved by the South African government in 2001, it had reached a 72% share of crops sown; and 99% of the Chinese papaya crop was genetically modified just five years after its approval in 2006 (Herring and Paarlberg 2016, p. 398). If GM crops are so harmful, we must wonder why they are so readily embraced by farmers. To date, engineered seeds have almost exclusively been approved for animal feed or industrial crops, however the limited evidence suggests that food crops are equally attractive to farmers. For instance, after Bt brinjal (eggplant) was approved for commercial release in Bangladesh in 2013, a trial during the 2016–2017 cropping season compared 505 Bt brinjal farmers with 350 non-Bt brinjal farmers. It found that the net returns for the GM crop were six times higher, and pesticide costs were reduced by 61%. Between the 2016 and 2017 seasons, the proportion of Bangladeshi brinjal farmers utilizing GM seeds jumped from less than 1% to 17% (27, 000 farmers) (Shelton 2018). Other research shows that GM crops have reduced the incidence of pesticide poisoning. For example, the introduction of Bt cotton has helped to avoid several million cases of pesticide poisoning in India every year (Kouser and Qaim 2011)

If the potential gains from biotechnology are so great, why is uptake restricted to a very small number of crops? Political scientists Ronald Herring and Robert Paarlberg have sought to explain biotech's failure with reference to the distribution of benefits and perceived risks. They argue that techological change can create pervasive uncertainty concerning potential risks. Even when evidence suggests that there is no specific hazard – as in the case of GMOs – it is impossible to prove safety scientifically. Consequently, risk has been 'socially constructed in hypothetical or anticipatory terms' (Herring and Paarlberg 2016, p. 398). If a technology's benefits for consumers are obvious, as in the case of cell phones, microwave ovens or medicines, early anxieties tend to fade. However, if there are few direct benefits for consumers, citizens may be persuaded to reject specific technologies on the basis of hypothetical risks. This logic resolves what might otherwise seem puzzling – why recombinant DNA technology has been normalized in medicine and pharmaceutical production for the synthesis of human insulin, hepatitis vaccines and gene therapy, while the same technologies have been widely rejected in food production. The key difference is that medical applications have direct benefits to consumers, so risks have been accepted. By contrast, it is producers who capture most benefits from biotech's application in agriculture, so GM food crops have been more vulnerable to consumer resistance. Consequently, the interests of producers have won out only in respect of industrial and feed crops such as cotton and oil, that are not sold directly to consumers.

If Herring and Paarlberg are correct, and the social acceptance of technologies turns on the distribution of perceived risks and benefits, another puzzle arises. It makes sense that consumer anxieties have closed the door to GM food in Europe, where agricultural producers make up a tiny proportion of society. But why have GM crops been rejected in developing countries where large proportions of the population are farmers who stand to benefit from improved crop varieties? This is where Western power and conditionality become relevant. In fact, I think the campaign against GM food is a classic example of what environmental politics scholar Elizabeth DeSombre (2000) has termed a 'Baptist and bootlegger' coalition. This prohibition era analogy refers to situations where ideologically motivated Green groups (Baptists) ally with corporations who stand to benefit from imposing environmental regulations on the world at large (bootleggers).

The first GM soy beans were licensed for import to the European Union in March 1996, with timing that turned out to be remarkably inauspicious. This was the same month that the UK acknowledged the existence of bovine spongiform encephalopathy (BSE), commonly known as 'mad cow disease' (Herring and Paarlberg 2016, p. 401). Cows contract BSE by eating body parts of other infected cows. BSE focused media attention on the practice of grinding up deceased animals for feed. Although mad cow disease has absolutely no connection with gene modification, it sensitized public opinion to the risks associated with industrialized agriculture. Green groups who opposed the hubris of biotechnology, seized the opportunity to turn opinion against it. So great was their success that the EU introduced strict labelling laws in 1997 and GM food production was soon regulated to the point of a virtual ban across many European countries (Herring and Paarlberg 2016, p. 401). Europe's large agricultural chemical industry was also threatened by the prospect of new crop varieties that required less chemical use, while European farmers welcomed an opportunity to shut out US agricultural exports (Juma 2016). A coalition of Baptists and bootleggers had assembled.

The early successes of the anti-GMO movement in Europe meant that European states, Green NGOs and chemical companies all shared an interest in resisting the adoption of GM crops internationally. The European campaign succeeded as it involved a pincer movement between civil society activism generating grass-roots resistance, and state power creating top-down pressure via diplomatic pressure and trade incentives. As Kenyan science and technology scholar Calestous Juma, who served as the executive secretary of the United Nations Convention on Biological Diversity in the late 1990s, explained: 'many African countries opted for a more precautionary approach partly because they had stronger trade relations with the EU and were therefore subject to diplomatic pressure' (Juma 2016, p. 241). However, it was the negotiation of the Cartagena Protocol on Biosafety to the Convention on Biological Diversity (2000) that created the strongest incentives for states to protect agricultural sales and reputation by ensuring that they remained GMO free. The Protocol governed the transboundary movement of living GMOs, and enshrined a 'precautionary approach' that allowed governments to restrict the release of products even if there was no existing conclusive evidence that they were harmful (Juma 2016, p. 239). GM foods required warning labels and exporters were required to gain prior informed consent from a designated 'biosafety authority' (Herring and Paarlberg 2016, p. 406). With GM foods being regulated like hazardous materials, there seemed to be a real possibility that agricultural products might be denied entry into Europe if there was any doubt concerning contamination. The EU's developing world trade partners now had strong incentives to ban GM foods or risk losing market access.

Energy

Energy infrastructure, unsurprisingly, is another area characterized by contending, morally charged narratives. I'll take up the story of Green energy conditionality in the 1980s when activist coalitions began to critique the World Bank for funding a series of projects such as India's Narmada Dam, and Nepal's Arun III Damn. Each project advanced national development goals, but required the relocation of large numbers of people and appeared to impose unacceptable environmental costs. After protracted transnational campaigns, the Bank withdrew its support from a series of projects. Political scientist Susan Park (2005) has demonstrated how Green NGOs were able to gain influence over World Bank decision-making both by lobbying states to require all projects to involve environmental impact assessments, and also through direct persuasion and 'socialization' of bank officials.

Over time, the 'Greening' of the World Bank group's agenda has made it increasingly difficult for developing world governments to gain international financing for a range of technologies – especially hydroelectricity and coal-fired power stations – that have been targeted by transnational environmental organizations. The World Bank group claims to have not funded any green-field coal projects since 2010 (World Bank 2016, p. 35), and in December 2017 it announced it would cease support for all upstream fossil fuel developments including oil and natural gas (Kim 2017). Some scholars have observed that the Bank gained a 'normative lustre' by tying loans to environmental and human rights and has thus been able to enhance its legitimacy in the Western states that fund and control it (Nelson 1996). Others have branded the reformed bank an agent of 'Green neoliberalism' (Goldman 2005) or recognized that sustainable development has been absorbed into a dominant discourse that reproduces social relations (Rootes 2014, p. 279).

Nevertheless, Green NGOs and scholars continue to promote lending practices that constrain developing world energy choices. Historically, the link between fossil fuel use and human development is incontrovertible. However, NGOs promoting Green conditionality often claim that recent advances in renewables mean fossil fuel development is no longer needed. For example, in 2015 Oxfam released a report which claimed that since 'renewable energy is a cheaper, quicker and healthier way to increase energy access', there is now 'no trade-off between improving lives and tackling climate change' (Bradshaw 2015). This report's central claim, that 'increasing coal consumption is incompatible with protecting the rights and interests of poor communities in developing countries', would have been entirely accurate had it focused on the rich world's coal consumption. However, given that energy access boosts both human development and resilience against climate harms, ecomodernists argue that it is immoral for Westerners to seek to constrict the developing world's choices.

Naomi Klein provides another example of this view that since fossil fuels are now 'unnecessary' Green conditionality will benefit developing world people. She writes (2015, p. 417):

[W]e need common agreement that having been wronged does not grant a country the right to repeat the same crime on an even grander scale. Just as having been raped does not bestow the right to rape ... having been denied the opportunity to choke the atmosphere with pollution in the past does not grant anyone the right to choke it today.

Klein holds up Mark Jacobson's 100% renewable energy plans as evidence that renewable energy now offers a viable alternative to 'extractivism'. Most commentary on Jacobson's work questions whether his proposed energy systems are practical – his modelling is certainly much more optimistic about the potential for renewable energy than is the Intergovernmental Panel on Climate Change. However, in order to make an all-renewable economy work, Jacobson assumes that today's patterns of deep global inequality must continue far into the future. Drill down into the spreadsheets that Jacobson publishes with his model, and we see, for example, that Ethiopians must make do with *less* energy in 2050 than they consume today. Meanwhile, each American is anticipated to consume more electricity than five Indians.[21] Since this seems to fit poorly with Klein's values, I assume her endorsement of Jacobson's work reflects a failure to engage with the challenging realities of electricity supply, rather than genuine support for such profound inequalities.

The fact that fossil fuels still supply around 80% of energy reveals a collective preference to prioritize energy

---

[21] These calculations are rough. However, Jacobson's tables for 2050 identify 996 GW/8,725 TWh of total end-use demand for India and 1,291.42 GW/11,313 TWh for the United States. According to the United Nations' 2017 world population prospects report, current US population is 324,459,000, and it is projected to grow to 389,592,000 by 2050, while the respective figures for India are 1,339,180,000 and 1,658,978,000. Using 2017 population ratios (which understate the likely per-capita disparity) this suggests a comparison of 0.744:3.979 kW per capita or 6.51:34.87 MWh per capita (meaning that US citizens use about 5.3 times as much electricity per capita). Downloaded 12 December 2017 from: https://esa.un.org/unpd/wpp/Publications/Files/WPP2017_KeyFindings.pdf; http://web.stanford.edu/group/efmh/jacobson/Articles/I/AllCountries.xlsx

abundance over climate mitigation. Ecomodernists' defence of autonomous energy choices seems to reflect a belief that all communities should have equal democratic self-determination, and that the developing world, in particular, needs the climate resilience that can be secured through wealth, development and energy access. Consequently, eco-modernists oppose Western financial institutions' efforts to control developing world energy choices (Pritzker 2016). For example, BI senior fellow and development expert Todd Moss (2018a) condemns the IEA's standard for 'energy access' of 50 kWh per person per year in rural areas. Moss observes that 'if people expect to use electricity for what economists call productive uses – and what regular people call jobs – they need a lot more than what small systems can currently deliver'. He outlines survey evidence which demonstrates that most African people with access to solar microgrids also want a conventional grid connection (Moss 2018b); meanwhile, the unreliability of the grid means that those who do have grid connections also commonly wish to secure renewable backup.

I observed earlier that debates over energy access seem to have a special emotional significance for ecomodernists. At the 2016 Breakthrough Dialogue when Samir Saran denounced World Bank and OECD rules that limited financing for India's coal-fired power stations as a neo-colonial mentality, and described 'poverty' as 'the world's chosen carbon mitigation option' (see Saran and Mohan 2016), the audience erupted in applause. Of course, ecomodernists seek a rapid transition away from fossil fuels, but they hope to achieve this by making clean energy so attractive that the third world chooses it willingly, not because conditionality denies developing world governments any alternative.

Conditionality and state-led development

The common thread connecting these debates is the worry that Green conditionality might close down the potential for national communities to choose their own destinies, including through state-led development. Indian philosophy of science scholar Meera Nanda has described earlier debates over the Green Revolution in terms that link back to my discussion of third-world state-led developmentalism and its opponents:

> While legions of radical critics of the Green Revolution have endlessly laid bare the self-interest (control of indigenous germplasm and access to 3rd world markets in seeds and farm chemicals) that motivated the US government and foundations to take the lead in the green revolution, these critics have paid very little attention to the other significant partners in this phase of agricultural modernization – the third-world governments themselves. (Nanda 1995, p. 25)

Nanda located India's participation in the Green Revolution within a long-term project of nation-building that was focused on creating scientific infrastructure that could conduct agricultural research appropriate to local crops and farming conditions. Nanda was also at pains to stress that the very idea of national development was something of an innovation. Historically, liberal trade theory's conception of comparative advantage had been focused on factors such as natural climate and natural endowments that were believed to be immutable. The new idea of national development suggested that natural endowments were not fixed but could be transformed by state policies such as those promoting agricultural innovation. However, Nanda also suggested that the window in which state-led development was possible lasted only between the end of the Second World War and the advent of the debt crisis. For example, she recounts how Mexico adopted policies that succeeded in almost doubling the rate of growth in agricultural production between 1980 and 1982. However, these policies were snuffed out by a World Bank negotiated structural adjustment loan that eliminated all price supports and privatized state agencies (Nanda 1995, p. 26). Today, state-led agricultural development again confronts Western resistance.

While my discussion of energy and biotechnology has advanced an ecomodernist perspective, I hope I have presented the Green perspective with sufficient generosity to make clear that it is probable that different communities – if left to their own devices – would make different choices. For example, some countries may choose combinations of zero-carbon energy such as wind and hydro-electricity, or nuclear and solar power. Some third-world countries may reject GM foods even without EU pressure. The key point is that Western activists and states have no justification for imposing their own preferences on the third world.

Conclusion

In his response to the *Ecomodernist Manifesto*, George Monbiot accused its authors of possessing neo-colonial instincts. Monbiot was most exercised by ecomodernism's claim that urbanization could spare space for nature. Allegedly this enthusiasm:

> [R]esonates with a long history of such proposals, from the enclosures in England and the Highland clearances in Scotland, the colonial seizures of land in Kenya and Rhodesia, the Soviet dispossessions and the villagization in Ethiopia to the current theft of farmland in poor nations by sovereign wealth funds and the rich world's financiers ... The poor of the world have long been subject to remote and confident generalizations by intellectuals of this stamp, and have suffered gravely. (Monbiot 2015)

Monbiot's rhetoric seems a little extravagant. Yes, the *Ecomodernist Manifesto* does claim that urbanization and agricultural intensification are both 'processes with a demonstrated potential to reduce human demands on the environment, allowing more room for non-human species'. However, the Manifesto's intent seems to be to challenge the metaphors that guide environmental activism, rather than to frog-march subsistence farmers and forest-dwelling people into high-density urban gulags. In fact, the Manifesto offers support for local self-determination noting that 'we recognize that many communities will continue to opt for *land-sharing*, seeking to conserve wildlife within agricultural landscapes' (Asafu-Adjaye et al. 2015, p. 27, original emphasis)

Nevertheless, Monbiot's point bears reflection. Although power is rapidly shifting 'East', trends in Western environmental thinking still have the potential to undermine third-world communities' autonomy. Were ecomodernism's enthusiasm for urbanization to become more politically influential it could potentially motivate coercive policies of the kind Monbiot imagines. It is also true that in their eagerness to defend the astonishing advances in human welfare of the last few decades, ecomodernists have often failed to recognize how wounding 'modernization' and 'progress' have been. Ecomodernists are correct that infant mortality is lower today, average life expectancy is higher, and health and caloric intake better than at any previous time for which we have data. However, they might also acknowledge that the other side of modernity's ledger includes the ongoing destruction of indigenous cultures, dispossession of traditional land-users, increases in national inequality, the loss of wild nature and the industrial-scale cruelties of intensive animal production.

Modernization and colonialism are analytically distinct. However, historically they have been so interconnected that those who celebrate the benefits of modernity risk seeming complicit if they do not also acknowledge the continuing wounds of colonial violence. Some ecomodernist scholars are at pains to recognize these complexities, as have been many previous materialist thinkers. For example, Marx's discussion of the transition from feudal to bourgeois society recognized how modernization inflicted hardships even if its aggregate impacts were progressive. At times, as in the Ecomodernist Manifesto's celebration of a 'great Anthropocene', ecomodernism seems to lose this balance. It is not just that ecomodernism would be more attractive if it struck a less triumphalist tone, but also that the Manifesto would be more faithful to its own humanist values if it were more attentive to the complexities of human experience.

However, in my view the Manifesto's greatest weakness is its inattention to how we might promote universal human development during the era of growing climate harms. Earlier, I discussed Raj Desai's observation that in per-capita income terms, contemporary Indonesia is as affluent as the United States was when it passed the Social Security Act in 1935, and China is richer today than was Britain when, in 1948, it established its National Health Service (Desai 2015, p. 315). A penny dropped for me when I read Desai's analysis. It is not just that some lower income countries are now, in historical terms, reasonably affluent. The world *as a whole* is also, on average, much richer than was Britain when it implemented comprehensive social security: average global per capita GDP on a purchasing power parity basis in 2017 was US $17,300. If all of humanity were a single political community, we would now be well past the point where we might expect development of universal welfare institutions. The barrier to universal provision of basic health care, education and old age pensions is not a lack of resources. Rather it is the absence of the kind of global solidarity that might support these forms of international social welfare. It is in this context that I propose that 'global social democracy' might be a useful metaphor to guide ecomodernist transition.

Ecomodernism is often accused of being an elitist and technocratic Western project. One of the reasons I began this chapter discussing the Third World Project was to demonstrate that ecomodernism shares its goal of state-led technological progress with this earlier radical anticolonial, third-world movement. Moreover, there is a continuity between ecomodernism's critique of Green conditionality and the Third World Coalition's rejection of both Malthusian logics and neo-colonial interference. While its origins are in the comparatively elite world of North American environmentalism, ecomodernism thus shares many of the concerns of the Third World Coalition. Yet the comparison with the Third World Project also underscores ecomodernism's limitations. While both movements have advocated universal human development and defended national self-determination, the Third World Project's demand for a New International Economic Order also set out a concrete programme of restitution and redistribution. If ecomodernism's commitment to universal human flourishing is to be substantive, ecomodernists must also develop an account of how to advance the welfare of vulnerable people during the coming era of mounting climate harms. In the next chapter I begin to explore what the metaphor of a 'global social democracy' might imply for the democratization of global climate governance.

6
Global Social Democracy and Geoengineering Justice

The year is 2023, and officials are gathering to review progress under the Paris Agreement. Five developing states, calling themselves the 'Geoengineering Justice Coalition', (GJC), have circulated an ultimatum. By 2025, rich countries must fulfil all pledges made in the Paris Agreement, including providing $US100 billion in annual assistance to the developing world. If these conditions are not met, the GJC will commence solar geoengineering. Through interventions that reflect a tiny proportion of the sun's energy back into space by spraying particles into the stratosphere, these developing states promise to halt global warming artificially. A spokesperson for the Geoengineering Justice Coalition addresses the press:

> It is now three and a half decades since, at a meeting in Toronto in 1988, developed countries first promised to cut greenhouse gas emissions by 20% by 2005. Today, we have reached a point where, even if all Paris Agreement pledges are fulfilled, warming this century is likely to exceed 3°C. As the climate has warmed, we have learned how heat waves, crop failures, rising seas, and extreme weather visit their worst harms on those who are already vulnerable. These harms to the world's poorest people are caused

– albeit indirectly and unintentionally – by the activities of the richest.

Thus, when our scientists tell us that the poorest people can be the greatest beneficiaries of solar geoengineering, we cannot dismiss them lightly (Bala and Gupta 2017). Today I invite all countries to join in designing a pro-poor plan of implementation. For developed countries, there is an admission price: they must first contribute their proportionate share of adaptation assistance to the Green Climate Fund. Geoengineering will commence only if the rich world does not fulfil its promises, and only with the approval of a majority of participating states. [22]

Admittedly, there is no significant constituency for either third-world radicalism or hubristic technological interventions. The idea of a Geoengineering Justice Coalition is fanciful. However, thinking about solar geoengineering from a developing world perspective serves a valuable purpose: it disrupts the idea that in the Anthropocene all share a common fate. In the case of geoengineering, that idea has been codified conceptually in the Oxford Principles, the most widely recognized ethical standards governing the research and implementation of geoengineering. The principles suggest that solar geoengineering must be regulated as a public good, and should only proceed with prior informed consent of all affected communities and, consequently, a universal governance arrangement to oversee implementation (Rayner et al. 2013).

Measured against the Oxford Principles, the Geoengineering Justice Coalition's actions would be unethical, because they would not be predicated upon a global democratic consensus. Most scholars agree. Some go further.

---

[22] This resembles the scenario that concludes Oliver Morton's book *The Planet Remade: How Geoengineering Could Change the World*, Princeton University Press, 2015; the important distinction is that here the threat of solar radiation is used as a bargaining chip.

Cambridge geographer Mike Hulme, for instance, has argued that any solar geoengineering would be 'undesirable, ungovernable, and unreliable'. Not only would it be impossible to achieve global agreement, but deployment would create international tensions. Once geoengineering commences, suspicious minds might see the hand of foreign saboteurs in any unfavourable weather pattern (Hulme 2014). For example, if India or Japan initiated geoengineering it seems likely that they might be blamed for the next Pakistani flood or Chinese drought.

The universal language of the Oxford Principles, however, conceals an inadvertent sleight of hand. These principles require that the rules governing intentional actions, through which developing countries might protect their people from climate harms, should be very different from the rules governing the unintentional actions that create those harms. It is the rich world that has benefited most from those unintentional actions, not least from the myriad ways in which fossil fuelled development has made citizens of those nations much more resilient to climate extremes than their counterparts in poor nations. For this reason, it is also the poor world that stands to benefit most from intentional actions to mitigate climate change, including geoengineering. Because the near-term threats of climate change primarily afflict developing world people, the rich and poor worlds may ultimately reach quite divergent conclusions about a flawed but functional techno-fix. In that eventuality, the universal ethical standards articulated by the Oxford Principles, well intentioned as they may be, might compound global injustice.

One of my goals in this book has been to reframe ecomodernism in more explicitly social democratic terms. Following Berman (2006), I understand social democracy as emphasizing the primacy of politics, the acceptance of democratic intervention to maximize social investments in human development and other collective goods, and the recognition of the national community as an effective source of identity and solidarity. To date, social democracy has been epitomized by advanced northern European states such as Norway, Sweden and Denmark. However, climate change interweaves the fates of national communities to such an extent as to pose an intrinsic challenge for communitarian social democracy at a national level. This is because the outcome of each national community pursuing its own conception of the public interest, will probably be the inadvertent wrecking of the shared global climate. Ideally, climate should figure much more strongly in national political deliberations so that the problem might be addressed through coordinated action. However, the pace of learning is much too slow. Climate harms, which are already overwhelming the limited resources of some more vulnerable communities, continue to accumulate. This reality poses multi-scalar challenges to social democracy: how to compensate or protect the poor world from harms that are now inevitable? How to better focus national democratic deliberation on global challenges? And, how to democratize decision-making on questions that are intrinsically global? My focus here – on solar geoengineering – concerns the third question. However, I conclude the chapter by examining potential sources of momentum towards a wider social democratic compact that might include the global provision of social services.

To begin, I try to think through the implications of recognizing that dangerous climate change is now all but inevitable, from the vantage of an ecomodernist politics that is committed to promoting human equality, freedom and democracy. My primary focus will be on solar geoengineering, in part because I think this technology's democratizing potential is seldom recognized. Against those who argue that solar geoengineering must not be implemented without a global, democratic governance regime, I argue that the process of discussing solar geoengineering may be a powerful spur towards democratization. Alternatively, it might become a bargaining chip in the hands of the less powerful, as the Geoengineering Justice Coalition scenario suggests. As we move further into the era of climate change, momentous political choices seem to be escaping deliberate democratic control. A more active international debate over 'earth systems governance' might help to reverse this trend.

Solar Geoengineering, Risk and Relative Vulnerability

Radical scholars often draw on Antonio Gramsci's concept of hegemony to explain how laws and norms expressed in universal terms can advance the interests of a dominant class (Cox 1983). The same insight is captured by Anatole France's quip that 'The law, in its majestic equality, forbids the rich as well as the poor to sleep under bridges.' The Oxford Principles' restrictions on solar geoengineering would make perfect sense if they only governed the West. Of course, rich countries and rogue billionaires should gain global consent before intentionally interfering with the earth system (Fuentes-George 2017). Even if we turn to climate intervention only as part 'of a symphony of actions harmonized for managing the global environment', Western-led geoengineering will only be ethical if it has wide international support (Long 2017, pp. 78–82).

But should the Oxford Principles dictate developing world responses to climate change? One of the most common tropes in the anti-geoengineering literature is the assertion that 'the world's most vulnerable people would likely be most affected' (Janos et al. 2017, p. 213) and that those who 'bear little or no responsibility for the problem of anthropogenic climate change' may be harmed (Svoboda and Irvine 2014). This is a rather curious distortion. What the evidence actually suggests is that solar geoengineering would – as a rule of thumb – bring poor communities and equatorial regions the greatest benefits (Reynolds 2014; Boucher et al. 2013 p. 630). Third-world people are the primary victims of climate change, both because poverty creates vulnerability and because equatorial regions are already close to the limits of thermal comfort. Since many poor countries are located in the tropics, they already experience roughly twice as many hot days as the rich world does, and that number of hot days is increasing twice as fast (Herold et al. 2017). It is true that solar geoengineering would impact equatorial regions disproportionately. But that effect would be beneficial: equatorial regions will cool much more than the poles. Solar geoengineering would therefore 'most affect' the poor much like public health insurance 'most affects' the sick.

Our knowledge of already existing climate harms is highly imperfect. Media attention focuses on dramatic cases, like Tuvalu and Kiribati, where entire nations are threatened by rising seas. Yet, crop failure, vector-born illness, heat waves, floods, and extreme weather events are already inflicting hardship on millions. In most cases the connection with climate change isn't apparent, even to the victims. Statistical analysis is needed to discern, probabilistically, what quantum of harm should be attributed to the changing climate amid incremental shifts in the everyday atrocities of global inequality (e.g. Mazdiyasni et al. 2017).

Enter solar geoengineering. The Intergovernmental Panel on Climate Change has concluded that what it terms solar radiation management (SRM) 'would generally reduce climate differences compared to a world with elevated greenhouse gas concentrations and no SRM' (Boucher 2013, p. 575). Sea-level rise would be slowed but not halted (Applegate and Keller 2015; Tokarska and Zickfeld 2015). The IPCC also emphasizes that geoengineering is no panacea. It carries considerable risks and its impacts on different regions will vary. Thus, it is entirely possible that some vulnerable people could be harmed – indeed, one early study found that a strategy designed to maximize global benefits might have adverse consequences for the Sahel region of West Africa (Ricke et al. 2010, p. 537). However, the same study also identified an alternative deployment strategy that would bring every region closer to preindustrial rainfall and temperature patterns. This finding has been confirmed by subsequent research (Kravitz et al. 2014).

Given this evidence, if a majority of developing world people and governments decide that solar geoengineering can advance their interests, should they wait for the rich world's permission? The Oxford Principles insist that they must – that powerful, polluting states should be able to veto an imperfect response. The principles are written in reasonable, impartial language and speak in abstract terms about the global public good. Those of us who speak in this privileged, universalist cadence should keep in mind that, despite our best intentions, we invariably project our own values and interests onto our image of the universal.[23]

Solar geoengineering conforms to the widely accepted public-health principle of 'harm minimization', which accepts that some activities (like drug use or greenhouse gas emissions) will not be eliminated immediately and that we should instead seek to reduce their negative impacts. Consequently, its implementation might be motivated by a desire to protect both human populations and ecosystems from climate harms (Talberg et al. 2018). It may thus come as a surprise that the potential ecological (and for that matter social) benefits of geoengineering are rarely discussed – Oliver Morton's wonderful book *The Planet Remade* is a rare exception (2015, p. 257). Perhaps the prohibition on intentional interference in nature – a defining norm of modern environmentalism – deters discussion of solar geoengineering's potential ecological advantages.

Estimates suggest as many as one in six animal species are at risk from climate change (Urban 2015). Humans are intervening to protect some of the most iconic species. However, among the less charismatic multitudes of threatened moths, spiders, fungus and fish, many have never been identified, and very few will be protected by dedicated conservation campaigns. This is why any intervention that

---

[23] Of course, this warning applies equally to ecomodernists and advocates of 'earth systems governance' as to the opponents of solar geoengineering.

reduces climatic stresses for all species could be so valuable – it might throw a lifeline to entire ecosystems and allow vulnerable species to migrate or adapt. Yet, threatened species, like impoverished people, are 'voiceless' in climate debates. This problem – of how affected non-humans and unborn generations can be represented in environmental decision-making – has long interested Green political theorists. For example, Robyn Eckersley has argued that since future generations and non-humans cannot speak for themselves, we should create constitutional provision for their representation. Eckersley proposed that an "Ecological Defenders Office" be created and granted specific powers to defend the interests of the voiceless (2004, p. 244). Yet, there's a hitch. As one reviewer of Eckersley's book noted, she fails to explain 'just how the "eco-defenders" would know what nonhuman nature or "countless generations" would prefer, or how one would be able to distinguish between these (nonpresent) "others"' preferences and what the "eco-defenders" themselves wanted' (Warren 2006, p. 377).

Still, what position should an 'Ecological Defenders Office' take in respect of solar geoengineering? Viewed from the perspective of biodiversity there are strong arguments both for and against. On the one hand, scientific modelling suggests that reducing solar radiation could potentially minimize ecological threats; on the other, sudden termination of geoengineering could spell disaster. To their credit, some environmental organizations have recognized this complexity and have adopted nuanced positions. Most, however, like *Greenpeace* and *Hands off Mother Earth* have pointed only to the risks.

In his expansive history, *The Progressive Environmental Prometheans*, William Meyer has traced how, after centuries in which European progressive politics had been characterized by a Promethean belief in humans' ability to enhance their biophysical environment, this position was reversed by the advent of modern environmentalism in the 1960s. Greens began to emphasize the 'danger of undesirable consequences produced by meddling in the complex system of nature' (Meyer 2016, p. 29). As a result, Prometheanism came to be associated with the environmental movement's conservative opponents. Naomi Klein reflects the taken-for-granted nature of this prohibition when she warns that if we try 'to fix the crud in our lower atmosphere by pumping a different kind of crud into the stratosphere', our geoengineering 'may cause the earth to go wild in ways we cannot imagine ... the last tragic act in this centuries-long fairy tale of control'. Here, Klein casually dismisses the predictions of climate scientists, and instead asserts that self-organizing, complex, adaptive systems such as the troposphere 'have emergent properties that simply cannot be predicted' (Klein 2015, p. 267). This is an inherently conservative position. Some Green theorists have acknowledged the Green movement's conservative associations and have sought to identify commitments that distinguish 'ecologism' from conservatism. For example, Andrew Dobson has identified respect for the intrinsic worth of nonhuman natures, concern for future generations (rather than with preserving the past), and belief in motivations other than self-interest as defining characteristics (Dobson 2007, pp. 161–2). Tellingly, hostility to solar geoengineering is not justified by any of these distinctly Green commitments.

To label Green advocacy of 'humility before nature' (Klein 2015, p. 267) as conservative is not to denigrate it. Green prudence provides an important corrective to the excesses of unreflective development. Its methodology of environmental impact assessment seeks to incorporate environmental values into decision-making about development. For example, in the United States, the National Environmental Policy Act of 1969 institutionalized 'environmental review'. By publishing a report on a project's possible environmental impacts and seeking public feedback, this approach has made a significant contribution to public policy. However, if respect for the complexity of nature (or the market or society) becomes an inviolable principle, it can quickly collapse into reactionary conservatism. Such conservatism is usually linked to deeply held commitments, the acceptance or rejection of which can render political perspectives mutually unintelligible. Consider anxiety over nuclear power in Merkel's Germany or over GMOs in the European Union. In both cases, a concern for purity has been mobilized by political elites to nurture anxieties that motivate cruel and irrational policies. The resulting harms (via increased gas emissions and restrictions on agricultural imports, most especially from sub-Saharan Africa) primarily afflict people who are excluded from the national community.

This process, wherein national elites stoke fears to mobilize and control public support for a certain policy position, is sometimes termed 'securitization' (Williams 2003). If a threat is chosen wisely, securitization may be beneficial. The Indonesian government's public burning of illegal foreign fishing vessels has usefully raised the profile of marine conservation (Busro 2017). More commonly, though, securitization promotes harmful self/other distinctions and is used to denigrate vulnerable minorities or outsiders. If developing countries were to commence solar geoengineering, it is likely that they would confront resistance from first-world Greens, and perhaps nationalists as well.

For many environmentalists, however, harm minimization is precisely the wrong approach. Climate change, in the view of some, has a redemptive purpose: like a planetary fever, warming will destroy the shallow materialist culture that is its cause. Clive Hamilton (2010, p. 218) writes wistfully of the possibility that 'fresh values will emerge in the era of the hot Earth – values of moderation, humility, and respect, even reverence, for the natural world. And in place of self-pity and instant gratification, we could see a resurgence of resourcefulness and selflessness.' Adherents of this view will probably oppose geoengineering because, by masking symptoms, it allows the disease to spread. In the belief that consumption harms both people and their environments, many traditional environmentalists argue that it would be a mistake for the developing world to emulate Western modernity. Nearly five decades after the

UN-sponsored Founex Report (Strong 1971) articulated the third world's position in preparation for the 1972 Stockholm Conference on the Human Environment, the conundrum is more intense that ever: vulnerable people's quest for development and adaptation will compound environmental harms and risks. Achievement of a universally good Anthropocene thus turns upon our capacity to recalibrate human impacts.

Ideally, decisions about both climate-change mitigation and solar geoengineering would be made democratically. In a global democracy developing world people would, by weight of numbers, dominate decision-making. However, despite promising green shoots of democratic practices, our capacity for reflective, democratically guided collective action remains limited. In this context, solar geoengineering may be attractive precisely because it can be implemented without necessitating deep transformations within every community globally. If national mitigation policy and technological innovation is proceeding too slowly to avert dangerous climate change, a global intervention like solar geo engineering might be useful in order to buy time. But might it also stimulate democratizing global reform?

'Termination shock' is one of the most commonly raised concerns about solar geoengineering. According to this argument, once initiated, geoengineering must continue indefinitely, as termination would produce intolerably rapid climatic change. It is true: climate models do predict that temperatures would rebound – in just a few years – to roughly where they would have been if solar geoengineering had never commenced. Any termination of solar geoengineering, therefore, would need to be gradual. Since climate impacts are tightly correlated with the rate of climatic change, the temperature bounce associated with unplanned termination would be much more damaging than would unmediated climate change. Given enough time, most species can migrate to new habitats or adapt to changing conditions. The same rule generally applies to humans – while our agricultural techniques and built infrastructure can be adapted in response to gradual climatic changes, they may be overwhelmed by more dramatic shifts.

Of course, 'termination shock' would only remain a problem for so long as atmospheric concentrations of greenhouse gases remain elevated. Ideally, geoengineering would be accompanied by aggressive mitigation measures so that intervention would only be necessary over the brief period in which atmospheric concentrations 'overshoot' safe levels. Unfortunately, this narrative is implausibly benign. Instead, current trends suggest that limiting warming to 1.5 °C (a level of warming that would occur eventually even if all emissions ceased tomorrow) is more likely to require centuries of solar geoengineering (Hansen et al. 2016). Few cooperative human projects continue over centuries. It seems hopelessly naive to believe that states could maintain a carefully modulated and cooperative solar geoengineering plan. At minimum, it would require that war and conflict among major powers were permanently banished.

So does the possibility of termination shock mean that solar geoengineering is too dangerous to contemplate? No doubt some will take this view. On the other hand, termination risks surround many human projects – earlier I discussed synthesized nitrogen fertilizer, on which about 40 percent of global agricultural production depends (Smil 2017). Others argue that geoengineering would necessitate an intolerable global social order. Sociologist Bronislaw Szerszynski worries it would require a 'centralized, autocratic, command-and-control world-governing structure' that sits 'in tension with the current, broadly Westphalian, international system based on national self-determination' (2013, p. 2812). By contrast, others speculate that a coalition of powerful states might seize control and impose a global planetary environment favourable to their interests (Ricke et al. 2013)

Langdon Winner distinguished between 'two ways that technologies can contain political properties'. In the first, a technology is deliberately designed, or unconsciously selected, in order to produce a particular set of political consequences – to weaken the power of organized labour, for example, or to exclude certain people from public places. In the second, certain technologies can be seen as inherently political, in that they promote or even necessitate certain social relations (Winner 1980, p. 123). What social relations would solar geoengineering promote? Most obviously, it would require an international organization with sufficient authority and power to maintain a global geoengineering effort. Doubtless, democratic control over this organization would be imperfect.

But any global geoengineering body would also quickly become a focus of political mobilization (see Horton et al. 2018). While terminating geoengineering would be complicated, its implementation could be constantly refined. Democratic pressure might shift the goal of climate intervention towards assisting the most vulnerable countries, preserving pre-industrial climate patterns, maximizing agricultural production or even executing a gradual phase-out. Debates over geoengineering might also promote better climate policies. Currently, the delay between emission of greenhouse gases and their full climate impact (approximately a decade) undermines effective policy-making. Solar geoengineering could transform the way this time-lag is perceived; the real possibility of 'termination shock' might make catastrophic climate impacts appear as a near-term risk, rather than as something associated with the far future. More immediate climate risks might create a much clearer connection between mitigation and its benefits.

In 1950, the American theologian Reinhold Niebuhr wrote an essay on the hydrogen bomb, which notes a potential silver lining of the technology: 'It increases the general horror of war and thereby presumably adds something to the power of the will of nations to achieve an orderly world.' Niebuhr adds, 'Each age of mankind brings forth new perils and new possibilities. Yet they are always related to what we have known before' (Niebuhr 1976, p. 235) Although it is likely that nuclear weapons have played a role in inhibiting great power conflict, the price has been the permanent threat of thermonuclear homicide. Were climate change and geoengineering to bring an equivalent cooperative benefit, the associated risks would be similarly vast. Nevertheless, the flipside of Szerszynski's argument is that, once implemented, solar geoengineering might potentially promote both international cooperation and democratization. For those who believe that democratic governance is only compatible with national politics, the 'inherently globalizing' aspect of solar geoengineering is necessarily problematic. For people who aspire to a global, social-democratic order, however, a more hopeful view might be in order (Karlsson 2017). Solar geoengineering would not, in itself, spell the end of the sovereign state. But it would presumably add something to the will to achieve a more orderly and democratic world.

Conventional wisdom has it that global democratic consensus is a precondition for any plausibly just and responsible geoengineering. But what if that formula has it exactly backwards? What if, in fact, developing world-led geoengineering might be the pre-condition for a just, responsible, and democratic response to climate change – a way out of the seemingly irresolvable collective action problems that have stymied effective climate action for a generation? It is possible to visualize a future in which the acute challenges associated with geoengineering motivate a serious global climate effort, including shared and equitable investments in clean energy innovation, infrastructure and adaptation aid. In the end, self-determination by the world's most affected nations might be the key not only to just geoengineering, but also to forcing the kind of coordinated global response necessary for an effective, democratic, and just effort to mitigate and adapt to climate change.

Towards Global Social Democracy

Today, there is little sign that mitigation efforts will succeed in shifting the trajectory of global GHG emissions on anything like the required scale, and little momentum towards implementing solar geoengineering. Consequently, the question of how to protect poorer communities from inevitable harm grows more pressing. This is the context in which I propose *global social democracy*, including public investments in global human development and service provision, as a useful metaphor for ecomodernist transition. A metaphor invites us to see or imagine something we don't fully understand as another more familiar entity, for the purpose of coming to understand the unknown. In this case, national social democracy is to be used as an aid to thinking about a potential global social democracy. Even in the absence of climate change there would be many potential reasons to support global investments in social services and human development – restitution for colonial harms, or the fostering of a humanitarian solidarity are among them. However, climate change generates new international connections. The world's poorest people, who are least responsible, are also the most vulnerable to climate-linked harms, and these harms are generated almost entirely by the activities of the world's more affluent people. Recognizing this basic injustice, many people argue a climate debt is owed to the world's poor in the same way that a social democratic state might argue that a social debt is owed to displaced workers when an industry closes down, or when an area in the state is affected by a catastrophic weather event.

In the social democratic model, investment in human development has also always been seen both as an end in itself, and also an enabler of continued social progress. Historically, universal service provision and welfare has been one of the most effective ways of advancing human development within states, and provision of primary health care is widely recognized as one of the most successful forms of international aid (Levine et al. 2004; Victor 2018). Investments in public health and education bring benefits to entire societies – for example, through increased economic productivity – as well as to individuals. Can global application of these social democratic ideas provide a template for addressing climate harms? For example, the link between universal basic health care and international disaster response services and climate harms is very clear. Moreover, if international assistance were channelled through state agencies it might support, rather than undermine, national sovereignty.

There is evidence that this kind of thinking is already underway. International institutions such as the *Green Climate Fund* have already been created with the goal of mobilizing funds to support adaptation and mitigation. To date though, international adaptation funding has been inadequate, and climate adaptation assistance faces all of the same difficulties as international aid more generally. Efforts to compensate climate-linked injustices need to navigate at least three challenges that have been elaborated by the rich literature propounding aid pessimism (see Rajan and Subramanian 2008). First is the problem of power and conditionality. The majority of mitigation and adaptation assistance is delivered through bilateral rather than multilateral schemes. Aside from the unnecessary complexity this creates, with recipient states needing to navigate a complex web of funding application and reporting processes, bilateral assistance also creates the potential for mitigation assistance to be used as a tool of political influence. Second, is the question of aid effectiveness. While aid is frequently effective, it is often least effective in places where governance is poorest and assistance is most needed (Victor 2018). Third is the problem of motivation. Climate-linked assistance that is conceptualized as aid is extremely politically vulnerable. The Trump Administration's cancellation of payments to the Green Climate Fund illustrates this point. While it seems morally clear that affluent communities owe the most vulnerable people protection against climate harms, we are making little progress towards this goal.

The social and political conditions for emergence of global democracy, let alone public support for a global social welfare system, do not yet exist. However, the ecomodernist goal of universal human flourishing will probably turn on our capacity to harness political momentum as it arises. There are considerable sources of contemporary momentum towards limited global social democratic practices. First, we are witnessing changes in how 'international community' is conceptualized. These changes are most clearly illustrated by the emergence of the 'Responsibility to Protect' (RtoP) norm which governs how the international community responds to genocide and mass atrocities (war crimes, ethnic cleansing, and crimes against humanity). While the RtoP norm is not directly connected to social democratic ideas, its international acceptance reflects an ongoing shift in the way in which 'sovereignty' and international responsibilities are understood. Sovereignty no longer simply refers to the legal identity of a state in international law and to the state's right to non-interference in internal affairs. Instead, the International Commission on Intervention and State Sovereignty (ICISS) that elaborated the RtoP norm proposed that we should think of 'sovereignty as responsibility' such that 'state authorities are responsible for the functions of protecting the safety and lives of citizens and promotion of their welfare' (ICISS, 2001, s.2.15). Where a state lacks the capacity to fulfil these responsibilities, the RtoP norm establishes that the international community has a responsibility to provide assistance.

A decade after the Responsibility to Protect norm was first adopted by the UN General Assembly, international relations scholar Alex Bellamy (2015, p. 161) noted that 'the principle has been unanimously reaffirmed in its entirety no fewer than four times by the UN Security Council and has informed more than twenty-five other Security Council resolutions; and RtoP is now being utilized by the wider community of UN member states'. Governments and other international organizations routinely act upon the norm, and they explain their behaviour with reference to it. By reconceptualizing sovereignty as involving the responsibility to protect human rights and human security, and by attributing a responsibility to the international community to assist states in upholding these rights, the RtoP norm has deepened the formal understanding of obligations owed internationally. This idea that the international community is collectively responsible for protection of human rights everywhere – although weak – is also articulated in a wide array of other international contexts. The articulation in 2015 of a set of 'Sustainable Development Goals' for cooperative implementation by 2030 is one of the clearer examples.

Advocates of the democratization of global governance commonly argue that although we should not expect global democratic institutions such as a world parliament, the emergence of *democratic practices* beyond the state can act as a stepping stone to greater democratization (Little and Macdonald 2013). Increasing accountability mechanisms in international organizations, and non-state efforts to govern environmental and labour standards across supply chains, are both examples. Analogously, tentative mechanisms of redistribution and investment in human development are appearing beyond the state. Advocates of universal human flourishing should nurture these *global social democratic practices*. Consider the major mechanisms through which redistribution occurs in national social democracies: employment regulation, progressive taxation, provision of public services (largely free at point of use), direct financial transfers through social security, regionally targeted economic development and migration (Jacobs et al. 2003). The foundation of the International Labor Organization in 1919, with the goal of establishing global employment regulation, was perhaps the earliest significant step towards internationalizing redistributive policies. A century later, there are plenty of newly emerging practices that ecomodernists can work to extend.

In their work on carbon and global inequality, Chancel and Piketty observe that although it would be desirable to fund climate adaptation via a global progressive taxation system, this seems politically infeasible. Since aviation is a good 'marker of high income and high CO2e emitting lifestyles', one of the more feasible (although still improbable) alternatives they consider would be to fund climate adaptation with a tax on aviation (Chancel and Piketty 2015, p. 38). In 2006, the French government tried to establish just such an international scheme. France hosted an international conference seeking to build support for a 'solidarity contribution' from plane tickets to finance a global health fund. Only Cameroon, Chile, the Republic of Congo, Madagascar, Mali, Mauritius, Niger and Korea joined France in imposing the tax, but the Solidarity Tax continues to generate revenue (approximately €200m per year) that is donated to UNITAID (a global health initiative focusing on infectious diseases such as HIV, malaria and tuberculosis) and the International Finance Facility for Immunization. Taxes range from €1 for economy flights within the EU to €40 for long-haul first-class flights. This solidarity contribution is just one of a range of innovative financing instruments for global health that demonstrate emerging global social democratic practices (see Atun et al. 2017).

Sustainable development goals create further momentum towards global health care. One of the targets of Goal 3 promises to achieve 'universal health coverage, including financial risk protection, access to quality essential healthcare services and access to safe, effective, quality and affordable essential medicines and vaccines for all' by 2030. In 2018, even so moderate an outlet as the liberal *Economist* magazine editorialized that 'universal health care, worldwide, is within reach' (2018, p. 9). The editorial observed that:

Chile and Costa Rica spend about an eighth of what America does per person on health and have similar life expectancies. Thailand spends $220 per person a year on health, and yet has outcomes nearly as good as in the OECD.

The idea of globalizing universal basic health care is feasible and, if focused on primary and community based care, has proven cost effective at a national level. Models in which international partners support low-income countries to deploy national schemes demonstrate the kind of 'nested' global social democratic practices that might make international solidarity consistent with national sovereignty and communitarian politics, and provide something to build on in relation to climate-change policies.

Conclusion

During the three decades in which the threat posed by climate change has been widely understood, the most significant human response has been a form of adaptation: rapid economic growth, especially in East and Southeast Asia, has dramatically improved the resilience of entire countries. Despite these remarkable advances, billions of people continue to experience levels of poverty that render them extremely vulnerable to climate harms. Meanwhile, the world economy as a whole remains on a trajectory in which warming far in excess of 2°C this century remains likely. Human impacts could be minimized through progressive global investments in social services that give communities everywhere a chance to adapt. Unfortunately, progress is slow. Meanwhile, climate modelling suggests that solar geoengineering, although as yet untested and uncertain, might dramatically reduce climate-linked harms. Most first-world Greens judge that the risks of interventions are too great, and evidence suggests that the general public in OECD countries may reach the same conclusion. However, if decisions about solar geoengineering were made democratically, these choices would belong to the more numerous communities of the third world. Ecomodernists have often discussed solar geoengineering in ways that suggest it is inevitable (Brand 2009). Perhaps a commitment to the primacy of politics over market forces would suggest another conclusion: that lower-income communities should have the freedom to exercise self-determination even in respect of climate interventions.

The two topics in this chapter – global provision of social services and planetary interventions to avert some impacts of climate change – are rarely considered together. However, a social democratic perspective advocates deployment of democratically garnered power in pursuit of collective goods. Interventions in climate systems and interventions in markets are two mechanisms through which social democrats might seek to advance human development amid mounting climate threats. In the words of sociologist Ulrich Beck, 'reality itself has become cosmopolitan' (2006, p. 341), well before the emergence of a thick bond of cosmopolitan solidarity. Given the continuing division of humanity into often rivalrous and insular national communities, the emergence of global social democratic practices is bound to be imperfect and piecemeal. However, increased international support for social services has the potential to build the kind of trust and solidarity that might also enable more effective climate governance.

Conclusion

Climate and its Metaphors

Writing in the early years of the AIDS epidemic, Susan Sontag worked to detach illness from its association with guilt and shame by interrogating and wearing out the metaphors through which AIDS was understood (Sontag 1989, pp. 54, 78, 94). 'Plagues' she observed, 'are invariably regarded as judgements on society' that suggest 'the immediate necessity of limitation, of constraint for the body and for consciousness'. Sontag believed that the attempt to separate calamity from moralizing metaphors is essential to a reasoned and humane response. Moreover, she observed that the societal response to AIDS was not simply an appropriate response to a new danger but that it also reflected a positive desire for external limitations. She wrote (1989, p. 93):

> There is a broad tendency in our culture, an end-of-an-era feeling, that AIDS is reinforcing; an exhaustion, for many, of purely secular ideals – ideals that seemed to encourage libertinism or at least not provide any coherent inhibition against it – in which the response to AIDS finds its place.

In viewing the climate crisis as a 'judgement on society', many Western Greens once again urge a retreat from the challenging complexity of modernity into simpler, more traditional patterns of life. The claim that interventions in natural systems should always be avoided, which is so distinctive of the modern Green movement, reflects one such a retreat. Yet, as was the case with AIDS, effective responses to climate change require a methodical, evidence-guided approach. If limitations and restraint are useful, they should be proposed as calculated responses to specific problems rather than viewed as a generalized cultural impera-tive. A blanket prohibition on 'hubristic' interventions – whether of solar geoengineering, genetic engineering or advanced nuclear technology – might offer a reassuring return to convention. However, such appeals to tradition risk undermining the concern for material welfare which has been the traditional focus of progressive politics.

Garrett Hardin's (1968) 'tragedy of the commons' has become one of the most influential metaphors of modern environmental politics, and it too deserves to be interrogated and worn out. Hardin's 'tragedy' is a moral fable describ-ing how the commonly owned land in a traditional English village is inevitably overgrazed and destroyed if villagers' cows have unrestricted access. Hardin famously described how each individual's interest in maximizing their personal utility conflicts with the collective interest in protecting a shared resource. He proposed that tragedy could be averted either through privatization or coercive government. Other scholars have emphasized that self-organized, collective governance systems often offer a better solution (see Ostrom 2012). When this analogy is applied to climate change, the earth's atmosphere is viewed as a shared resource that is threatened by excess GHG emissions, and the global com-munity needs to find a way to allocate the remaining emis-sions budget fairly. Accordingly, many analysts propose carbon pricing, regulated emissions standards, voluntary non-state mitigation initiatives, and target setting by states and other organizations. Useful as these policies undoubt-edly are, if the time in which we might have spared the commons has already passed, then the tragedy of the commons may not offer a useful guide.

If we are already at the tragedy's denouement, then the metaphor of limits is also exhausted. Instead, villagers will have no choice but to innovate and identify alternative sources of income and sustenance. Tellingly, Hardin raised and rejected the possibility that improved technologies (grain varieties) might offer a resolution to the tragedy. He developed his analysis of 'common-pool resources' as part of an essay whose central claim was that the 'freedom to breed is intolerable' and that governments must severely limit human reproduction (Hardin 1968, p. 1246). Needless to say, the rapid agricultural productivity gains of the intervening decades have proven Hardin's analysis wrong in the case of food supply. However, the Malthusian imagery of limits and overpopulation still stalks climate discourse at a time when the material demands of over seven billion people are clearly irreconcilable with planetary limits, unless those limits are transcended through technological change.

New metaphors are needed to guide our transition towards a technologically sophisticated yet biodiverse future. I have proposed that 'global social democracy' should join 'mission-oriented innovation' and 'separation' from dependence on natural ecosystems as a central ecomodernist metaphor. However, Emma Marris's (2013) description of the future earth as a 'rambunctious garden' or Holly Jean Buck's (2015) suggestion that through practices of 'rewilding', 'crafting' biophilic cities and 'planetary gardening' we might yet achieve a 'charming Anthropocene' also strike me as promising ways of conceptualizing the future.

Ecomodernism, Innovation and Heresy

This book set out to examine the relationship between ecomodernism, environmentalism and other political traditions, and to reflect on a politics that might best respond to the climate crisis. Of course, there is no single ideal climate politics. Differently situated communities will experience and perceive climate threats differently. This is why it is not productive to view climate harms as a consequence of elite corruption, societal hubris or alienation from nature. Rather, climate change should, ideally, come to be seen simply as an unintended consequence of human activities, and we should aspire to a response that is as scientifically informed, as democratic and as attentive to global scales as possible. Similarly, interventions such as solar geoengineering deserve careful, democratic deliberation rather than presumptive rejection. This critique of Green cultural values alienates many environmentalists. Believing that our capitalist society's estrangement from nature is the root cause of climate harms, many Greens are horrified by ecomodernism's call for more deliberate *separation* from nature, more public-good focused innovation and more attentive application of technology.

In the conclusion to *Green Delusions*, which might be regarded as the earliest book-length statement of ecomodernist thinking, Martin Lewis observed that the environmental movement 'must devise realistic plans and concrete strategies for avoiding ecological collapse and for reconstructing an ecologically sustainable economic order' (1994, p. 250). Lewis went on to speculate that our 'best hope' might lie in a 'coalition in which moderate conservatives continue to insist on efficiency and prudence, and where liberals forward an agenda aimed at social progress and environmental protection' (Lewis 1994, p. 250). In the ensuing decades, however, climate change has been invested with intense partisan associations in the United States. Consequently, Lewis's aspiration now seems hopelessly naive. Among those for whom either denying the importance of climate change or asserting the inherent virtues of renewable energy is a marker of political identity, it is hard to imagine how a stable consensus supporting effective policies might emerge. To be sure, the Obama Administration generally pursued technologically neutral and innovation-focused climate policies, despite a polarized political culture. However, the Obama Administration's ecomodernist agenda is now rejected by both the Trumpian right and by much of the activist left (e.g. Bernie Sanders' prioritization of closing nuclear power stations over GHG emission reductions (Nordhaus 2016)).

It is perhaps not surprising that people would disagree over a challenge that is as abstract and far-reaching as climate change. However, once an issue becomes polarized, the deadlock can be difficult to unwind. Polarization over climate change has been carefully nurtured, and vested interests have deliberately promoted denial and scientific confusion. This is not the Green movement's work. Nevertheless, these are the circumstances in which advocates of ambitious mitigation must try to win broad support. Unfortunately, the Green movement's insistence that climate action must be consistent with Green cultural values has only exacerbated these divisions. If conservatives are told that the zero-carbon technologies they typically like – such as nuclear power and hydroelectricity – must be excluded from the climate response, then the psychological appeal of denial will inevitably increase.

This book has deliberately drawn a stark contrast between 'Greens' and other progressives (primarily ecomodernists) in relation to climate change. Many people, of course, embrace both Green and scientific ideals, and will be drawn to paths that integrate both. Inevitably, society will also follow some middle way. However, I have drawn sharp distinctions because I think it is important to clarify how impulses towards humility and localism can undermine climate ambition, equality and human development. My hope is that if climate mitigation efforts were to be seen as slightly more distinct from the pursuit of Green values, this might help to reduce political polarization, and perhaps allow broader coalitions to support more ambitious climate action.

Given that climate change is a long-term, global challenge, clarity around policy goals is especially important. Not only is there roughly a decade's delay between emissions and their full impact, but local policies generally make only a minimal contribution to global outcomes – so, policy-makers can easily be distracted from the goal of emissions reduction. This is why ecomodernists often condemn Germany's *Energiewende* policy: the decision to close zero-carbon nuclear power while continuing to utilize carbon-intensive lignite and coal (even building new plants), is a clear example of a 'Green' (local) policy that is producing adverse *global* climate impacts. The same disconnection applies at an individual level too. A home with vegetables growing in the yard and solar panels on the roof will feel Green (even if the solar panels are backed up by a diesel generator) in ways that a societal choice to construct a zero-carbon nuclear grid, to develop synthetic milk and meat, or invest in synthesizing jet fuel might not. Yet, it is the deliberate choice of *collective* zero-emissions technologies, rather than the aesthetic of rustic self-sufficiency, that will minimize climate harms.

A fundamental argument of this book is that low-carbon innovation must become a central focus of climate policy. This argument is by no means new. The case for an innovation-focused climate response has been made repeatedly by scholars, by economic reports and by scientific bodies (e.g. Prins and Rayner 2007). Their arguments have seldom been rebutted. Instead, the argument for innovation-led mitigation has largely been defeated through inattention. 'Zero-carbon innovation' has failed to gain traction among proponents of climate action as it doesn't fit with Green conceptions of environmental transition. Meanwhile, state investment in mission-oriented innovation contradicts prevailing economic ideology. Consequently, an innovation-focused climate strategy has never been implemented at scale.

Zero-carbon innovation may simply be too abstract an idea. It seems that anyone who has heard of ecomodernism remembers that these are 'pro-nuclear environmentalists'. Yet fewer recall ecomodernism's most urgent, practical argument – that state-directed low-carbon innovation must be at the heart of our climate response. Perhaps this perspective is too dull to gain attention. In this case, Calestous Juma may be correct to argue that human society's fate hangs on the capacity of political leadership, that much impugned elite, to navigate the inherent tensions between innovation and continuity by charting 'new paths while at the same time maintaining continuity, social order, and stability' (Juma 2016, p. 7). This however, would not be political leadership of just any kind. It would need to weave global challenges and shared human interests into narratives capable of gaining sustained support within national communities.

A Social Democratic Climate Response

Social democracy embodies the idea that the future should be deliberately and democratically chosen and shaped in the service of some collective good, rather than be allowed to emerge from the ungoverned working of markets. Historically, social democracy has also been communitarian and embedded in specific national projects. Since climate change is a global process operating outside the boundaries of any single democratic community, climate responses often seek to promote global solidarity rather than national loyalty. Nevertheless, utilizing democratic power to redirect the energies of a capitalist economy towards the provision of public goods is a classic social democratic position. Ecomodernism's defence of national self-determination in energy and environmental policy is also consistent with a social democratic politics. However, I have argued that ecomodernists should go further and embrace *global social democracy* as an organizing metaphor. This is primarily because ecomodernism's goal of universal human development will, during an era of mounting climate harms, be impossible without a basic level of global social services. I have also argued that decisions about climate engineering and other forms of earth systems governance will need to be democratized if they are to reflect the interests of more vulnerable populations, rather than the cultural preferences of the affluent groups that dominate global civil society.

While global social democracy holds obvious attractions, its feasibility seems doubtful. The most challenging question here, then, is identifying the sources of solidarity that might ground a more redistributive ecomodernist project. I don't have a confident answer to this question. For the foreseeable future, national communities will remain the most effective source of political solidarity. For this reason, it would be more useful and effective to work to make the provision of global public goods a goal of *national* politics. That is, to use the metaphor of global social democracy in national politics and policy-making to promote public engagement with international initiatives like Mission Innovation, and to seize opportunities to globalize social services as they arise. I have pointed to the way in which great power rivalries have motivated states to prioritize innovation in the past, and how some of these innovations have brought social benefits beyond their initial application. The recent development of the Responsibility to Protect norm reflects a wider momentum towards global solidarity. National communities have proven capable of at least limited collective responses towards global challenges.

Ecomodernists are correct to point to astonishing human progress in the last half century, and they are probably correct that universal human flourishing remains possible on a warming planet. However, given the deep inequalities, injustices and ecological catastrophes that characterize our era, a 'good' or 'charming' Anthropocene can seem improbable. It is populist localism rather than progressive globalism that is now politically ascendant. There is likelihood, of which Meera Nanda warned in a landmark study of Hindu nationalism (2003, xvi), that if left-wing anti-Enlightenment movements succeed in severing the historical association between science and progressive, secular politics, they may 'unwittingly contribute to the ugly phenomenon of reactionary modernism'. Climate change only amplifies this risk. And yet for most people in the first world, climate change presents as either an unimportant abstraction or a distant catastrophe. Consequently, moral gestures and small-scale, local initiatives dominate Western climate responses. Ecomodernists, though, ask us to think on a larger scale, and they ask us to do this in the name of universal human flourishing as well as environmental care. If eight billion people are to enjoy modestly prosperous lives on an ecologically vibrant planet, then energy production must be dramatically expanded, even as emissions are reduced to zero. It seems improbable that a self-consciously 'ecomodernist' agenda will amass sufficient power to achieve this goal. However, in interrogating the metaphors of limits and in advocating for bolder and more systemic global responses, ecomodernism may help to catalyse a more effective climate politics.

References

Acemoglu, D. 2002. Directed technical change. *The Review of Economic Studies*, 69(4).

Adorno, T. W. and Horkheimer, M. 1979. *Dialectic of Enlightenment*. tr. Cumming, J., Verso.

Aklin, M. and Urpelainen, J. 2018. *Renewables: The Politics of a Global Energy Transition*. MIT Press.

Andersson, J. 2009. *The Library and the Workshop: Social Democracy and Capitalism in the Knowledge Age*. Stanford University Press.

Ang, B. W. and Su, B. 2016. Carbon emission intensity in electricity production: A global analysis. *Energy Policy*, 94.

Applegate, P. J. and Keller, K. 2015. How effective is albedo modification (solar radiation management geoengineering) in preventing sea-level rise from the Greenland ice sheet? *Environmental Research Letters*, 10.8:084018.

Arias-Maldonado, M. 2016. *Real Green: Sustainability after the End of Nature*. Routledge.

Asafu-Adjaye, J., Blomquist, L., Brand, S., Brook, B. W., DeFries, R., Ellis, E., Foreman, C., Keith, D., Lewis, M., Lynas, M. and Nordhaus, T. 2015. *An Ecomodernist Manifesto*. http://www.ecomodernism.org/manifesto-english/

Atkinson, R., Chhetri, N., Freed, J., Galiana, I., Green, C., Hayward, S., Jenkins, J. et al. 2011. Climate Pragmatism: innovation, resilience and no regrets. The Hartwell analysis in an American context. The Hartwell Group. https://thebreakthrough.org/blog/Climate_Pragmatism_web.pdf

Atun, R., Silva, S. and Knaul, F. M. 2017. Innovative financing instruments for global health 2002–15: a systematic analysis. *The Lancet Global Health*, 5(7).

Ausubel, J. H. 1996. Can technology spare the earth? *American Scientist*, 84(2).

Bala, G. and Gupta, A. 2017. Geoengineering and India. *Current Science*, 113(3).

Ball, J. 2018. Why carbon pricing isn't working: Good idea in theory, failing in practice. *Foreign Affairs*, 97(134). https://www.foreignaffairs.com/articles/world/2018-06-14/why-carbon-pricing-isnt-working?cid=otr-author-why_carbon_pricing_isnt_working-061418

Barmann J. 2016. Dozens of pro-nuclear protesters march to resist Diablo Canyon Closure. *SFist*, 24 June. http://sfist.com/2016/06/24/dozens_of_pro-nuclear_protesters_ma.php

Battistoni A. 2015. How to change everything. *Jacobin*. https://www.jacobinmag.com/2015/12/naomi-klein-climate-change-this-changes-everything-cop21

Bauman, Z. 2000. *Modernity and the Holocaust*. Cornell University Press.

Bazilian, M. D. 2015. Power to the poor: Provide energy to fight poverty. *Foreign Affairs*, 94.

Beck, U. 2006. Living in the world risk society: A Hobhouse Memorial Public Lecture given on Wednesday 15 February 2006 at the London School of Economics. *Economy and Society*, 35(3)

Bedjaoui, M. 1979. *Towards a New International Economic Order*. Holmes and Meier.

Berkowitz, R., Callen, M. and Dworkin, R. 1983. *How to Have Sex in an Epidemic: One Approach*. News From the Front Publications. https://joeclark.org/dossiers/howtohavesexinanepidemic.pdf

Berman, S. 2006. *The Primacy of Politics: Social Democracy and the Making of Europe's Twentieth Century*. Cambridge University Press.

Bernstein, J. and Szuster, B. 2018. Beyond unidimensionality: Segmenting contemporary pro-environmental worldviews through surveys and repertory grid analysis. *Environmental Communication* 12(8).

Block. F. 2011. Daniel Bell's prophecy. *Breakthrough Journal* Summer. https://thebreakthrough.org/index.php/journal/past-issues/issue-1/daniel-bells-prophecy

Block. F. 2018. Seeing the State. *Breakthrough Journal*. https://thebreakthrough.org/index.php/journal/no.-9-summer-2018/seeing-the-state

Bookchin, M. 1989. *Remaking Society* (Vol. 23). Black Rose Books.

Boucher, O., Randall, D., Artaxo, P., Bretherton, C., Feingold, G., Forster, P., Kerminen, V. M., Kondo, Y., Liao, H., Lohmann, U., Rasch, P., Satheesh, S. K., Sherwood, S., Stevens, B. and Zhang, X. Y. 2013. Clouds and aerosols. In *Climate Change 2013: The Physical Science Basis. Contribution of Working Group I to the Fifth Assessment Report of the Intergovernmental Panel on Climate Change*. Stocker, T. F., Qin, D., Plattner, G. K., Tignor, M., Allen, S. K., Boschung, J., Nauels, A., Xia, Y., Bex, V. and Midgley P. M. (eds). Cambridge University Press.

B. P. Global. 2018. BP statistical review of world energy. 2017. https://www.bp.com/en/global/corporate/energy-economics/statistical-review-of-world-energy.html

Bradshaw, S. 2015. *Powering Up Against Poverty, Why Renewable Energy in the Future*. Oxfam. https://www.oxfam.org.au/wp-content/uploads/2015/07/coal_report_lowres_web2.pdf

Bramwell, A. 1990. *Ecology in the 20th Century: A History*. Yale University Press.

Brand, S. 2009. *Whole Earth Discipline*. Atlantic Books Ltd.

Breakthrough Energy Coalition. 2018. http://www.b-t.energy/

Bronner, S. 2006. *Reclaiming the Enlightenment: Toward a Politics of Radical Engagement*. Columbia University Press.

Brook, B. W., Edney, K., Hillerbrand, R., Karlsson, R. and Symons, J. 2016. Energy research within the UNFCCC: A proposal to guard against ongoing climate-deadlock. *Climate Policy*, 16(6).

Brookes, G., Taheripour, F. and Tyner, W. E. 2017. The contribution of glyphosate to agriculture and potential impact of restrictions on use at the global level. *GM Crops and Food*, 8(4).

Brundtland, G. H. 1987. *Report of the World Commission on Environment and Development: 'Our Common Future'*. United Nations.

Buck, H. J. 2015. On the possibilities of a charming Anthropocene. *Annals of the Association of American Geographers*, 105(2).

Bull, H. 1979. The State's positive role in world affairs. *Daedalus*, 108(4).

Bush, V. 1945. *Science – The Endless Frontier*. US Government Printing Office.

Bush, G.W. 2003. *Iraq War Ultimatum Speech*. Washington, DC, 18 March 2003.

Busro, Z. M. 2017. Burning and/or sinking foreign fishing vessels conducting illegal fishing in Indonesia. *Asia-Pacific Journal of Ocean Law and Policy*, 2(1).

Cao, J., Cohen, A., Hansen, J., Lester, R., Peterson, P. and Xu, H. 2016. China–US cooperation to advance nuclear power. *Science*, 353(6299).

Carr, E. H. 2001. *The Twenty Years' Crisis 1919–1939: An Introduction to the Study of International Relations*. Macmillan.

Carson, R. 1962. *Silent Spring*. Houghton Mifflin.

Carvalho, D. O., McKemey, A. R., Garziera, L., Lacroix, R., Donnelly, C. A., Alphey, L. et al. 2015. Suppression of a field population of *Aedes aegypti* in Brazil by sustained release of transgenic male mosquitoes. *PLoS Negl Trop Dis*, 9(7).

Cass, O. 2018. *Testimony of Oren M. Cass before the House Committee on Science, Space, and Technology*. 16 May 2018 https://www.manhattan-institute.org/sites/default/files/Cass-Testimony-May2018.pdf

Chancel, L. and Piketty, T. 2015. *Carbon and Inequality from Kyoto to Paris: Trends in the Global Inequality of Carbon Emissions (1998–2013) and Prospects for an Equitable Adaptation Fund*. Paris School of Economics. http://piketty.pse.ens.fr/files/ChancelPiketty2015.pdf

Charbit. Y. 2009. Capitalism and population: Marx and Engels against Malthus. In *Economic, Social and Demographic Thought in the XIXth Century*. Springer.

Chen, G., Huang, S. and Hu, X. 2018. Backpacker personal development, generalized self-efficacy, and self-esteem: Testing a structural model. *Journal of Travel Research*. https://doi.org/10.1177/0047287518768457

Chibber, V. 2014. *Postcolonial Theory and the Specter Of Capital*. Verso Books.

Clack, C. T., Qvist, S. A., Apt, J., Bazilian, M., Brandt, A. R., Caldeira, K., Davis, S. J., Diakov, V., Handschy, M. A., Hines, P. D. and Jaramillo, P. 2017. Evaluation of a proposal for reliable low-cost grid power with 100% wind, water, and solar. *Proceedings of the National Academy of Sciences*, 114(26).

Collard, R. C., Dempsey, J. and Sundberg, J. 2015. A manifesto for abundant futures. *Annals of the Association of American Geographers*, 105(2).

Cowan, R. 1990. Nuclear power reactors: A study in technological lock-in. *The Journal of Economic History*, 50(3).

Cox, R. W. 1983. Gramsci, hegemony and international relations: An essay in method. *Millennium*, 12(2).

Crist, E. 2015. The reaches of freedom: A response to an ecomodernist manifesto. *Environmental Humanities*, 7(1).

Crutzen, P. and Stoermer, E. 2000. The 'Anthropocene', *Global Change Newsletter*, 41(2000).

Cullather, N. 2014. Stretching the surface of the earth: The foundations, neo-Malthusianism and the modernising agenda. *Global Society*, 28(1).

Danforth, W. H. 1991. *The AIDS Research Program of the National Institutes of Health*. National Academies, 1991. Ch. 4. Available: http://www.ncbi.nlm.nih.gov/books/NBK234085/

Davis, Steven J., Lewis, Nathan S., Shaner, Matthew, Aggarwal, Sonia, Arent, Doug, Azevedo, Inês L., Benson, Sally M. et al. 2018. Net-zero emissions energy systems. *Science* 360(6396).

Davis, S. J., Lewis, N. S. and Caldeira, K. 2017. Achieving a near-zero carbon emissions energy system, *Eos*, 98. https://doi.org/10.1029/2017EO064017

de Castro, C. and Capellán-Pérez, I. 2018. Concentrated solar power: Actual performance and foreseeable future in high penetration scenarios of renewable energies. *BioPhysical Economics and Resource Quality*, 3(3).

DeFrancesco, L. 2013. How safe does transgenic food need to be? *Nat. Biotechnology*, 31.

DeFries, R. 2014. *The Big Ratchet: How Humanity Thrives in the Face of Natural Crisis*. Basic Books.

Desai R. 2015. Social policy and the elimination of extreme poverty. In L. Chandy, H. Kato and H. Kharas, eds, *The Last Mile in Ending Extreme Poverty*. Brookings Institution Press.

DeSombre, E. 2000. *Domestic Sources of International Environmental Policy*. MIT Press.

Diamond, J. 2005. *Collapse*. Viking.

Dobson, A. 2007. *Green Political Thought*. 4th edn. Routledge.

Dryzek, J. S. 2013. *The Politics of the Earth: Environmental Discourses.* 3rd edn. Oxford University Press.

Eckersley, R. 1992. *Environmentalism and Political Theory: Toward an Ecocentric Approach.* Suny Press.

Eckersley, R. 2004. *The Green State: Rethinking Democracy and Sovereignty.* MIT Press.

Economist. 2018 (26 April). Universal health care, worldwide, is within reach. *The Economist Group.* https://www.economist.com/news/leaders/21741138-case-it-powerful-oneincluding-poor-countries-universal-health-care-worldwide

Edler, J. and Georghiou, L. 2007. Public procurement and innovation: Resurrecting the demand side. *Research Policy,* 36.

Ehrlich, P. 1968. *The Population Bomb.* Ballantine Books.

France, D. 2016. *How to Survive a Plague: The Story of How Activists and Scientists Tamed AIDS.* Picador Books.

Frank, T. 2016. *Listen, Liberal: Or, Whatever Happened to the Party of the People?* Macmillan.

Fremaux, A. and Barry, J. 2019. The 'good Anthropocene' and green political theory: Rethinking environmentalism, resisting ecomodernism. In F. Biermann and E. Lövbrand, eds, *Anthropocene Encounters. New Directions in Green Political Thinking.* Cambridge University Press.

Fuentes-George, K. 2017. Consensus, certainty, and catastrophe: Discourse, governance, and ocean iron fertilization. *Global Environmental Politics,* 17(2).

Gates, B. 2015. Energy innovation: Why we need it and how to get it. *Breakthrough Energy Coalition.*

Garnaut, R. 2008. *The Garnaut Climate Change Review.* Cambridge University Press. http://garnautreview.org.au/

Geden, O. 2016. The Paris Agreement and the inherent inconsistency of climate policy-making. *Wiley Interdisciplinary Reviews: Climate Change,* 7(6).

Gerasimova, K. 2016. Debates on genetically modified crops in the context of sustainable development. *Science and Engineering Ethics,* 22(2).

Gilbert, D. 2006. If only gay sex caused global warming. *Los Angeles Times,* 2.

Gilman, N. 2015. The new international economic order: A reintroduction. *Humanity: An International Journal of Human Rights, Humanitarianism, and Development,* 6(1).

Goldman, M. 2005. *Imperial Nature: The World Bank and Struggles for Social Justice in the Age of Globalization*. Yale University Press.

Golub, P. S. 2013. From the new international economic order to the G20: How the 'global south' is restructuring world capitalism from within. *Third World Quarterly*, 34(6).

Gore, A. 2007. *The Assault on Reason*. Bloomsbury.

Gottlieb, R. 2005. *Forcing the Spring: The Transformation of the American Environmental Movement*. Island Press.

Grant, R.W. 2011. *Strings Attached: Untangling the Ethics of Incentives*. Princeton University Press.

Greenpeace International 2015. *Why our Food and Farming System is Broken*. https://www.greenpeace.org/archive-international/en/campaigns/agriculture/problem/

Haas P. M. 1992. Banning chlorofluorocarbons: Epistemic community efforts to protect stratospheric ozone. *International Organization*, 46.

Hamilton, C. 2010. *Requiem for a Planet*. Earthscan.

Hamilton, C. 2013. *Earthmasters: The Dawn of the Age of Climate Engineering*. Yale University Press.

Hamilton, C. 2015. The technofix is in: A critique of 'An Ecomodernist Manifesto'. *Earth Island Journal*, 21.http://www.earthisland.org/journal/index.php/elist/eListRead/the_technofix_is_in/

Hansen, J. et al. 2008. Target atmospheric CO_2: Where should humanity aim? *The Open Atmospheric Science Journal*, 2. doi:10.2174/1874282300802010217

Hansen, J. et al. 2016. Young people's burden: Requirement of negative CO_2 emissions. *arXiv:1609.05878*.

Hardin, G. 1968. The tragedy of the commons. *Science*, 162.

Hardin, G. 1974. Lifeboat ethics: The case against helping the poor. *Psychology Today*, September, http://www.garretthardinsociety.org/articles/art_lifeboat_ethics_case_against_helping_poor.html

Hartmann, B. 1997. Population control I: Birth of an ideology. *International Journal of Health Services*, 27(3).

Harvey, D. 2003. *The New Imperialism*. Oxford University Press.

Hasan, M. 2018. Dear Bashar al-Assad apologists: Your hero is a war criminal even if he didn't gas Syrians, *The Intercept*, 20 April. https://theintercept.com/2018/04/19/dear-bashar-al-assad-apologists-your-hero-is-a-war-criminal-even-if-he-didnt-gas-syrians/

Herold, N., Alexander, L., Green, D. and Donat, M. 2017. Greater increases in temperature extremes in low versus high income countries. *Environmental Research Letters*, 12(3).

Herring, R. and Paarlberg, R. 2016. The political economy of biotechnology. *Annual Review of Resource Economics*, 8.

Hesketh, T., Zhou, X. and Wang, Y., 2015. The end of the one-child policy: Lasting implications for China. *Jama*, 314(24).

Hiltzik, M. 2010. *Colossus: Hoover Dam and the Making of the American Century*. Simon and Schuster.

Horton, J. B., Reynolds, J. L., Buck, H. J., Callies, D., Schäfer, S., Keith, D. W. and Rayner, S., 2018. Solar geoengineering and democracy. *Global Environmental Politics*, 18(3).

Hulme, M. 2014. *Can Science Fix Climate Change? A Case Against Climate Engineering*. John Wiley and Sons.

ICISS. 2001. International Commission on Intervention, State Sovereignty and International Development Research Centre (Canada). *The Responsibility to Protect: Report of the International Commission on Intervention and State Sovereignty*. IDRC.

IPCC. 2014a [core writing team, R. K. Pachauri and L. A. Meyer (eds)], *Climate Change 2014: Synthesis Report, contribution of Working Groups I, II and III to the Fifth Assessment Report of the Intergovernmental Panel on Climate Change (2014)*, IPCC, Geneva, Switzerland. Table 2.2, https://www.ipcc.ch/pdf/assessment-report/ar5/syr/SYR_AR5_FINAL_full_wcover.pdf

IPCC. 2014b [O. Edenhofer, R. Pichs-Madruga, Y. Sokona, E. Farahani, S. Kadner, K. Seyboth, A. Adler, I. Baum, S. Brunner, P. Eickemeier, B. Kriemann, J. Savolainen, S. Schlömer, C. von Stechow, T. Zwickel and J. C. Minx (eds)], Summary for Policymakers. In *Climate Change 2014: Mitigation of Climate Change: Contribution of Working Group III to the Fifth Assessment Report of the Intergovernmental Panel on Climate Change*. Cambridge University Press.

IPCC. 2014c: Annex II: Glossary [K. J. Mach, S. Planton and C. von Stechow (eds)]. In *Climate Change 2014: Synthesis Report. Contribution of Working Groups I, II and III to the Fifth Assessment Report of the Intergovernmental Panel on Climate Change* [Core Writing Team, R. K. Pachauri and L. A. Meyer (eds)]. IPCC, Geneva, Switzerland, http://www.ipcc.ch/pdf/assessment-report/ar5/syr/AR5_SYR_FINAL_Annexes.pdf

IPCC. 2018 [Myles Allen (UK) Global warming of 1.5 °C, an IPCC special report on the impacts of global warming of 1.5 °C above pre-industrial levels and related global greenhouse gas emission pathways, in the context of strengthening the global response to the threat of climate change, sustainable development, and efforts to eradicate poverty]. IPCC, Geneva, Switzerland, http://www.ipcc.ch/report/sr15/

Inhofe, J. M. 2012. *The Greatest Hoax: How the Global Warming Conspiracy Threatens Your Future.* WND Books.

International Energy Agency (IEA). 2013. Tracking Clean Energy Progress: IEA input to the Clean Energy Ministerial. http://www.iea.org/publications/tcep_web.pdf

International Energy Agency (IEA). 2018. Tracking clean energy progress. http://www.iea.org/tcep/

Ito, A. 2013. Global modeling study of potentially bioavailable iron input from shipboard aerosol sources to the ocean. *Global Biogeochemical Cycles*, 27(1).

Jacobs, M., Lent A. and Watkins, K. 2003. *Progressive Globalisation: Towards International Social Democracy.* Fabian Society.

Jacobson, M. Z., Delucchi, M. A., Bauer, Z. A., Goodman, S. C., Chapman, W. E., Cameron, M. A., Bozonnat, C., Chobadi, L., Clonts, H. A., Enevoldsen, P. and Erwin, J. R. 2017. 100% clean and renewable wind, water, and sunlight all-sector energy roadmaps for 139 countries of the world. *Joule*, 1(1).

Janos P., Scharf, C. and Schmidt. K. U. 2017. How to govern geoengineering? *Science*, 21. 357 (Jul), Issue 6348: 231; DOI 10.1126/science.aan6794

Jenkins, J., Devon, S., Borofsky, Y., Aki, H., Arnold, Z., Bennett, G., Knight, C. et al. 2010. Where good technologies come from: Case studies in American innovation. *Breakthrough Institute*, 5 December.

Juma, C. 2016. *Innovation and its Enemies: Why People Resist New Technologies.* Oxford University Press.

Kahan, D. M. 2015. The politically motivated reasoning paradigm, part 1: What politically motivated reasoning is and how to measure it. *Emerging Trends in the Social and Behavioral Sciences: An interdisciplinary, searchable, and linkable resource.* John Wiley and Sons. pp.1–16.

Kahan, D. M. and Corbin, J. C. 2016. A note on the perverse effects of actively open-minded thinking on climate-change polarization. *Research and Politics*, 3(4).

Karlsson, R. 2013. Ambivalence, irony, and democracy in the Anthropocene. *Futures*, 46.

Karlsson, R. 2016. Three metaphors for sustainability in the Anthropocene. *The Anthropocene Review*, 3(1).

Karlsson, R. 2017. The environmental risks of incomplete globalization. *Globalizations*, 14(4).

Kealey, T. and Nelson, R. 1996. *The Economic Laws of Scientific Research*. Macmillan.

Kennedy, A. 2015. Powerhouses or pretenders? Debating China's and India's emergence as technological powers. *The Pacific Review*, 28(2).

Kim, J. Y. 2017. High-Level Session Opening Remarks by World Bank Group President Jim Yong Kim. *The World Bank*. Dec. 12. http://www.worldbank.org/en/news/speech/2017/12/12/high-level-session-opening-remarks-by-world-bank-group-president-jim-yong-kim

Klein, N. 2007. *The Shock Doctrine: The Rise of Disaster Capitalism*. Macmillan.

Klein, N. 2015. *This Changes Everything: Capitalism vs. The Climate*. Simon and Schuster.

Kloor, K. 2012. The great schism in the environmental movement. *Salon*, 12 Dec. http://www.slate.com/articles/health_and_science/science/2012/12/modern_green_movement_eco_pragmatists_are_challenging_traditional_environmentalists.single.html

Klümper, W. and Qaim, M. 2014. A meta-analysis of the impacts of genetically modified crops. *PloS one* 9(11).

Kouser, S. and Qaim, M. 2011. Impact of Bt Cotton on pesticide poisoning in smallholder agriculture: A panel data analysis. *Ecological Economics*, 70(11).

Kravitz, B., MacMartin, D. G., Robock, A., Rasch, P. J., Ricke, K. L., Cole, J. N. S., Curry C. L. et al. 2014. A multi-model assessment of regional climate disparities caused by solar geo-engineering. *Environmental Research Letters*, 9.7.

Kurtz, L. R. 1983. The politics of heresy. *American Journal of Sociology* 88(6). https://doi-org.simsrad.net.ocs.mq.edu.au/10.1086/227796

Lachapelle, E., MacNeil, R. and Paterson, M. 2017. The political economy of decarbonisation: From green energy 'race' to green 'division of labour'. *New Political Economy*, 22(3).

Lai, J. 2012. *Financial Crisis and Institutional Change in East Asia*. Springer.

Lamb, W. F. and Rao, N. D. 2015. Human development in a climate-constrained world: what the past says about the future. *Global Environmental Change*, 33.

Lang, P. A. 2017. Nuclear power learning and deployment rates: Disruption and global benefits forgone. *Energies*, 10(12).

Latour, B. 2011. Love your monsters. *Breakthrough Journal*, 2(11).

Lavery, T. J., Roudnew, B., Gill, P., Seymour, J., Seuront, L., Johnson, G., Mitchell, J. G. and Smetacek, V. 2010. Iron defecation by sperm whales stimulates carbon export in the Southern Ocean. *Proceedings of the Royal Society of London B: Biological Sciences*.

Leiss, William. 1978. *The Limits to Satisfaction: On Needs and Commodities*. Marion Boyars.

Levine, R. and 'The What Works Working Group' with Molly Kinder. 2004. Millions saved: Proven successes in global health. Center for Global Development.

Lewis, M. W. 1994. *Green Delusions: An Environmentalist Critique of Radical Environmentalism*. Duke University Press.

Lewis, M. W. 1993. On human connectedness with nature. *New Literary History*, 24(4).

Little, A. and Macdonald, K. 2013. Pathways to global democracy? Escaping the statist imaginary. *Review of International Studies*, 39.4.

Long, J. 2017. Coordinated action against climate change: A new world symphony. *Issues in Science and Technology*, 33(3), http://issues.org/33-3/coordinated-action-against-climate-change-a-new-world-symphony/

Lynas, M. 2018. *Seeds of Science: Why We Got It So Wrong On GMOs*. Bloomsbury Publishing.

McDonnell J. 2017. Speech to IPPR conference. Tuesday 14 November 2017. https://labour.org.uk/press/john-mcdonnell-speech-to-ippr-conference/

Macy, J. 1991. *Greening of the Self*. Parallax Press.

Maher, B. 2018. Why policymakers should view carbon capture and storage as a stepping-stone to carbon dioxide removal. *Global Policy*, 9(1).

Malthus, T. R. 1888. *An Essay on the Principle of Population: Or, a View of its Past and Present Effects On Human Happiness*. Reeves and Turner.

Mann, C. C. 2018. *The Wizard and the Prophet: Two Ground-breaking Scientists and Their Conflicting Visions of the Future of Our Planet*. Pan Macmillan.

Markandya, A. and Wilkinson, P. 2007. Electricity generation and health. *The Lancet*, 370(9591).

Marris, E. 2013. *Rambunctious Garden: Saving Nature in a Post-Wild World*. Bloomsbury Publishing USA.

Marris, E. 2013. Humility in the Anthropocene. In *After Preservation: Saving American Nature in the Age of Humans*. University of Chicago Press.

Marris E. 2017. Can we love nature and let it go? *Breakthrough Journal*. https://thebreakthrough.org/index.php/journal/past-issues/issue-7/can-we-love-nature-and-let-it-go

Mazdiyasni, O., AghaKouchak, A., Davis, S. J., Madadgar, S., Mehran, A., Ragno, E., Sadegh, M., Sengupta, A., Ghosh, S., Dhanya, C. T. and Niknejad, M. 2017. Increasing probability of mortality during Indian heat waves. *Science Advances*, 3(6).

Mazur, C., Contestabile, M., Offer, G. J. and Brandon, N. P. 2015. Assessing and comparing German and UK transition policies for electric mobility. *Environmental Innovation and Societal Transitions*, 14.

Mazzucato, M. 2015. *The Entrepreneurial State: Debunking Public vs. Private Sector Myths*. Anthem Press.

Mazzucato, M. and Semieniuk, G. 2017. Public financing of innovation: New questions. *Oxford Review of Economic Policy*, 33(1).

Meyer, W. B. 2016. *The Progressive Environmental Prometheans: Left-Wing Heralds of a 'Good Anthropocene'*. Springer.

Milanovic, B. 2011. *Worlds Apart: Measuring International and Global Inequality*. Princeton University Press.

Miller, D. 2012. *Consumption and its Consequences*. Polity.

Mingardi, A. 2015. A critique of Mazzucato's entrepreneurial state. *Cato Journal*, 35.

Monbiot G. 2015. Meet the ecomodernists: Ignorant of history and paradoxically old-fashioned. *Guardian*. https://www.theguardian.com/environment/georgemonbiot/2015/sep/24/meet-the-ecomodernists-ignorant-of-history-and-paradoxically-old-fashioned

Morgan, M. G., Abdulla, A., Ford, M. J. and Rath, M. 2018. US nuclear power: The vanishing low-carbon wedge. *Proceedings of the National Academy of Sciences*, 115(28).

Morton O. 2015. *The Planet Remade: How Geoengineering Could Change the World*. Princeton University Press.

Moss, T. 2018a. Bravo to power Africa for moving up the energy ladder. *Center for Global Development*. https://www.cgdev.org/blog/bravo-power-africa-moving-energy-ladder

Moss, T. 2018b. On-grid or off-grid electricity? African consumers say...We want both. *Center for Global Development*. https://www.cgdev.org/blog/grid-or-grid-electricity-african-consumers-say-we-want-both

Najam, A. 2005. Developing countries and global environmental governance: From contestation to participation to engagement. *International Environmental Agreements: Politics, Law and Economics*, 5(3).

Nanda, M. 1995. Transnationalisation of Third World state and undoing of Green revolution. *Economic and Political Weekly*, PE20–PE30.

Nanda, M. 2003. *Prophets Facing Backwards: Post-Modem Critiques of Science and Hindu Nationalism in India*. Rutgers University Press.

Nelson, P. 1996. NGO Networks and the World Bank's expanding influence. *Millennium Journal of International Studies*, 25(3).

Nickerson, R. S. 1998. Confirmation bias: A ubiquitous phenomenon in many guises. Review of general psychology, 2(2).

Niebuhr, R. 1976. *Love and Justice*, edited by D. Robertson. Peter Smith.

Niemann, Michelle. 2017. Hubris and humility in environmental thought. In Ursula K. Heise, Jon Christensen and Michelle Niemann, eds, *The Routledge Companion to the Environmental Humanities*. Taylor and Francis.

Nisbet, M. C. 2014. Disruptive ideas: Public intellectuals and their arguments for action on climate change. *Wiley Interdisciplinary Reviews: Climate Change*, 5(6).

Nordhaus, T. and Shellenberger, M. *The Death of Environmentalism: Global Warming Politics in a Post-environmental World* 2004.

Nordhaus, T. and Shellenberger, M. 2007. *Break Through: From the Death of Environmentalism to the Politics of Possibility*. Houghton Mifflin.

Nordhaus, T. 2016. Don't let the planet Bern. *USA Today*. 10 March. https://www.usatoday.com/story/opinion/2016/03/10/

bernie-sanders-energy-plan-anti-emissions-reduction-nuclear-natural-gas-column/81500436/

Oakeshott, M. 1991. On being conservative. *Rationalism in Politics and Other Essays*. Liberty Press.

Obama, B. 2010. *State of the Union Address*. Jan. 28. http://edition.cnn.com/2010/POLITICS/01/27/sotu.transcript/index.html

O'Neill, D. W., Fanning, A. L., Lamb, W. F. and Steinberger, J. K. 2018. A good life for all within planetary boundaries. *Nature Sustainability*, 1(2).

Ostrom, E. 2012. Nested externalities and polycentric institutions: must we wait for global solutions to climate change before taking actions at other scales? *Economic Theory*, 49(2).

Ostrom, E. 2015. *Governing the Commons*. Cambridge University Press.

Paarlberg, R. 2010. *Food Politics*. Oxford University Press.

Palmer, G. 2014. Germany's Energiewende as a model for Australian climate policy? *Brave New Climate*. https://bravenewclimate.com/2014/06/11/germany-energiewende-oz-critical-review/

Park, S. 2005. Norm diffusion within international organizations: A case study of the World Bank, *Journal of International Relations and Development*, 8(2).

Parry, D. 2017. Naval Research Laboratory receives patent for carbon capture device – a key step in synthetic fuel production from seawater. *Phys.org.*, Oct 10. https://phys.org/news/2017-10-nrl-patent-carbon-capture-devicea.html#jCp

Pascoe, B. 2014. *Dark Emu Black Seeds: Agriculture or Accident?* Magabala Books.

Pershing, A. J., Christensen, L. B., Record, N. R., Sherwood, G. D. and Stetson, P. B. 2010. The impact of whaling on the ocean carbon cycle: Why bigger was better. *PloS one*, 5(8).

Peters, G. P. 2018. Beyond carbon budgets. *Nature Geoscience*, 11(6).

Peters, G. P., Le Quéré, C., Andrew, R. M., Canadell, J. G., Friedlingstein, P., Ilyina, T., Jackson, R. B., Joos, F., Korsbakken, J. I., McKinley, G. A. and Sitch, S. 2017. Towards real-time verification of CO2 emissions. *Nature Climate Change*, 7(12).

Pfeiffer, A., Hepburn, C., Vogt-Schilb, A. and Caldecott, B. 2018. Committed emissions from existing and planned power plants and asset stranding required to meet the Paris Agreement. *Environmental Research Letters*, 13(5).

Phillips, L. 2015. *Austerity Ecology and the Collapse-Porn Addicts: A Defence of Growth, Progress, Industry and Stuff*. John Hunt Publishing.

Pinker, S. 2018. *Enlightenment now: The case for Reason, Science, Humanism, and Progress*. Penguin.

Prashad, V. 2007. The Third World idea. *The Nation*, 4 June. https://www.thenation.com/article/third-world-idea/

Prashad, V. 2008. *The Darker Nations: A People's History of the Third World*. The New Press.

Prebisch, R. 1962. The economic development of Latin America and its principal problems. *Economic Bulletin for Latin America*.

Prins, G. and Rayner, S. 2007. Time to ditch Kyoto. *Nature*, 449(7165).

Pritzker, R. 2016. Recognizing India's Energy Independence. *Stanford Social Innovation Review*. https://ssir.org/articles/entry/recognizing_indias_energy_independence

Qvist, S. and Brook, B. 2015. Potential for worldwide displacement of fossil-fuel electricity by nuclear energy in three decades based on extrapolation of regional deployment data. *PLoS One*, 10(5): e0124074. doi:10.1371/journal.pone.0124074

Rajan, R. G. and Subramanian, A. 2008. Aid and growth: What does the cross-country evidence really show? *The Review of Economics and Statistics*, 90(4).

Randall, T. 2015. Fossil fuels just lost the race against renewables. *Bloomburg*, 15 April. https://www.bloomberg.com/news/articles/2015-04-14/fossil-fuels-just-lost-the-race-against-renewables

Rayner, S., Heyward, C., Kruger, T., Pidgeon, N., Redgwell, C. and Savulescu, J. 2013. The Oxford principles. *Climatic Change*, 121(3).

Ren21. 2018. Global status report. *REN21 secretariat, Paris*. http://www.ren21.net/wp-content/uploads/2018/06/17-8652_GSR2018_FullReport_web_final_.pdf

Reynolds, J. 2014. Response to Svoboda and Irvine. *Ethics, Policy and Environment*, 17(2).

Ricke, K. L., Granger-Morgan, M. and Allen, M. R. 2010. Regional climate response to solar-radiation management. *Nature Geoscience*, 3(8).

Ricke, K. L., Moreno-Cruz, J. B. and Caldeira, K. 2013. Strategic incentives for climate geoengineering coalitions to exclude broad participation. *Environmental Research Letters*, 8(1).

Roberts, D. 2011. Why I've avoided commenting on Nisbet's 'Climate Shift' report. *Grist*, 27 April. https://grist.org/climate-change/2011-04-26-why-ive-avoided-commenting-on-nisbets-climate-shift-report/

Rockström, J., Steffen, W., Noone, K., Persson, Å., Chapin III, F. S., Lambin, E. F., Lenton, T. M., Scheffer, M., Folke, C., Schellnhuber, H. J. and Nykvist, B. 2009. A safe operating space for humanity. *Nature*, 461(7263).

Rootes, C. 2014. *Environmental Movements: Local, National and Global*. Routledge.

Rosling, H., Rönnlund, A. R. and Rosling, O. 2018. *Factfulness: Ten Reasons We're Wrong about the World – and Why Things are Better Than You Think*. Flatiron Books.

Samir, K. C. and Lutz, W. 2017. The human core of the shared socioeconomic pathways: Population scenarios by age, sex and level of education for all countries to 2100. *Global Environmental Change*, 42.

Saran, S. and Mohan, A. 2016. Indian climate policy in a post-Paris world. *The Strategist*. https://www.aspistrategist.org.au/indian-climate-policy-in-a-post-paris-world/

Schumacher, E. F. 1973. *Small is Beautiful: A Study of Economics as if People Really Mattered*. Blond and Briggs.

Schumpeter, J. A. 2010. *Capitalism, Socialism and Democracy*. Routledge.

Sepulveda et al. 2018. The role of firm low-carbon electricity resources in deep decarbonization of power generation, *Joule*. https://doi.org/10.1016/j.joule.2018.08.006

Shellenberger, M. 2018. How Trump's nuke bailout may help America meet Paris climate commitments. 6 June 2018, https://www.forbes.com/sites/michaelshellenberger/2018/06/06/trumps-bail-out-of-nuclear-plants-could-allow-us-to-meet-its-paris-climate-commitments/

Shelton, A. M., Hossain, M., Paranjape, V. and Azad, A. K. 2018. Bt eggplant project in Bangladesh: History, present status, and future direction. *Frontiers in Bioengineering and Biotechnology*, 6.

Shuba, E. S. and Kifle, D. 2018. Microalgae to biofuels: 'Promising' alternative and renewable energy, review. *Renewable and Sustainable Energy Reviews*, 81.

Siddiqui, M. Z., Goli, S., Reja, T., Doshi, R., Chakravorty, S., Tiwari, C., Kumar, N. P. and Singh, D. 2017. Prevalence of anemia and Its determinants among pregnant, lactating, and nonpregnant nonlactating women in India. *SAGE Open*, 7(3).

Sivaram, V. 2018. *Taming the Sun: Innovations to Harness Solar Energy and Power the Planet*. MIT Press.

Smalley, R. E. 2005. Future global energy prosperity: The terawatt challenge. *MRS Bulletin*, 30(6).

Smil, V. 2017. *Energy and Civilization: A History*. The MIT Press.

Snow, C. P. 1959. *The Two Cultures and the Scientific Revolution*. Cambridge University Press.

Somanathan, E., Sterner, T., Sugiyama, T., Chimanikire, D., Dubash, N. K., Essandoh-Yeddu, J. K., Fifita, S., Goulder, L., Jaffe, A., Labandeira, X. and Managi, S. 2014. National and sub-national policies and institutions. In O. Edenhofer et al. (eds) *Climate Change 2014: Mitigation of Climate Change. Contribution of Working Group III to the Fifth Assessment Report of the Intergovernmental Panel on Climate Change*, Cambridge University Press. http://www.ipcc.ch/pdf/assessment-report/ar5/wg3/ipcc_wg3_ar5_chapter15.pdf

Sontag, S. 1989. *AIDS and its Metaphors* (Vol. 1). Farrar, Straus and Giroux.

Specter, M. 2015. How not to debate nuclear energy and climate change. *The New Yorker*, 18 December. https://www.newyorker.com/news/daily-comment/how-not-to-debate-nuclear-energy-and-climate-change

Srnicek, N. and Williams, A. 2015. *Inventing the Future: Post-capitalism and a World without Work*. Verso Books.

Stern D. 2014. Censored IPCC summary reveals jockeying for key UN climate talks. *The Conversation*, 24 April. https://theconversation.com/censored-ipcc-summary-reveals-jockeying-for-key-un-climate-talks-25813

Stern, N. 2006. *Stern review on the economics of climate change*. HM Treasury.

Stiglitz, J. E. 2002. *Globalization and its Discontents* (Vol. 500). New York.

Strong, M. 1971. *The Founex Report of development and the environment*. https://www.mauricestrong.net/index.php/the-founex-report?showall=1&limitstart=

Subramanian, A. 2015. India is right to resist the West's carbon imperialism. *Financial Times* (27 November). https://www.ft.com/content/0805bac2-937d-11e5-bd82-c1fb87bef7af

Svensson, J. 2000. When is foreign aid policy credible? Aid dependence and conditionality. *Journal of Development Economics*, 61(1).

Svoboda, T. and Irvine, P. 2014. Ethical and technical challenges in compensating for harm due to solar radiation management geoengineering. *Ethics, Policy and Environment*, 17(2).

Symons, J. and Karlsson R. 2018. Ecomodernist citizenship: rethinking political obligations in a climate-changed world. *Citizenship Studies*, 22(7).

Symons, J. 2018. Geoengineering justice: Who gets to decide whether to hack the climate? *Breakthrough Journal*, 8. https://thebreakthrough.org/index.php/journal/past-issues/no.-8-winter-2018/geoengineering-justice

Sweeney, S. 2012. Resist, reclaim, restructure: Unions and the struggle for energy democracy. *Discussion Document prepared for Global Union Roundtable, Energy Emergency: Developing Trade Union Strategies for a Global Transition*. http://unionsforenergydemocracy.org/wp-content/uploads/2014/05/resistreclaimrestructure_2013_english.pdf

Szerszynski, B., Kearnes, M., Macnaghten, P., Owen, R. and Stilgoe, J. 2013. Why solar radiation management geoengineering and democracy won't mix. *Environment and Planning A*, 45(12).

Talberg, A., Christoff, P., Thomas, S. and Karoly, D. 2018. Geoengineering governance-by-default: An earth system governance perspective. *International Environmental Agreements: Politics, Law and Economics*, 18(2)

Tanigawa, K., Hosoi, Y., Hirohashi, N., Iwasaki, Y. and Kamiya, K. 2012. Loss of life after evacuation: Lessons learned from the Fukushima accident. *The Lancet*, 379(9819).

Taylor, M. 2012. Toward an international relations theory of national innovation rates. *Security Studies*, 21(1).

Tokarska, K. B. and Zickfeld, K. 2015. The effectiveness of net negative carbon dioxide emissions in reversing anthropogenic climate change. *Environmental Research Letters*, 10(9).

Torgeson, D. 1999. *The Promise of Green Politics: Environmentalism and the Public Sphere*. Duke University Press.

Trainer, T. 2010. Can renewables etc. solve the greenhouse problem? The negative case. *Energy Policy*, 38(8).

Trembath, A. 2015. The dramatic shift in our climate thinking, quietly, we've moved to relying on technological innovation, not efficiency, to save the planet. *Zocal Public Square*, 9 December. http://www.zocalopublicsquare.org/2015/12/09/the-dramatic-shift-in-our-climate-thinking/ideas/nexus/

Tsing, A. L. 2015. *The Mushroom at the End of the World: On the Possibility of Life in Capitalist Ruins*. Princeton University Press.

UNEP. 2017. The Emissions Gap Report 2017. United Nations Environment Programme (UNEP) Nairobi. www.unenvironment.org/resources/emissions-gap-report

UNFCCC. 2015a. Report on the structured expert dialogue on the 2013–2015 review. *UNFCCC Subsidiary Body for Scientific and Technological Advice*. http://unfccc.int/resource/docs/2015/sb/eng/inf01.pdf

UNFCCC. 2015b. Synthesis report on the aggregate effect of the intended nationally determined contributions. FCCC/CP/2015/7. http://unfccc.int/resource/docs/2015/cop21/eng/07.pdf

UN General Assembly. 1974. Resolution adopted by the General Assembly 3201 (S-VI) Declaration on the Establishment of a New International Economic Order 29. U.N. Doc. A/9559

UN General Assembly. 1983. A/RES/38/161 Process of preparation of the Environmental Perspective to the Year 2000 and Beyond. https://www.un.org/documents/ga/res/38/a38r161.htm

Urban, M. 2015. Accelerating extinction risk from climate change. *Science* 348.

Uscinski, J., Douglas, K. and Lewandowsky, S. 2017. Climate change conspiracy theories. *Oxford Research Encyclopedia of Climate Science*. DOI: 10.1093/acrefore/9780190228620.013.328

Victor, D. G. 2011. *Global Warming Gridlock: Creating More Effective Strategies for Protecting the Planet*. Cambridge University Press.

Victor, D. G., Akimoto, K., Kaya, Y., Yamaguchi, M., Cullenward, D. and Hepburn, C. 2017. Prove Paris was more than paper promises. *Nature*, 548(7665).

Victor, D. 2018. Foreign aid for capacity building to address climate change. In *Aid Effectiveness for Environmental Sustainability* (pp. 17–49). Palgrave Macmillan.

Warren, W. A., 2006. A review of: 'Eckersley, Robyn. 'The Green State'. *Society and Natural Resources* 19(4).

Weiss, L. 2000. Developmental states in transition: Adapting, dismantling, innovating, not 'normalizing'. *The Pacific Review*, 13(1).

Weiss, L. 2014. *America Inc.?: Innovation and Enterprise in the National Security State*. Cornell University Press.

Wendt, A. 2003. Why a world state is inevitable. *European Journal of International Relations*, 9(4).

Whyte, J. 2017. The invisible hand of Friedrich Hayek: Submission and spontaneous order. *Political Theory*: https://doi.org/10.1177/0090591717737064

Williams, A., and Srnicek, N. 2013. *Accelerate Manifesto for an Accelerationist Politics. Critical Legal Thinking*. http://criticallegalthinking.com/2013/05/14/accelerate-manifesto-for-an-accelerationist-politics/

Williams, M. 1993. Re-articulating the Third World coalition: The role of the environmental agenda. *Third World Quarterly*, 14(1).

Williams, M. C. 2003. Words, images, enemies: Securitization and international politics. *International Studies Quarterly*, 47(4).

Winner, L. 1986. *The Whale and the Reactor: A Search for Limits in an Age of High Technology*. University of Chicago Press.

Winner, L. 1980. Do artifacts have politics? *Daedalus*, 109(1).

Wissenburg, M. 1998. *Green Liberalism: The Free and the Green Society*. UCL Press.

World Bank, IFC, and MIGA. 2016. *World Bank Group Climate Change Action Plan 2016–2020*. World Bank.

World Bank, Ecofys and Vivid Economics. 2017. State and trends of carbon pricing 2017 (November), by World Bank, Washington, DC. Doi: 10.1596/978-1-4648-1218-7

World Bank. 2018. *World Development Indicators* http://data.worldbank.org/data-catalog/world-development-indicators

Wright, C. and Nyberg, D. 2015. *Climate Change, Capitalism, and Corporations*. Cambridge University Press.

Yan, W., Fehrmann, R., Kegnæs, S., Mielby, J. J., Stenby, E. H., Fosbøl, P. L. and Thomsen, K. 2018. Carbon capture innovation challenge. In *Accelerating the Clean Energy Revolution – Perspectives on Innovation Challenges: DTU International Energy Report 2018* (ch. 7, pp. 55–61). Technical University of Denmark.

Index